Intervention Narratives

War Culture

Edited by Daniel Leonard Bernardi

Books in this series address the myriad ways in which warfare informs diverse cultural practices, as well as the way cultural practices—from cinema to social media—inform the practice of warfare. They illuminate the insights and limitations of critical theories that describe, explain, and politicize the phenomena of war culture. Traversing both national and intellectual borders, authors from a wide range of fields and disciplines collectively examine the articulation of war, its everyday practices, and its impact on individuals and societies throughout modern history.

Tanine Allison, *Destructive Sublime: World War II in American Film and Media*

Purnima Bose, *Intervention Narratives: Afghanistan, the United States, and the Global War on Terror*

Brenda M. Boyle and Jeehyun Lim, eds., *Looking Back on the Vietnam War: Twenty-First-Century Perspectives*

Jonna Eagle, *Imperial Affects: Sensational Melodrama and the Attractions of American Cinema*

H. Bruce Franklin, *Crash Course: From the Good War to the Forever War*

Aaron Michael Kerner, *Torture Porn in the Wake of 9/11: Horror, Exploitation, and the Cinema of Sensation*

David Kieran and Edwin A. Martini, eds., *At War: The Military and American Culture in the Twentieth Century and Beyond*

Delia Malia Caparoso Konzett, *Hollywood's Hawaii: Race, Nation, and War*

Nan Levinson, *War Is Not a Game: The New Antiwar Soldiers and the Movement They Built*

Matt Sienkiewicz, *The Other Air Force: U.S. Efforts to Reshape Middle Eastern Media Since 9/11*

Jon Simons and John Louis Lucaites, eds., *In/visible War: The Culture of War in Twenty-First-Century America*

Roger Stahl, *Through the Crosshairs: The Weapon's Eye in Public War Culture*

Mary Douglas Vavrus, *Postfeminist War: Women and the Media-Military-Industrial Complex*

Simon Wendt, ed., *Warring over Valor: How Race and Gender Shaped American Military Heroism in the Twentieth and Twenty-First Centuries*

Intervention Narratives

. . . .

Afghanistan, the United States, and the Global War on Terror

PURNIMA BOSE

Rutgers University Press

New Brunswick, Camden, and Newark, New Jersey, and London

Library of Congress Cataloging-in-Publication Data

Names: Bose, Purnima, 1962- author.
Title: Intervention narratives: Afghanistan, the United States, and the
  Global War on Terror / Purnima Bose.
Description: New Brunswick: Rutgers University Press, 2020. | Includes index.
Identifiers: LCCN 2019007365| ISBN 9781978805989 (pbk.) | ISBN 9781978805996
  (cloth) | ISBN 9781978806009 (ePUB) | ISBN 9781978806016 (ePDF)
Subjects: LCSH: Afghan War, 2001- | United States—Relations—Afghanistan. |
  Afghanistan—Relations—United States. | War on Terrorism, 2001-2009. |
  Imperialism. | Intervention (International law) | Afghan War,
  2001—Literature and the war. | Afghan War, 2001—Mass media and the war.
Classification: LCC DS371.412 .B67 2020 | DDC 958.104/7—dc23
LC record available at https://lccn.loc.gov/2019007365

A British Cataloging-in-Publication record for this book is available from the British Library.

www.rutgersuniversitypress.org

Manufactured in the United States of America

Typesetter: Nord Compo

For Barbara Harlow, who is missed long after the final cigarette has been extinguished.

Contents

Acronyms

AVMA American Veterinary Medical Association

CIA Central Intelligence Agency. US's premier intelligence agency.

COIN Counterinsurgency

DoD Department of Defense

EIT Enhanced Interrogation Techniques. A euphemism for torture coined by the G.W. Bush Administration.

FOB Forward Operating Base. A military installation that is geared toward tactical support without featuring full support services.

IED Improvised Explosive Device. IEDs are popular with insurgents and are a leading cause of combat fatalities in Afghanistan and Iraq.

ISAF International Security Assistance Force. Security forces, consisting of forty-two countries under NATO command, and disbanded in 2014.

ISI Inter-Services Intelligence. Pakistan's premier intelligence agency.

LBGL Louis Berger Group. A New Jersey-based engineering and construction corporation, which has scored reconstruction contracts.

LCSF Limited Contingent of Soviet Forces. Soviet forces serving in Afghanistan during its military occupation from 1979 to 1989.

MWD Military Working Dog

NGO Non-governmental Organization. Non-profit, voluntary group that can operate at the local, national, or international levels.

NSC National Security Council. A group that advises the US President on national security, consisting of the Vice President, the Secretary of State, the Secretary of the Treasury, the Secretary of Defense, and the Assistant to the President for National Security Affairs. Not to be confused with the National Security Agency, which gathers intelligence.

PTSD Posttraumatic Stress Disorder. A serious mental disorder as a result of experiencing trauma. Often associated with combat or the operation of drones, and recently acknowledged as a condition afflicting Military Working Dogs.

RMA Revolution in Military Affairs. Long-distance warfare that is dependent on communications technology and sophisticated weaponry.

RSM Resolute Support Mission. The NATO security force that is the successor to ISAF.

SALW Small Arms and Light Weapons trade.

SIGAR Special Inspector General for Afghanistan Reconstruction. Created by Congress to exercise oversight over Afghanistan's reconstruction, SIGAR audits, inspects, and issues periodic reports on reconstruction projects and activities.

SSD Specialized Search Dog. Military dogs trained to search for explosives off leash.

TFBS Task Force for Business and Stability Operations. A DoD organization that was founded in 2006 to stabilize the Iraqi economy; its mandate expanded to include Afghanistan in 2010.

UNAMA United Nations Mission in Afghanistan.

USAID United States Agency for International Development. A government agency that provides development assistance to foreign countries.

Intervention Narratives

Introduction

● ●

Intervention Narratives and Geopolitical Fetishism

Prologue

As the United States military intervention in Afghanistan inches toward its eighteenth year, a profound disjunction characterizes the American public experience of this conflict and the actual realities of war.[1] The number of casualties for Afghans is notoriously difficult to ascertain, but one estimate is that from October 2001 through August 2016, 111,000 Afghans, of whom 31,000 were civilians, died. For US armed forces, the Pentagon places the death toll, from 2001 to May 5, 2017, at 2,216.[2] Notwithstanding these casualties, the war in Afghanistan no longer features prominently on the front page of the national dailies with the exception of the more excessive instances of military atrocities such as the 2012 massacre of Afghan civilians by Staff Sergeant Robert Bales. Rarely do the nightly newscasts of network journalism cover the conflict, and the 2012 and 2016 presidential candidates only sparingly referenced it in their political speeches.

Given the invisibility of the Afghan war, it is not surprising that many Americans have little knowledge of the conflict. I take four factors to be the most salient in contributing to the general ignorance of the war among the US public: the absence of a universal military draft in the US and restriction of the direct experience of war to a very small percentage of the citizenry; the lack of governmental demands from the general public for shared sacrifice in the way of rationing goods and services; the ongoing US military interventions in a number of countries (Iraq, Pakistan, Yemen, Syria, and Libya) of which Afghanistan is only one; and the general dearth of meaningful information for understanding the conflict. The advent of cable news, the consolidation of media outlets to a handful of corporations, the transformation of serious journalism into sensational entertainment over the last two decades, and the decline in resources for foreign reporting all contribute to this knowledge deficit.[3]

Even as the Afghan war has faded from print and broadcast media, narratives about the conflict have emerged in mass culture in the form of memoirs by soldiers and intelligence agents, espionage novels, and the odd Hollywood film. These cultural artifacts are the subject of *Intervention Narratives: Afghanistan, the United States, and the Global War on Terror*, which analyzes the different stories that have circulated in the United States about its clandestine and overt military operations in Afghanistan from 1979 to the present. As would be expected, these narratives almost always present the conflict as it is experienced by Americans, such that Afghans recede into the background of their history and the political economy of the war is obscured. Afghanistan and the war appear in the US public sphere as what Jean Baudrillard calls "hyperreality," a series of signifiers and simulacra, a pastiche created from remnants of British Orientalism, figurations of neoliberal subjectivity, and expressions of US imperial hubris.[4] These representations do not necessarily communicate knowledge of actual conditions on the ground in Afghanistan so much as they affirm mainstream American assumptions and feelings about the conflict.

Contradictory and competing narratives about US intervention proliferate in the public sphere and are under examination in this project. My book offers a taxonomy of the war's narrative forms to analyze a cultural discourse about sentiment that substitutes for political analysis among the public. These narratives involve projecting Afghans as brave anti-communist warriors who suffered the consequences of our disengagement with the region following the end of the Cold War (the premature-withdrawal narrative); as victimized women who can be empowered through enterprise (the capitalist-rescue narrative); as stray dogs who are innocent bystanders and need saving by US soldiers (the canine-rescue narrative); and as terrorists who deserve punishment for 9/11 (the retributive-justice narrative). *Intervention Narratives* explores the significance of the tropes and narrative forms, along with the discursive absences and historical erasures, which allow these narratives to function as what Gillian Whitlock calls "soft weapons" of empire, the ideological justifications of an imperial foreign policy.[5] Together the four narratives demonstrate that contemporary imperialism, like its nineteenth- and twentieth-century precursors, does not function on an ideologically unified cultural terrain, but rather occupies a whole range of political sensibilities and projects. I am interested in exploring the contradictions that inhere in the casting of Afghans as both warriors and terrorists. I also explore the juxtaposition of a humanist story focused on saving women with a post-humanist tale centered on canine rescue. Together, these narratives illuminate the contours of contemporary US imperial culture.

Intervention Narratives focuses on US cultural texts, with occasional references to South Asian materials, rather than on Afghan cultural production, as an ethical response to Edward Said's injunction in *Orientalism* that US scholars must confront the fact of their citizenship in an imperial country.[6] My motivation for this project thus derives from my status as a US citizen and my outrage and sorrow over the devastation my country has wrought in the long arc of US foreign policy from the Cold War to the present. I have sought to understand those cultural currents that enable the stark disconnect between the rhetoric of support for democracy and respect for human rights at "home" (however lofty an aspiration that might be in reality), and the actual practices of a state that has demonstrated regard for neither in its treatment of people "abroad."

That disconnect, I believe, emanates from the dysfunctional structure of a state characterized by intelligence and security apparatuses that have long operated with impunity in the absence of oversight from Congress, coupled with several successive recent administrations who have been seduced by the partnering of covert operations and techno warfare. Moreover, both the legislative and executive branches of government have been hijacked by a neoliberal ruling class consensus. This consensus has resulted in the increasing privatization of the armed forces, the rapid erosion of the welfare state in the last twenty years, along with a concurrent commitment from the state to robustly and more blatantly serve the interests of the wealthy than in the three decades immediately following World War II. One consequence of this dynamic has been that the Afghan conflict has acquired its own momentum: perpetual war is now the norm and not the exception.[7] Too many individuals, government officials, and corporate entities profit from the military-industrial-(non)governmental complex and have a stake in the war's continuance for there to be a complete withdrawal of US forces any time soon, particularly in the absence of a vociferous anti-war movement. For Afghans under American occupation, the prospects of the right to life, liberty, and the pursuit of happiness seem increasingly bleak.

In the current political climate, the burden of cultural criticism has shifted insofar as "facts" and "knowledge" seem to have even less weight among the public and policy makers than they once did. The adequacies of ideology critique are in question because so much of public political life now involves affect rather than knowledge, feelings rather than facts. Yet the analysis of ideology does not end when we recognize the limitations of earlier iterations of cultural criticism to speak to the political conditions of the present. One consequence of the dearth of meaningful information about the Afghan war has been that the US population understands the conflict largely through stories and films that draw on familiar tropes of heroism, entrepreneurship, family, and terrorism. Reflecting this kind of public engagement with the war, the state too formulates foreign policy on the basis of a phantasmagorical Afghanistan populated by Orientalist tropes and cultural fictions, which, in turn, generate new fictions that give the illusion of US military gains and progress in reconstruction. The urgency of attending to the complexities of imperial citizenship requires that we develop an understanding of the work of ideology today and of how people are primed to "feel" what they think they "know." In our present moment, cultural analysis entails both historicizing and analyzing the production of sentiment in support of the war by asking what fictions and fantasies enable Americans to feel better about ourselves, the state of our union, and our place in the world.

The impulse to historicize presents its own challenges, given the constantly changing contour of contemporary events. Over the span of the last five years, organized resistance to the United States in Afghanistan has taken the form of Al Qaeda (which may or may not still be active); a revivified Taliban and its Pakistani offshoot; and groups that are called variously Islamic State, ISIS-K (Islamic State in Iraq and Syria, Khorasan), Daesh, and ISIL-KP (Islamic State in Iraq and the Levant, Khorasan Province)—not to mention the various organizations such as the Haqqani Network and Lashkar-e-Taibi operating out of Pakistan. US policy has also fluctuated over three administrations from troop surges to drawdowns to the redeployment of forces. Indeed, the prognosis for a stabilization in US policy now appears even more unlikely given the erratic and impetuous character of the current Commander-in-Chief, Donald J. Trump, a person who has a tenuous grasp of global history and often reverses his policy declarations within the same news cycle.

The challenges of historicizing have also been amplified by the lack of transparency in military operations and defense accounting practices, along with the circumvention of the law by several presidents and the Pentagon. The security forces consist of a bewildering array of soldiers, Marines, Special Operations Forces, intelligence branches, International Security Assistance Force [ISAF] (officially disbanded in 2014 but still present in smaller numbers in its successor organization, the Resolute Support Mission), and private contractors who now outnumber US troops by three to one or ten to one, depending on the source consulted.[8] Although the privatization of the US military dates back to the Vietnam War, former Secretary of Defense Donald Rumsfeld drove the outsourcing engine at full throttle, and the Obama administration enthusiastically took over the wheel, in part, because these forces did not have to be included in official "boots-on-the-ground" counts.[9] Given the chaotic and haphazard accounting practices at the Department of Defense [DoD], no one really knows how many private contractors work for the US. All of these factors complicate the twin tasks of historical analysis and cultural interpretation.

Notwithstanding these interpretive difficulties, the historical context matters to my analysis of the four intervention narratives that constitute the individual chapters of this book, enabling a different way to engage our "feelings" about the Afghan conflict that focuses on the effects and logic of actions rather than on causes and intentions. To that end, I parse out the history that these cultural narratives evacuate in a version of what we might call "geopolitical fetishism": the obfuscation of the political economy of the current Afghan war in terms of its dual logics of territoriality and capital.

Geopolitical Fetishism

The generalized ignorance in the United States regarding the Afghan conflict contributes to a form of fetishism in the Marxist sense, which I will call "geopolitical fetishism." "Commodity fetishism," for Marx, signifies the dual processes by which social relations become obscured in capitalist societies and commodities are reified as "mysterious things" with "metaphysical subtleties."[10] Marx drew on the concept of the "fetish" that had been articulated by European proto anthropologists, who described how West African natives worshipped objects and invested them with religious powers.[11] Significantly, cross-cultural contact between the Portuguese and Africans provided the framework for the original conceptualization of the "fetish." I mean the neologism "geopolitical fetishism" to conjure both the dynamics of unequal power between metropole and periphery that permitted the production of knowledge about natives, and the attribution of religious practices and beliefs to them. The identification between Afghans (as well as Arabs) and Islam is overdetermined and has become the explanation for decades of civil war in quasi-mystical terms. Religious differences serve as an alibi to pronounce conflict in Afghanistan as intractable and very difficult to understand, characterizations that slide too easily into an atemporal register whereby several decades of civil war acquire the weight of being an "ancient" and "enduring" conflict and, thus, beyond resolution.[12]

Against such ahistorical formulations, it is important to recognize that geopolitical fetishism is imbricated in a capitalist system of exchange, which functions at a level larger than the relationships among commodity, individual producer, and consumer, to encompass those among states, corporations, and transnational and supranational entities. Geopolitical fetishism substitutes for a number of material realities, including the human consequences of military intervention, the geostrategic motivations of imperial states, the profit drive of corporations, and the operations of what David Harvey terms "the new imperialism," which he dates to about 2002 and associates with the US.[13]

According to Harvey, a dialectic between the logics of territoriality and of capital constitutes the new imperialism in which each logic is "distinct" but simultaneously "intertwine[d] in complex and sometimes contradictory ways."[14] The two logics can be differentiated on the basis of their agents and motivations, along with their temporalities and spatial locations. For Harvey, the logic of territoriality inheres in "imperialism as a distinctively political project," generally pursued by states "whose power is based on a command of a territory and a capacity to mobilize [their] human and natural resources towards political, economic, and military ends."[15] In democratic states, this project is enacted by politicians and statesmen who "typically seek outcomes that sustain or augment the power of their own state vis-à-vis other states."[16] They act *outside* of the territorialized space of the nation-state and *inside* the temporality governed by election cycles, a crucial point in relationship to the US military intervention in Afghanistan, which I will return to later.

In contrast to the logic of territoriality, Harvey connects the logic of capital to discrete "processes of capital accumulation in space and time" that render a more dispersed form of imperialism in which the control and manipulation of capital is prioritized over territorial objectives.[17] Where the logic of territoriality is bound to specific geographical entities, the logic of capital exceeds territorial limits and geopolitical boundaries, and is characterized by movement. The logic of capital consists of "production, trade, commerce, capital flows, money transfers, labour migration, technology transfer, currency speculation, flows of information, cultural impulses, and the like."[18] Economic power is not spatially bound and can flow multi-directionally to and from territorial entities.

Capital logic plays a crucial role in what Harvey terms "accumulation by dispossession." Whereas Marx posited primitive accumulation—the expulsion of peasants from their land and their transformation into wage laborers, and the enclosure of the commons—as comprising the pre-history of capitalism, Harvey views these processes as ongoing and actively present today. His conceptualization of accumulation by dispossession names the earlier processes of privatizing land, enclosing the commons, and commodifying labor while identifying other mechanisms for the transfer of wealth from the many to the few and the consolidation of capital among a small number of elites—mechanisms that have become ubiquitous under neoliberalism. In addition to privatization, accumulation by dispossession occurs through financialization, the manipulation and management of crises by federal and international banking units, and policies devised by the state to redistribute wealth (for example, by restructuring tax codes). The state functions as the primary agent for the redistribution of wealth, given its superior capacity to organize "institutional arrangements," in Harvey's words, "to preserve that pattern of asymmetries in exchange that are most advantageous to the dominant capitalist interests working within its frame."[19]

The logics of territoriality and capital are obscured by geopolitical fetishism. Laura E. Lyons has argued for the necessity of grounding analyses of globalization and geopolitical relations in actually existing land, but it is precisely this dimension that disappears in representations of the US military intervention in Afghanistan.[20] Whereas in older forms of imperialism, territorial expansion through direct military seizure and political domination from the metropole were front and center of the colonial project, the status of land in the new imperialism and its ownership are occluded. Although Harvey's formulation of the new imperialism does not treat the issue of land in quite this way, we can extrapolate to a consideration of military installations abroad. The new imperialism does not strive for direct control of the totality of Afghan territory but instead asserts dominion over discrete pockets of land for the establishment of military bases. While it is difficult to ascertain the exact number of US military bases in the world and in Afghanistan, given the secrecy surrounding the Pentagon's properties overseas, some analysts estimate that by 2009, the US military had acquired control of over 795,000 acres, housing around 190,000 troops on more than 1,000 bases worldwide.[21]

In the last decade and a half, the DoD has undertaken a systematic geographic realignment of US military forces and bases overseas, precipitated by the end of the Cold War and a foreign policy orientation no longer directed toward containment. Michael T. Klare identifies three concerns motivating this realignment: the recognition of the increasing importance of different US geopolitical interests, such as controlling other countries' access to resources; "a shift from defensive to offensive operations"; and an uncertainty about "the future reliability of long-term allies, especially those in 'Old Europe.'"[22] To address these concerns, the US military is scaling back on the number of conventional military bases it operates in Germany, Japan, and South Korea in favor of establishing new facilities in Eastern Europe, Central Asia, Southeast Asia, and Africa.[23] In the continental migration of military installations, we see territorial elements of the new imperialism at work.

Reluctant to term these facilities "military bases"—a designation which signifies large-scale operations with permanent barracks, family housing, recreation facilities, and arsenals—the Defense Department prefers the vocabulary of "enduring camps," a name which in itself suggests semi-permanence.[24] Unlike military bases that require the negotiation of elaborate treaties with host countries, the new facilities, because of their apparent flexibility and alleged impermanence, can bypass the usual protocols requiring congressional approval for their establishment; instead, the president can exert his prerogative to secure "partnership agreements" without consulting Congress. These new facilities are geared toward enabling the rapid deployment of troops to conflict zones, and they come in two varieties: those that contain weapons stockpiles and logistical facilities (such as airstrips or port complexes), and bare-bones facilities that are assembled on an as-needed basis in response to specific crises. Staffed by "a small permanent crew of US military technicians," the first type of installation, "forward operating bases" [FOBs], typically do not house large combat units. The second type of installation, called "cooperative security locations," or the more benign, almost cute-sounding "lily pads," are run by "military contractors and host-country personnel."[25]

Geopolitical fetishism is aided by the changing status of Afghanistan in the US calculation and the Pentagon's lack of transparency over military installations. As Nick Turse explains, determining the US base count in Afghanistan has always been difficult, bedeviled by conflicting tallies, the military's shoddy accounting practices, and confusion on how to demarcate the boundaries between US facilities and ISAF ones.[26] At its highest count, in 2012, estimates of the base count in Afghanistan fluctuated from 400 to 700, depending on the calculation of the size of the facilities and amenities available for troops.[27] These facilities varied from rustic Combat Outposts, Camps, and FOBs consisting of tents in compounds made of mud and straw to mega-bases like the one at Bagram that "resemble small American towns" and house fast food franchises, including Burger King and Popeyes.[28] By 2017, the majority of these facilities had been closed, though an exact tally is hard to ascertain given the ambiguity over the definition of a base. In *Base Nation*, David Vine puts the number of US bases in Afghanistan at nine, as of 2015.[29]

Even though the US and Afghanistan signed an "Enduring Strategic Partnership Agreement" in 2012, which was to lay the groundwork for an eventual US withdrawal from Afghanistan, the US had already dedicated millions of dollars toward the construction of additional military facilities in Afghanistan and the renovation of existing ones such as Bagram Airfield. According to Air Force Lieutenant Colonel Daniel Gerdes of the US Army Corps of Engineers, these structures would be "concrete and mortar, rather than plywood and tent skins."[30] The durability of these construction materials augurs a longer-term presence of US military forces in Afghanistan than is indicated by former President Barack Obama's now past 2014 timetable for the withdrawal of US forces. Indeed, when journalist Douglas A. Wissing visited Bagram Air Field in 2013, he was puzzled by the ongoing construction at the base and a mood that he describes as "bipolar": "For a dozen years military orders have alternated between 'Don't build anything permanent; we're not going to be here long,' and 'We are going to be here a very long time, so build a fortress.'"[31]

Such contradictions plague both military policy and mainstream coverage of Afghanistan. Michael Shaw has remarked on the narrative structure of mainstream media representations of the war in Afghanistan, which he notes are "largely unironic" inversions of reality. He identifies a series of "mock" figures and scenarios that together constitute the media's construction of a "narrative of pretend" about the Iraq and Afghan wars. The visual images of the wars present, as Shaw explains, "a mock version of reality showing mock-progress, in mock-relationship with our mock-allies, by way of mock media access depicting mock front lines. . . no one is going to question these photos, or the often Grand Canyon-sized gap between pictures and reality [. . .] so long as the images make our cause *appear* just and our warriors *appear* heroic."[32]

Shaw's use of the word "mock" sublimely captures the imitative and ridiculous quality of such narratives, as well as the corporate media's contempt for the US public's ability to discern the real consequences of the conflict signaled by their use.

To Shaw's repertoire of narratives, we can add the "mock withdrawal," evidenced by the bilateral "Security and Defense Cooperation Agreement" signed by the two countries on September 30, 2014.[33] The agreement simultaneously avers "the United States does not seek permanent military facilities in Afghanistan" *and* grants the US "exclusive use" over a number of agreed upon military facilities into the future.[34] Article Seven of the agreement, "Use of Agreed Facilities and Areas," spells out the US's rights to these facilities, including "the right to undertake new construction works" by its forces or by private contractors. Subsequent articles cover "Property Ownership" (Article Eight) and "Contracting Procedures" (Article Eleven). This bilateral agreement, significantly, does not specify the permissible number of US troops who can remain in Afghanistan, nor does it name a definitive expiration date, stipulating that it "shall remain in force till the end of 2024 *and beyond*" (my emphasis).[35] New construction will be geared, most likely, toward light-footprint warfare and oriented around special operations units, which largely work in secrecy.[36] 2014 represents a mock withdrawal given the wording of this bilateral agreement that permits a US military presence in perpetuity with the added irony that the total number of US soldiers on the ground could very well decrease even as technological warfare and covert operations increase. Given the resilience of US military bases and their tendency to persist many decades after conflicts are declared over, it is worth probing the geostrategic aims of maintaining a semi-permanent military presence in Afghanistan, aims that contain geographical aspects—in other words, the logic of territoriality—but also slide into the logic of capital.

The territorial and economic logics of establishing and maintaining military bases in this embattled country, I believe, are tied to three primary American objectives. One: the US hopes to stabilize the region and check the growth of Islamic militancy in Iran, Afghanistan, and Pakistan. Two: the presence of US military bases in Afghanistan further erodes the influence of Russia in the region and curbs the potential challenge of a strong China and India. These two objectives are referenced in a recent publication by the US Army War College, "US Policy and Strategy toward Afghanistan After 2014," which identifies the need to pursue counter-terrorism measures against Al Qaeda and prevent the proliferation of weapons of mass destruction in the region, and also warns of the "emergence of a multipolar scramble for Central Asia in which all the regional powers are taking part."[37] The document is explicit about the urgency to "forestall rising peer competitors in the region," namely China, India, and Russia.[38] The third and final objective is connected to natural resources, but the details of that objective have changed over the course of seventeen years of occupation, shifting from the desire to secure access to oil and gas reserves in Central Asia to the goal of establishing *control over* access to these energy sources, particularly for rapidly growing Asian economies, and to an interest in the untapped mineral deposits in Afghanistan itself. As Harvey observes of the Middle East in an assessment that could be applied to Central Asia, "whoever controls the global oil spigot can control the global economy, at least for the near future."[39]

Global oil production and distribution have long been a consideration of US foreign policy going back to the late 1970s when President Jimmy Carter declared that the US would use "any means necessary, including military force," to ensure its access to oil reserves in the Persian Gulf, in what became known as the doctrine that bore his name.[40] The US is the largest consumer of oil and at the beginning of the twenty-first century, imported roughly half of its energy requirements. A significant portion of this oil originated in the Middle East; the region's chronic instability necessitated that the US diversify its sources of imported oil to avoid the potential interruption of oil delivery in the Gulf. It had turned its attention, consequently, to the last untapped reserves of energy in the world today in Central Asia. The Central Asian Republics of Azerbaijan, Kazakhstan, Turkmenistan, and Uzbekistan are purported to possess considerable oil and gas reserves. Because these countries are landlocked, Afghanistan became strategically important. As the US government Energy Information fact sheet on Afghanistan notes, the country's "significance from an energy standpoint stems from its geographic position as a potential transit route for oil and natural gas exports from Central Asia to the Arabian Sea. This potential includes proposed multi-billion dollar oil and gas export pipelines through Afghanistan."[41]

By 2001, successive US administrations and various corporate executives of UNOCAL (now Chevron) and CentGas (an international consortium of six corporations) had conducted on-again/off-again negotiations with Afghan officials over the construction of gas and oil pipelines. Much was made in the American left-leaning press of the ties between G.W. Bush-era officials and the oil industry, and the consensus among progressives was that the 2001 invasion of Afghanistan, along with the 2003 Iraq war, had been launched because of the desire to gain control over these natural resources.[42] One popular sign at anti-war demonstrations in the early days of both conflicts read, "How did our oil get under their soil?"[43] An American-made pipeline failed to materialize for a number of reasons outlined in audits conducted by the Special Inspector General for Afghanistan Reconstruction [SIGAR], including rampant corruption, lack of infrastructure, and a worsening security situation.[44] When Barack Obama assumed the presidency, peak oil consumption in the US, which was during the period 2001–2007, had begun to decline. Through a combination of diversifying domestic energy production such as fracking and increasing fuel efficiency standards, the Obama administration presided over a significant decrease in net foreign petroleum imports, reducing them from one half to a quarter of US energy consumption.[45] More recently, the US Energy Information Administration estimates that the US is most likely now the top producer of oil in the world, having overtaken Saudi Arabia and Russia in 2018.[46] The US's declining dependence on foreign oil probably has made a pipeline less attractive and the oil motive no longer seems a credible rationale for ongoing military engagement in the region. Nor does the US appear particularly bothered at the development of the Trans-Afghanistan Pipeline, a collaboration between Turkmenistan, Afghanistan, Pakistan, and India, which is slated for completion in 2019, in spite of the US's concern with checking peer competitors in the region.[47]

Another economic motivation inheres in the Pentagon's determination of about a trillion dollars of untapped mineral wealth in Afghanistan, including iron, copper, cobalt, and industrial metals like lithium (one Pentagon internal memo describes Afghanistan's potential to be "the Saudi Arabia of lithium," a crucial material for manufacturing batteries for laptops and smartphones).[48] While these resources were initially discovered by the Soviets in the 1980s, the US Geological Survey conducted an extensive subterranean study in 2007. The DoD's Task Force for Business and Stability Operations [TFBS] and United States Agency for International Development [USAID] were assigned the task of "developing the extractive industries of Afghanistan," investing nearly $488 million in the effort.[49] To date, this effort has not been successful for what has become a familiar litany: widespread corruption, poor infrastructure, and a precarious security situation.[50] SIGAR also flags the almost complete lack of coordination between TFBS, which closed shop in December 2014, and USAID as a factor, and it is pessimistic overall about Afghanistan's capacity to develop these resources. In spite of the bleak prognoses for developing the country's mining industries by previous US administrations, President Trump is intrigued by the money to be made from this possibility, which he has discussed with executives from American Elements, Blackwater International, and Dyncorp International.[51] It remains to be seen whether the Trump administration will attempt to develop Afghanistan's extractive industries. Given the pervasiveness of the resource curse whereby countries rich in natural resources tend to be poorer in economic growth and development and to experience a deficit in democracy, Afghanistan might benefit more in the long run if its minerals remain unmined.

From an economic perspective, one point seems notable. Just as the scramble for oil might have inspired the initial US invasion and have been the impetus to maintain hostilities through 2007, the desire to exploit mineral resources could very well have been a motive for the US's operations till April 2015, when SIGAR released its first audit of the mining industries. In this period, 2001–2015, the two logics of the new imperialism converge insofar as the territorial dimensions of intervention map on to the capitalist logic of resource exploitation, together becoming the means of accumulation by dispossession. As M. Nazif Shahrani points out, the US and its coalition partners "have empowered" jihadist and "Western-educated technocratic elites. . . who have seriously mismanaged, misappropriated, and criminalized Afghanistan's common resources—that is, pasture, water, minerals, forests, state-owned lands, and more."[52]

Oil pipelines alone after 2008 no longer present convincing economic explanations for the occupation, though the possibility of exploiting Afghanistan's mineral resources does under the Trump administration. Other financial motivations for the continuance of the war seem most evident in the US reconstruction effort, thus far, characterized by corruption, lack of oversight, and subpar workmanship, which has resulted in hazardous new highways; schools, clinics, and hospitals that are crumbling and that have not been built to withstand the chronic earthquakes in the region; and medical facilities that lack adequate clean water delivery or waste removal systems. While billions of dollars have been channeled toward Afghan reconstruction by numerous countries—the US has spent approximately $113.1 billion since 2002—most of this aid does not make it into the hands of ordinary Afghans.[53] Instead, as Fariba Nawa reveals, the US and donor countries "have a system, through world financial institutions, that treats the country like a massive money laundering machine. The money rarely leaves the countries that pledge it; USAID gives contracts to American companies (and the World Bank and IMF give contracts to companies from their donor countries) who take huge chunks off the top and hire layers and layers of subcontractors who take their cuts, leaving only enough for sub-par construction."[54]

To cite just one example of many, USAID and the Pentagon have awarded more than a few no-bid, open-ended contracts to the Louis Berger Group [LBG], a privately held, New Jersey-based engineering and consulting corporation, charged with constructing schools, medical clinics, and highways. Contracted by the UN via USAID to build the Shiberghan Highway in northern Afghanistan, LBG partnered with a Turkish firm which, in turn, hired an Afghan-American construction company for the actual construction. By construction time, the money for the highway had gushed through so many agencies and contractors that very little trickled down for high-quality building materials, and the highway started to disintegrate before it had even been completed. After all the contractors and sub-contractors had taken their cuts—varying from six to twenty percent—not much money remained for materials to build decent highways let alone to fund the annual maintenance required to keep them functioning.[55]

In Marx's account of the circulation of capital in the production process, profits from production—after the cost of inputs and labor have been subtracted—are ideally reinvested in the production process both to make it more efficient and to finance a market expansion. Capital expands in this process and ideally creates new opportunities for investment and economic growth. In Afghanistan, however, because so much of reconstruction is funneled through US and international corporations—at the expense of contracting directly with local Afghan businesses—the process of capital expansion typically associated with production has been transformed to its opposite, a capital contraction, or rather, its redistribution by the US government in another example of accumulation by dispossession. Capital aggregation occurs in the metropole in the profits of transnational corporations rather than at the site of production. Where colonial modes of accumulation derived from the extraction of raw materials from the periphery and the creation of a network of railways to facilitate resource exploitation, accumulation now occurs on the basis of the *disintegration* of the native infrastructure. Afghans, in the process, are dispossessed of the majority of aid earmarked for them, a dispossession that includes losing opportunities to create the infrastructure necessary for commodity production, a market economy, and modern relations of exchange.

Harvey links election cycles to the territorial dimensions of the new imperialism, which help explain capital contraction and the limitations of reconstruction efforts in Afghanistan. Construction of the Kabul to Kandahar Highway, along with other infrastructure projects, were rushed under pressure from the G.W. Bush and Karzai administrations to demonstrate progress in reconstruction ahead of crucial elections for both politicians. As Peggy O'Ban, a spokeswoman for USAID acknowledges, reconstruction involves "cultural and political imperatives. The quality [of a highway] may be affected if it's between one layer of asphalt or two, for example. [The Kabul to Kandahar Highway] wasn't just to build a road but to show that the transitional government can get things done. Free society is the goal."[56] The need to demonstrate progress for political purposes rather than as a commitment to improving Afghanistan's infrastructure suggests that the goal of creating the illusion of progress is more important than its actualization. To paraphrase Michael Shaw, mock reconstruction has become the occasion to trumpet mock progress in Afghanistan.[57]

As a counter to both such mock narratives and the general ignorance of the Afghan war among the public, I have attempted to historicize the conflict in terms of its territorial and economic dimensions. The mock narratives, along with other narratives about the intervention, exist at the center of geopolitical fetishism, constituting the simulacra that substitutes for political analysis in the public sphere and often becomes the basis for US policy in Afghanistan, as I show in the following chapters. These fictions, feelings, and fantasies perform a kind of reparative work. Americans do not want "to know"; we just want reassurances that we are good people and are having a positive impact on the world. Intervention narratives enable these affective delusions and foster a collective national stupidity about the impact of our actions in Afghanistan. The stories Americans tell ourselves involve projecting Afghans as brave anti-communist warriors who suffered the consequences of our disengagement with the region following the end of the Cold War and as terrorists who deserve punishment for 9/11. Intervention narratives also feature the dueling figurations of the humanist and post-humanist stories in which Afghan women need to be inducted into capitalist modernity and canines require that they be absorbed into neoliberal articulations of pet-love. Organized around these four narratives, each chapter of this book surveys a range of cultural texts to disclose how US imperialism marshals affect and sentiment into support for military intervention.

Warriors, Entrepreneurs, Canines, and Terrorists

Chapter 1, "The Premature-Withdrawal Narrative," analyzes three accounts of covert operations and Mujahideen resistance to the Soviet occupation during the 1980s: the Hollywood film, *Charlie Wilson's War* (2007); CIA agent Milton Bearden's espionage novel, *The Black Tulip* (1998); and Pakistani Brigadier Mohammad Yousaf's memoir, *Afghanistan—The Bear Trap* (1992).[58] While from different genres and national contexts, all three texts share a similar structure of feeling that posits hegemonic masculinity as the driver of history and invokes an Orientalist repertoire to represent Afghans. The achievement of the Soviet withdrawal and, by extension, the end of the Cold War is primarily credited to the actions of an American politician, a CIA operative, and the Pakistani intelligence services in each of these texts, respectively. Of these narratives, the American texts construct the liberal humanist subject as the locus of historical agency and, consequently, present covert operations as a form of humanitarianism; in the process, these fictions validate the practices and policies of Congress and the CIA.

All three of these texts are constrained by the ideological assumptions of the Cold War and the view of the USSR as the Evil Empire. In spite of their Cold War triumphalism, *Charlie Wilson's War* and *The Bear Trap* conclude by expressing dismay over the Afghan civil war that followed the Soviet withdrawal, a sentiment voiced by Milton Bearden in interviews as well. But they assign blame for the subsequent hostilities to the premature withdrawal of US engagement from the region and its unwillingness to invest in Afghan civil society at that crucial juncture. What the premature-withdrawal narrative cannot admit is the possibility that covert operations themselves were the problem, proving instrumental in the destabilization of Afghanistan.

Whereas the first chapter treats the *male* liberal humanist subject, chapter 2, "The Capitalist-Rescue Narrative: Afghan Women and Micro-Entrepreneurship," turns to its *female* counterpart in a reading of two mainstream American feminists' accounts of Afghan women and their empowerment: Gayle Tzemach Lemmon's *The Dressmaker of Khair Khana* (2011) and Deborah Rodriguez's *Kabul Beauty School* (2007).[59] Following 9/11, the post-colonial, academic feminist analysis of the US intervention in Afghanistan as an updated version of Gayatri Chakravorty Spivak's formulation of nineteenth-century British imperialism of "white men saving brown women from brown men" became ubiquitous. The popularity of Spivak's analysis coincided with the coming-of-age of Third Wave feminism and its insistence on intersectionality and the demand that the category of "women" be expanded to include women of color, plural gender and sexual identities, and the poor. Against this conjoining of feminist concerns, many US feminists roundly condemned, in the terms set by Spivak, the Bush administration's retaliatory air campaign against Afghanistan and criticized women's organizations such as the Feminist Majority Fund for condoning the US attacks in the name of gender liberation.[60]

These feminist debates have filtered into the public sphere with the result that some mainstream feminists have learned the lesson that Afghan women are not passive victims of native patriarchy in need of saving by Westerners. Indeed, mainstream American feminists are at pains to demonstrate Afghan women's agency and their self-empowerment in their non-fictional accounts of women's entrepreneurship. The agent of empowerment in these biographies of individuals and enterprises is American-style capitalism with its attendant production arrangements and consumer practices. By mapping Fordist modes-of-production onto a home tailoring business, Lemmon's *The Dressmaker of Khair Khana* represents women's clandestine entrepreneurship during the Taliban regime; Rodriguez's *Kabul Beauty School* describes training Afghan beauticians in the aftermath of the US invasion and inculcating them into the consumption of American beauty products and techniques.

Both texts rest on the assumption that Afghan women's entry into modernity requires their embrace of US-style capitalism, which will eventually lead to Afghanistan's integration into the global economy and Afghan women's employment in the NGO sector. Insofar as the US invasion and occupation provide the conditions of possibility for this capitalist teleology of gender progress, such accounts provide a legitimization of imperialism. Through a critical reading of these works, I show how they, in effect, posit the emergence of Afghan women as a new quasi-comprador class. In the capitalist rescue narrative, the female liberal humanist subject melds with the neoliberal one: contemporary US imperialism gives birth to new subjectivities that bear a remarkable resemblance to the old ones. That is to say, the emphasis on agency in the liberal humanist conception of the subject finds expression in the entrepreneurial self at the heart of neoliberalism.

In chapter 3, "The Canine Rescue Narrative," I shift from the previous chapter's emphasis on elaborating the *agent* of rescue to focusing on an *object* of rescue: dogs. Over the last decade, a new genre of memoir has emerged that represents the relationship between US soldiers and Marines in Afghanistan and Iraq and their dogs. Two variations characterize this genre of life writing: one narrates the rescue of a stray native dog and the other recounts the challenges of safeguarding a loyal "American" Military Working Dog [MWD] through his or her tour of duty. This chapter reads an example of each subgenre, along with a novel based on a narrative film: Christine Sullivan's *Saving Cinnamon: The Amazing True Story of a Missing Military Puppy and the Desperate Mission to Bring Her Home* (2009), Maria Goodavage's *Top Dog: The Story of Marine Hero Lucca* (2015), and Jennifer Li Shotz's novel, *Max: Best Friend, Hero, Marine* (2015).[61] Examining the mechanisms by which these texts solicit a sentimental identification with their canine subjects, I argue that canine rescue functions as a post-humanist articulation of humanitarianism in order to present a kinder, gentler side of the US intervention.

The rendering of dogs as highly visible tropes for objects of US humanitarianism is informed by two parallel processes: the humanization of dogs in the US toward the end of the twentieth century and the invisibility, in the public sphere, of Afghan civilians in the twenty-first century. Largely intertwined with late capitalism, canine personhood in the US has been materialized in consumer culture through the creation of a panoply of pet products and services oriented toward canine care. Dogs have become what Lauren Berlant describes as "infantile citizens," enabling a sentimental understanding of war and feel-good endings of a military intervention that has wrought death and destruction in Iraq and Afghanistan.[62] Like the capitalist rescue narrative, the canine rescue narrative is also structured as a teleology where the end goals are the dog's return to the home front, integration into the American family, and investiture of US citizenship, all, of course, with references to manifest destiny and pet exceptionalism overlaid with Christian piety.

I supplement my analysis of the memoirs *Saving Cinnamon* and *Top Dog* with an interpretation of the novel *Max*, a narrative that shares many of the clichéd conventions of American family life that infuse the other texts. At the same time, however, the novel, and the film on which it is based, provide a critique of the Global War on Terror by demonstrating how the violence of the battlefront eventually heads home. *Max* also exposes one aspect of the political economy of the US military intervention by representing the illicit transnational trade in small arms and drugs, an unintended consequence of the war, to be sure, but one that is a salient characteristic of imperialism and late twentieth-century American wars.

In contrast to the other chapters' analyses of sympathetic characters (brave warriors, entrepreneurial women, and heart-warming canines), chapter 4, "The

Retributive-Justice Narrative," examines representations of Osama bin Laden, whom I read as a displacement for Afghans, following the logic of the US government when it invaded Afghanistan to punish him for the 9/11 attacks. Retributive justice, the idea that some crimes are so heinous as to require "proportionate punishment" by a "legitimate" agent of the state, was a leitmotif among politicians and media pundits in the US following the 9/11 attacks. I trace this theme in President George W. Bush's speeches, alongside Osama bin Laden's justifications for terrorist acts against the US. For bin Laden, the US's history of military violence, its unconditional support for the Israeli Occupation, and its alliances with countries engaged in oppressing Muslims legitimized "reciprocal violence" against it. Both Bush and bin Laden relied on a similar logic of reciprocity and violent punishment of which the best outcome could only be the establishment of a terrible, bloody equilibrium. Such a logic suggests similarities and synergy between terrorism and war.

The chapter then turns to Mark Owen's memoir, *No Easy Day: The First-hand Account of the Mission that Killed Osama bin Laden* (2012).[63] A member of the SEAL team that assassinated bin Laden in 2011, Owen articulates retributive justice with techno-military masculinity. I analyze the gendered and raced aspects of this subjectivity in conjunction with its reliance on technological prostheses such as surveillance equipment and sophisticated weaponry. A crucial aspect of techno-military masculinity is its simultaneous invocation of retributive justice and its contempt for the rule of law as evidenced by the extrajudicial killing of bin Laden. The post-publication history of the memoir that involves bickering among SEAL Team Six members over the credit for firing the fatal bullet demonstrates the fragility of the combat community asserted in Owen's account.

The rhetoric of retributive justice and the Global War on Terror, more generally, is exposed as a "fiction" in Abhishek Sharma's Indian independent film *Tere Bin Laden* (2010).[64] A Bollywood-style comedy, the plot involves a second-rate Pakistani journalist staging fake footage of Osama bin Laden as a way to generate income and to finance his immigration to the US. The film features collusion among the ISI, CIA, and segments of Pakistani civil society in the creation of videos purporting to be from bin Laden, thus riffing on rumors that circulated in many parts of the world that the US government had faked footage of bin Laden in order to justify bombing Afghanistan. The screenplay draws on bin Laden's actual speeches to highlight convergences between the Global War on Terror and terrorism, showing how war generates its own momentum. *Tere bin Laden* ends on a hopeful premise: the "fiction" of the Global War on Terror, embodied in fake bin Laden tapes, can be rewritten to bring this conflict to a close.

While it is beyond the scope of this book to contextualize contemporary US ideology within the long arc of US imperialism, readers will recognize continuities with and differences from older American imperial cultural forms. Imperialism has long been an integral aspect of the American experience; the US has its origins in settler colonialism and the extermination of natives to facilitate westward expansion, augmented later with the acquisition of territory in the Pacific, wars waged in Asia, and covert operations in support of repressive, pro-capitalist governments in other parts of the world. As Tom Engelhardt notes, the essential narrative elements of the "American war story" derive from the originary violence of settler colonialism: the plot generally coheres around numerically disadvantaged white settlers who must defend themselves against attack from "Indians."[65] In this plot, the colonial subject is never the aggressor and is always the aggrieved victim of violence from racialized others. The brutality of colonial conquest thus becomes coded as a necessary and justified response, a legitimate form of self-defense, to savagery projected onto the dispossessed.

This basic plot animates the mainstream media coverage and political speeches that accompanied the initial US bombing of Afghanistan in 2001: Arab terrorists had attacked the US, killing a large number of people, necessitating a military response against Afghans for harboring the mastermind of the operation. Never mind that Afghans were not Arabs; the epidermal similarity of brown skin would provide a sufficient alibi for military action. The unleashing of lethal firepower constituted retributive justice for the 9/11 attacks, according to this narrative logic. Indeed, the vocabulary of the frontier and Indian Wars surfaced then as well, as they did in the 2003 invasion of Iraq. Engelhardt observes that George W. Bush's pronouncements on the Global War on Terror invoked references to the "triumphalist frontier mythology" screened in the John Wayne movies of his youth.[66] The resilience of settler colonial violence is also signaled by the naming of bin Laden "Geronimo" by the SEAL team sent to assassinate him.

Ashley Dawson and Malini Johar Schueller point out that "contemporary US imperialism can be understood only through the conjuncture of the specific imperial politics of the present and the various political, religious, racial, and economic practices and rhetoric that have contributed to imperial culture in the past."[67] A belief in American exceptionalism, they emphasize, constitutes a stable ideological element from past to present and explains the widespread, if naïve and uninformed, view that the US has been and will be the beacon of freedom for the world.[68] A version of American exceptionalism acts as the palimpsest for gunboat democracy, underwriting attempts at nation-building in Iraq and Afghanistan. Several other aspects of earlier imperial ideology make appearances in the intervention narratives I analyze, namely, articulations of hegemonic masculinity and the fetishization of technological warfare, both of which figured in the discourse of the Vietnam War and are present in the Iraq War as well.

But there are likewise subtle differences between imperial ideology then and now that can be attributed to the neoliberal, post-Civil Rights context of the US intervention in Afghanistan. The intensification of consumption for pets under neoliberalism has contributed to canine personhood, resulting in an updated version of the captivity narrative of yore: native dogs have displaced white women as abject objects in need of rescue. And after the gains of second-wave feminism, white women have emerged as new imperial subjects, not only becoming eligible to serve in combat, but becoming civilian agents of rescue of Afghan women by introducing them to the joys of entrepreneurship. While the post-humanist humanitarianism of the canine rescue narrative also occurs in Iraq, I have not found versions of the capitalist rescue narrative there. It may be that the relatively high status of Iraqi women prior to the Gulf War in 1991 foreclosed the possibility of this narrative, which was more easily imposed on Afghan women who had endured repression under the Taliban. In addition, the UN's twenty years of brutal economic sanctions on Iraq, lifted only in 2010, made it highly unlikely that American women could initiate capitalist uplift projects for Iraqi women. The expansion of imperial ideology to incorporate these new narrative forms attests to its capacity to adapt to changing historical circumstances.

Part of this ideological adaptability is evident in the differential interpellation of imperial citizens. Imperial culture, as Melani McAlister demonstrates, hails citizens in different ways that are grounded in their political, racial, and religious identifications.[69] The clarion call for contemporary US imperialism contains themes that resonate with dominant ideological strands in US culture: belief in the power of individual agency, affirmations of entrepreneurship, pet love, and vigilantism. These themes play well to different constituencies across the political landscape. Appealing to liberals is the centrality of the liberal humanist subject in both the premature withdrawal and capitalist rescue narratives. As chapter 1 explicates, the de-Republicanization of the Cold War in *Charlie Wilson's War*—and publicity interviews for the film by Tom Hanks, Mike Nichols, and Julia Roberts about the power of individuals to affect change—ventriloquized 2007 presidential campaign rhetoric that resonates with liberals and Democrats.

Afghan women's self-empowerment through capitalism, the subject of chapter 2, has a receptive audience among a broad group: feminists, liberals, and free-market fundamentalists. Feminists and liberals will be cheered by this inspiring narrative confirmation of the power of individuals to scale the economic ladder provided that they are given the opportunity. Free-market fundamentalists can applaud the articulation of faith and entrepreneurship, which showcases the capacity of capitalism to reward hard work, thus demonstrating the essential morality of markets. In contrast, the muscular idiom of militarism and targeted assassination that I treat in chapter 4 is alluring to Republicans and the hard-core right, who tend to support violent responses to political violence and to subscribe to Islamophobia.

As for the puppies and military working dogs, the subject of chapter 3, their appeal in the US transcends domestic politics and party affiliations, as demonstrated by the 2016 presidential election. A television spot during the election season, "A vote for good," featured voters affirming the universality of canine love. "I love that apparently when it comes to dogs, there's no political party," says a bemused Hillary Clinton supporter while a Donald J. Trump supporter emphatically states, "We have our differences but everyone loves dogs."[70] For many Americans, as chapter 3 contends, canine lives matter in a way that human lives, particularly of the black, brown, and foreign kind, do not.

I have argued that the ideological work of these four intervention narratives is reparative and aimed at generating positive feelings about the Afghan war. Telling ourselves that we supported the "good guys" against evil communists, we inspired Afghan women to become entrepreneurs, we rescued adorable dogs, and we eliminated the "bad guys" contributes to the fantasy that we are on the right side of history. The resilience of intervention narratives and their appeal to Americans across the ideological spectrum require a more honest and sober appraisal of our military campaign and geostrategic motivations in the region—and the actual toll of US intervention in creating misery. In the meantime, casualties on all sides continue to mount.

Chapter 1

The Premature-Withdrawal Narrative
● ●
Hegemonic Masculinities and the Liberal Humanist Subject

Introduction

The George W. Bush administration's refusal to recognize the historic role of United States foreign policy in the emergence of terrorism helps explain the liberal-left counter-narrative of the war in Afghanistan. Thematically concerned with "blowback," the premature-withdrawal narrative attempts to contextualize the 2001 US intervention in terms of Cold War policy and the emergence of a global jihad in the 1980s. The Central Intelligence Agency [CIA] uses the term "blowback" to signify the unintended and violent consequences of covert operations that are visited on the civilian population of the metropole. As Chalmers Johnson elucidates, "the concept 'blowback' does not just mean retaliation for things our government has done to and in foreign countries. It refers to retaliation for the numerous illegal operations we have carried out abroad that were kept totally secret from the American public. This means that when the retaliation comes—as it did so spectacularly on September 11, 2001—the American public is unable to put the events in context."[1] The public consequently supports "acts intended to lash out against the perpetrators, thereby most commonly preparing the ground for yet another cycle of blowback."[2] In the left-liberal counter-narrative of the war, the 9/11 attacks are blowback from US covert operations in Afghanistan and Pakistan during the Cold War, a massive effort to arm and supply the Mujahideen in their campaign against the Soviet Occupation.

Blowback serves as the palimpsest for the premature-withdrawal narrative and its explanation of the historical causality of modern-day terrorism. The premature-withdrawal narrative diagnoses the current problem of Islamic terrorism as due to the US's hasty and ill-considered disengagement from Afghanistan following the defeat of the Soviet Union. The distinguishing characteristic of this genre consists of its tripartite narrative sequence: insurgency-triumphalism-prognostication. Representations of Afghan insurgency constitute the longest segment of this narrative and become the staging ground to showcase different forms of masculinity. Triumphalism at the Soviet withdrawal is followed by dire prognostications of future violence, which anticipate the terrorism to come and Afghanistan's status as a failed state. My concern in this chapter is to analyze three very different premature-withdrawal narratives to consider how the continuities in narrative structure nevertheless yield contradictory understandings of agency and geopolitics, which is to say that each narrative invests particular agents of the state (American, Pakistani, and Russian) with the power to alter history. In spite of competing versions of agency, however, all three of the premature-withdrawal narratives share an ideological cohesion in their implacable opposition to communism.

Commenting on the "representational features of the Vietnam War," Susan Jeffords astutely notes that they "are structurally written through relations of gender, relations designed primarily to reinforce interests of masculinity and patriarchy."[3] Jeffords's insights regarding the structuring of representations of the Vietnam War through gender resonate for Afghanistan as well. The Hollywood film *Charlie Wilson's War* and former CIA agent Milton Bearden's novel *The Black Tulip* present two of the three premature-withdrawal narratives that are the focus of this chapter; they promote different versions of hegemonic masculinity that not only reinforce patriarchy but also affirm capitalist ideology and American geopolitical supremacy.[4] My use of the term "hegemonic masculinity" draws on R.W. Connell and James W. Messerschmidt's contention that a particular version of masculinity becomes normative as a cultural ideal, requiring "all other men to position themselves in relation to it."[5] Within a patriarchal gender regime, hegemonic masculinity presumes the existence of multiple subordinated masculinities, whose secondary status derives in part from their association with culturally derived forms of "femininity" that both cause subordination and become its consequence.

In *Charlie Wilson's War* and *The Black Tulip*, hegemonic masculinity assumes the racialized form of elite white males engaged in clandestine activities on behalf of the US state: a member of Congress, who channels money and munitions to the Afghan insurgency, and a CIA operative, who provides them with combat support. Hegemonic masculinity is constituted by the protagonists' proximity to state power by virtue of their professions and their racial difference from African Americans, Asians, Russians, and Afghans. Condescending and

Orientalist representations of racial and national difference shore up white hegemonic masculinity. This instantiation of the premature-withdrawal narrative articulates hegemonic masculinity with the liberal humanist subject as the primary driver of historical change. Both texts figure covert operations as a vehicle to save women and children, in other words, a type of civilian rescue. Covert operations, in effect, become a form of humanitarianism in response to the brutality of the USSR.

The third premature-withdrawal narrative that I analyze in this chapter, Brigadier Mohammad Yousaf's memoir *Afghanistan—The Bear Trap*, offers a version of hegemonic masculinity associated with the elite corporatized body of the Pakistani Inter-Services Intelligence [ISI], which is asserted against the subordinated masculinities of Afghan insurgents, Russian soldiers, and American CIA operatives. I have found it illuminating to analyze a Pakistani memoir alongside the American narratives for several reasons. First, many journalistic accounts of the Mujahideen rely on *The Bear Trap* as a primary and transparent source on the resistance to the Soviets without probing its problematic assumptions about Afghans, which emanate from a distinctly South Asian context and are holdovers of the colonial theory of the martial races. Second, the American narratives present the CIA as a competent body, which Yousaf's account casts in doubt, raising basic questions seldom asked in American public discourse about the value of the agency, given its failure to anticipate the Soviet withdrawal and the impending dissolution of the USSR. Third, Pakistan's close but contentious relationship with the US makes it prudent to examine perspectives aligned with its military branches, which are largely running the state.

The juxtaposition of *The Bear Trap, Charlie Wilson's War,* and *The Black Tulip* suggests that geopolitical conflicts are simultaneously contestations about gender, consisting of a competition among multiple masculine subjects to establish their sovereignty over territory and social relations. While different versions of hegemonic masculinity populate these texts, all three depict Afghan men as being pre-modern warriors with little capability to lead the struggle against the Soviet Occupation. Thus, Afghan men function as minor and supporting characters, if they play a role at all, in their historical drama. In the premature-withdrawal narrative, subordinate Afghan masculinity takes a backseat to hegemonic American and Pakistani masculinities.

The power of the premature-withdrawal narrative resides in its ongoing resilience as an explanation for the existence of Al Qaeda, offshoots of Islamic State and the Taliban, and as a policy directive for the US government to attend to unfinished business in the aftermath of the Soviet withdrawal by winning the hearts and minds of Afghans. Even as the US government attempts to build the institutions of civil society, the American military is conducting a counterinsurgency campaign against those groups that challenge its occupation— and in the process, blurring the lines between development and militarism.

Seventeen years into the current US occupation and with over $900 billion spent in military training and reconstruction, Afghanistan remains a failed state. New policies are clearly in order.

Charlie Wilson and Hegemonic Masculinity

Based on George Crile's 2003 eponymous book, the Hollywood blockbuster *Charlie Wilson's War* charts the congressman's conversion to the Mujahideen cause and his clandestine efforts on its behalf. Wilson threw himself into the campaign motivated by his hatred of the Soviets and a desire to avenge the Vietnam War. As he explained in *The Washington Post*, "There were 58,000 dead in Vietnam and we owe the Russians one . . . I have a slight obsession with it, because of Vietnam. I thought the Soviets ought to get a dose of it. . . ."[6] In his desire to draw the rival superpower into a Vietnam-like quagmire, Wilson was not alone. US policy was initially geared toward this end; the government covertly routed antiquated World War I weapons and a five million dollar appropriation—considered a pittance for this kind of operation—to the Mujahideen, outsourcing these support services to Pakistan's ISI. Over time in his capacity as a member of the Defense Appropriations subcommittee, Wilson increased congressional funding for covert activities in Afghanistan to one billion dollars, matched in kind by Saudi Arabia. The massive increase in appropriations, which among other things enabled the purchase of a range of sophisticated weapons, including Stinger missiles, helped turn the military tide in favor of the Mujahideen. On February 15, 1989, the last Soviet troops withdrew from Afghanistan.[7]

References to the US "defeat" in Vietnam periodically appear in mass culture, generally in relation to other armed conflicts. Indications of a close association between masculinity and militarism surface in invocations of the Vietnam Syndrome. Wilson's admission of Vietnam as a motivating factor, along with George H. Bush's February 1991 declaration that "we've kicked the Vietnam Syndrome once and for all" to prematurely signal the end of the Iraq War, hint at a national injury experienced as an affront to American masculinity that can only be cured by unleashing lethal military power on other countries.[8] *Charlie Wilson's War* subscribes to this patriarchal equation, showing how the success of the Afghan insurgency depends on a version of hegemonic masculinity embodied by Representative Charlie Wilson.

In one sense, the film's representation of Wilson casts him in the idiom of conventional masculinity. A number of scholars have pointed out that masculinity is a performance, constituted through quotidian acts that gain their power through repetition.[9] As the vocabulary of performance indicates, such "signifying practices" require "props" and standard scripts that conform to normative gendered behavior. The performance of masculinity also evokes the necessity of having an "audience"—others who recognize and affirm this identity through their interactions.[10] In the film, many of these interactions are heterosexual. Scene after scene features flirtation and seduction; young, attractive women—Wilson's legislative aides and lovers—serve as props to signify his masculinity, which stands in stark contrast to Wilson's co-conspirator, CIA operative Gust Avrakotos, who has no luck with the ladies. More significant than this conventional register of heterosexuality, American masculinity requires demonstrating the capacity "to make things happen" and to "exert control" over others.[11] Wilson's masculinity is of the hegemonic variety insofar as his wheeling and dealing in Congress and his ability to close transnational weapons sales evidence his power. His status as a member of Congress and his ability to surreptitiously channel money to the insurgency (in other words, his control over capital) are key elements informing the film's gloss on hegemonic masculinity.

Tom Hanks portrays a sanitized version of the film's central character, Democratic Congressman Charlie Wilson. Prior to representing the Texas 2nd District in the US House, Wilson served in the state legislature for twelve years, where his support of the Equal Rights Amendment, reproductive choice, Medicaid, and the regulation of utilities, among other positions, earned him the moniker of "the liberal from Lufkin" (Crile 28). But he was also a firm believer in Second Amendment rights and an anti-communist ideologue. His nickname changed during his tenure in the House of Representatives to "Good Time Charlie" for his insatiable appetite for women and whiskey, which resulted in a messy personal life that involved simultaneous relationships with several women and at least one DUI and a hit-and-run accident for which he was never convicted. These uncomfortable details appear nowhere in the film.

Instead, the film's version of Wilson's character presents him as a hard-drinking and fun-loving but essentially decent man who lacks the odor of insincerity and hypocrisy wafting from many US politicians. *Charlie Wilson's War* cleverly codes his womanizing as a deliberate performance to provide cover for his clandestine activities. Apart from an early scene in a Vegas hot tub surrounded by strippers—and here too, Wilson is more riveted by *60 Minutes* footage of Dan Rather interviewing Mujahideen than by his beautiful companions—the film implies that once Joanne Herring enters his life and his bed, his womanizing comes to an end. In actuality, the real Charlie Wilson was very much a ladies' man and seemed incapable of living without female companionship. While on an early visit to Islamabad, he "had vowed never to return to Pakistan without an American girl in tow" and, even during his short-lived wedding engagement to Herring, he was accompanied on his various trips to South Asia by women who were belly dancers or beauty queens with titles such as "Miss Sea and Ski," "Miss Northern Hemisphere," and "Miss Humble Oil," and colorful nicknames such as "Snowflake," "Firecracker," and "Sweetums" (Crile 138).[12]

These absences in the film are significant insofar as they contribute to the impression that Wilson is playing the part of a playboy and that his surface propensity for women and whiskey masks a deeper commitment to hard work, grasp of geopolitics, and humanitarian impulses. The film establishes Wilson's benevolent credentials by first constructing the Soviet invasion of Afghanistan as a humanitarian crisis. On a visit to Pakistan, urged by Herring, Wilson confronts the anger of two of Zia's aides, Brigadier Rashid and Colonel Mahmood, who are furious with the United States for providing inadequate military assistance to fight the Soviets. They frame their outrage over the paltry CIA appropriations for Afghanistan and the failure of the Americans to sell radars for F-16s to Pakistan by emphasizing the sheer magnitude of the Afghan refugee crisis. An angry Rashid lashes out at Wilson, "Three million Afghan refugees are living like poorly treated livestock. Another two million have fled to Iran." (Mahmood interjects, "And two million more angry men is just what the doctors ordered for Iran, don't you think?") "People are dying by the tens of thousands. And the ones that aren't are crossing into Pakistan every day. . . One fifth of Afghanistan now lives in Pakistan's North-West Frontier Province." President Zia, who is represented as an elderly statesman rather than a tyrannical dictator, is left to smooth things over in this awkward encounter, which is accomplished by his managing to persuade Wilson to visit the Afghan refugee camp in Peshawar.

The next scene opens with Wilson and his aide touring the refugee camp and hearing stories of Soviet atrocities. The scene intersperses reverse angle shots between Wilson and different Afghan refugees who recount the targeting and brutalization of civilians, particularly children. Tales of Russian soldiers slitting the throats of children, bulldozing army defectors with tanks, and disguising land mines as toys and candy horrify him.[13] But Wilson is clearly most moved by the injured children, whose facial scars and missing limbs testify to Soviet savagery. The final minutes of the scene feature Wilson on a hill, and through a point-of-view shot we see him watching a woman weeping over a grave. He then turns around, and the camera zooms out in another point-of-view shot from Wilson's perspective, showing the immensity of the refugee crisis; the camp extends as far as the eye can see. In the following scene, an impatient Wilson badgers Howard Hart, the CIA's chief of station in Pakistan, who is portrayed as overly cautious and insufficiently committed to the Afghan cause. "Have you been to these refugee camps?" Wilson irately asks him, "Have you heard these stories?" The encounter with Afghan refugees, particularly the maimed children and sorrowful women, functions as a conversion experience of sorts for Wilson, whose involvement with the guerrillas deepens from this point and acquires a humanitarian sheen. The provision of logistical support to brave Mujahideen fighters is no longer his sole motive for aiding the insurgency. Rather, Wilson's actions are driven by the desire to save Afghan women and children. At the ideological level, the premature-withdrawal narrative merges here with the rescue narrative to justify covert operations.

Covert Operations as Democratic Practice

Wilson's covert operations are also implicitly presented in the guise of democracy through the film's sequencing of scenes and the shift from the Afghan refugee camp to the CIA offices in Pakistan and then to the plane ride back to the US. Immediately after his tense interaction with Hart, while aloft in the aircraft, the Congressman describes his entry into politics to his aide; he attributes his political consciousness to a childhood trauma involving the death of his beloved canine, Teddy. Wilson's neighbor and city council member Charles Hazard ground up glass and fed it to Teddy in order to eliminate the dog's forays into his flower garden. In revenge for Teddy's excruciatingly painful death, the thirteen-year-old Wilson, using his farm vehicle operator's license, shuttled carloads of African American voters to the polls, telling them, "I don't mean to influence you, but I think you should know Mr. Charles Hazard has intentionally killed my dog." Hazard lost the election by sixteen votes. Wilson reminisces, "About 400 ballots were cast in that election. I drove ninety-six of them to the polls. . . And that's the day I fell in love with America."

This revelation establishes Wilson's conviction that Americans, when confronted with acts of cruelty, will side with the victims of violence rather than with the social elites who perpetrate them. It also aligns him with subaltern minorities by showing his willingness to drive African American voters to the polls, thereby increasing this politically underrepresented group's participation in the electoral process. In this sentimental tale, mainstream electoral politics becomes the means to right wrongs committed against the least powerful: pets, whose symbolic valence as family members I treat in chapter 3, and children. At the same time, the anecdote reveals two aspects of Wilson's character that resonate with his later covert activities: first, that the desire for revenge is a prime motivation for his actions, inspiring him as a child to punish Hazard for the murder of his pet and as an adult to finance a secret war to exact revenge on the Soviets for Vietnam; and second, the use of the farm vehicle operator's license by the thirteen-year-old Wilson, in the context of increasing the electoral participation of a targeted demographic, violates the spirit of the law if not its letter.

This incident has acquired its own biographical momentum, appearing in Crile's text, The History Channel's documentary *The True Story of Charlie Wilson*, and even the *New York Times* obituary of Wilson. Crile recounts the incident in some detail, significantly following it with a paragraph on Wilson's solidifying conviction of the righteousness of the Mujahideen cause.

> Thirty-six years later, something about the mujahideen's appeal to stop the Soviet gunships brought back memories of his dog. "I started to think to myself: Where are all the congressmen who are always talking about humanitarian aid, and the human-rights activists? Where are they now?" In the fall of 1982, the mujahideen had no congressional champions. In fact, they had no one in position of power who believed that they had a chance for victory. Wilson had no logical reason to believe that he could help these tribesmen fight a ruthless superpower. But he felt the same rush of anger and clarity that had made it possible for a thirteen-yearold boy to bring down his dog's murderer. Surrounded by these determined men, Wilson saw a path to honor, if not victory. "It began to dawn on me right then and there that I didn't know what was going to happen, but with my rage and their courage I knew we were going to kill some Russians." (112)

Elsewhere in the same chapter, Crile claims that "Wilson's whole sense of himself rested on his self-image as a champion of the underdog" (110). The recounting of the origins of Wilson's political consciousness thus creates a chain of signifiers that link "underdogs" to the murdered pet dog "Teddy" to the "Mujahideen." The film's sequencing of scenes from the Afghan refugee camp to the CIA office in Pakistan to Wilson's trip down memory lane in the plane correspondingly weaves a web of signification that includes the Afghan refugee crisis, covert operations, and democratic processes. The net effect of this sequence is to imply that a democratic response to the humanitarian refugee crisis necessitates covert operations.

The film's construction of Wilson as a humanitarian at heart plays off the tension between surface and depth. While on the surface, the Texas representative is "Good Time Charlie," we see the depth and complexity of his personality, witnessing his seriousness of purpose and earnestness in supporting what he perceives as a just cause as he exploits his congressional authority to negotiate arms deals between states outside officially sanctioned channels. Indeed, Avrakotos, Wilson's CIA conspirator, remarks on the fortuitousness of Charlie's playboy reputation, which provides a perfect cover for their clandestine activities. As Wilson and Avrakotos attempt to persuade Zvi Rafiah, a former Israeli diplomat and arms dealer to collaborate with Egypt to ship weapons to the Mujahideen, the CIA agent assures Rafiah that Wilson's $35.5 million appropriation for the weapons will not result in any awkward questions from the press. Rather the media will be fixated on rumors of Wilson's cocaine use and weekend flings with strippers. "The press is going to be busy asking about a weekend in Vegas," Avrakotos explains. "As long as the press sees sex and drugs behind the left hand, you can park a battle carrier behind the right hand and no one's gonna fucking notice." In his biography of Wilson, Crile reveals how the Representative's Dionysian activities on the eve of an important trip to Afghanistan with a congressional delegation resulted in a hit-and-run accident and Wilson's fleeing the scene, behavior that almost jeopardized the mission. A technicality over the jurisdiction of the accident and the quick intervention of Wilson's very competent staff enabled him to elude arrest and make his flight with the delegation (185). The film, however, presents Wilson's addictions to alcohol and women not as a liability but as an asset and the ideal disguise for covert operations. It is as if masculinity-as-performance, for Wilson, becomes a performance of masculinity as a diversionary tactic to achieve humanitarian ends by deflecting media attention from his nefarious weapons deals.

Surface and Depth: Public Diplomacy and Covert Operations

The play between surface and depth informs the very nature of covert operations. Formed in 1947, the Central Intelligence Agency expanded its activities from conducting propaganda and covert political campaigns such as influencing the outcome of elections abroad to engaging in economic and paramilitary operations.[14] Primarily oriented toward checking the growth of communism—even when it emerged organically in different contexts—the CIA's authority to intervene was sanctioned by the National Security Council [NSC] in 1948 in a document NSC 10/2, which outlined measures to contain the influence of the Soviet Union: "Propaganda, economic warfare; preventive direct action, including sabotage, anti-sabotage, demolition and evacuation measures; subversion against hostile states, including assistance to underground resistance movements, guerrillas and refugee liberation groups, and support of indigenous anti-communist elements."[15] NSC 10/2 was crafted to insure plausible deniability for the US government. Covert operations, in other words, were to provide a "third option" between diplomacy and open warfare. President Reagan's innovation, as Loch K. Johnson notes, was to place "responsibility for key covert action operations in the hands of NSC staffers in the White House, outside normal procedures, and. . . to raise funds from private Americans and foreign heads-of-state for further 'off-the-shelf, self-sustaining, stand-alone' secret operations."[16] Such measures created a gap between surface diplomacy and the depth of US geopolitical machinations through its covert operations.

Covert operations depend on the creation and maintenance of secrecy, a secrecy which *Charlie Wilson's War* and the film's actors take for granted.[17] In the roughly two decades between the sharp escalation of US covert operations in Afghanistan in 1985 and the film's release in 2007—given the tabloidization of mainstream news and the American public's unfortunate tendency toward historical amnesia—this assumption is understandable, if not naive. However, the premise of secrecy does not stand up to historical scrutiny of public discourse about covert operations during the 1980s, when such operations attracted a great deal of attention because of the Iran-Contra scandal. The morality of covert operations was debated in Congress, analyzed in academic writing, and referenced in the mainstream media. While much of the public discourse about covert operations coalesced around the extent of the involvement of William Casey, the CIA, and National Security Agency staff such as Lieutenant Colonel Oliver North in destabilizing the Sandinistas and negotiating secret arms deals with Iran for the release of American hostages in Lebanon, the Iran-Contra debacle only constituted one of about forty or so covert actions during the mid-1980s. Writing in 1987, Gregory F. Treverton, who served on the Church Committee in 1975-1976 and on Carter's National Security Council, asserts that "at least half [of these covert actions] have been the subject of some press account."[18] He elaborates, "Yet only a few were controversial enough so that the first leaks became continuing stories. Most of the others were open secrets, more unacknowledged than unknown; they were that because most members of Congress thought they made sense, as did most Americans who knew or thought about them—and, no doubt, most of the journalists who reported them."[19] Treverton, in effect, acknowledges an ideological consensus about the righteousness of covert operations among government officials, journalists, and the news-reading public, the social segments that are important constituents of the professional-managerial class.

The CIA's destabilization of Nicaragua and support for the Salvadoran military in the 1980s resulted in the founding of US grassroots organizations in solidarity with the Sandinistas and Farabundo Martí National Liberation Front, such as the Central American Peace Initiative and the Committee in Solidarity with the Peoples of El Salvador. However, no comparable groups emerged to challenge US covert operations in Afghanistan.[20] One consequence of this absence was that there was almost universal support for the Mujahideen—in contrast to the CIA's activities in Central America, which were debated robustly and to some extent reined in because of public pressure. In Afghanistan, Treverton reports, "The secret was open; the American role was not so much covert as, by tacit agreement, unacknowledged."[21] Indeed, Crile describes how Wilson exploited his Democratic congressional colleagues' skittishness over the public reaction to the CIA's covert operations in Nicaragua to lobby additional support for the Mujahideen by arguing that the Afghan struggle enabled them to prove they were tough on communism (167).

In spite of the general consensus in the US regarding the legitimacy of aid to Afghan insurgents, the CIA and Reagan administration maintained the facade of non-involvement, primarily to avoid triggering an outright conflict with the Soviets and to protect Pakistan, which was the conduit for the delivery of money, mules, and munitions, from a retaliatory attack from the Soviets as well. Initially, the desire to maintain deniability took the form of insuring that only Soviet-made weapons reached the Mujahideen. As Avrakotos explains to Wilson in the film, "When an Afghan freedom fighter gets captured, it can't be with an American-made weapon on him. That's how a cold war turns into an actual war, and that's something you want to keep a good eye on. So anything that we give them has to look like it could have plausibly been captured from the Soviets." To this end, he and Wilson broker an arms deal among Israel, Egypt, and Pakistan—two states which did not recognize Israel's right to exist at the time.[22]

Charlie Wilson's War acknowledges but does not dwell on the question of the legality of the congressman's wheeling and dealing with the Israelis, Egyptians, and Pakistanis. In one scene, Zia asks Wilson if he has the "authority" to buy Israeli weapons and channel them to the Mujahideen via Pakistan. Wilson replies, "None whatsoever. In fact, I'm pretty close to violating the Logan Act." Zia's response to Wilson ("Well, I don't know what that is.") does not prompt an explanation of the legislation, the implications of which the film refuses to engage. Dating back to 1799, the Logan Act is a federal statute that prohibits unauthorized citizens from conducting negotiations with foreign governments; it stipulates that "[a]ny citizen of the United States, wherever he may be, who, without authority of the United States, directly or indirectly commences or carries on any correspondence or intercourse with any foreign government or any officer or agent thereof, in relation to any disputes or controversies with the United States, or to defeat the measures of the United States, shall be fined under this title or imprisoned not more than three years, or both."[23] The qualification that communications with foreign governments are of concern *when* they contradict the US's policies creates some maneuvering room in the law's interpretation insofar as it opens the space for private negotiations when those are conducted in concert with the desires of the state. It is perhaps this linguistic ambiguity that explains Crile's reluctance to charge Wilson outright with violating this act. Although there have been no prosecutions of the Logan Act as of 2016, a number of judicial decisions and two opinions rendered by the State Department have referenced it.[24]

Charlie Wilson's War presents the boundaries between public diplomacy and private negotiations, decision-making transparency and covert operations, and secrecy and disclosure as fairly clear-cut. Historically, however, these categories blur into one another; what might start out as a secret covert operation can generate its own momentum and become much larger and eventually public, as happened with the Afghan insurgency. By 1985, Steve Coll writes, the CIA's secret war was public knowledge: "Spurred by Charlie Wilson's romanticized tales and envious of his battlefield souvenirs, more and more congressional delegations toured Pakistan and the frontier."[25] Print media and television documentaries made Afghan covert operations general knowledge.[26] The film maintains the illusion of secrecy for dramatic effect to augment Wilson's role in covert operations; the cloak-and-dagger representation of his actions contributes to the construction of hegemonic masculinity, which, in turn, paves the way for the liberal humanist subject.

"Change": The Power of Individuals

The major ideological thrust of the film is to propose a liberal humanist interpretation of historical processes and geopolitical relationships in which individual agency trumps the power of larger institutional and governmental structures to alter international alignments and to bring down communism. As the film demonstrates, American citizens, specifically those who are elite on the basis of their wealth or access to political power, matter and make history. The film credits three Americans—Charlie Wilson; his wealthy right-wing, socialite lover, Joanne Herring; and the maverick CIA operative, Gust Avrakotos—as the architects of covert operations in Afghanistan. In the bonus scenes, Julia Roberts and Mike Nichols articulate this ideological formulation of American individualism explicitly, as does Hanks in a 2007 interview on the *Oprah Winfrey Show*. "I think people are very reluctant to believe that we can assist change so powerfully as an individual," Roberts earnestly states, "which I think these three people [Wilson, Herring, and Avrakotos] demonstrate perfectly." Nichols more volubly elaborates, "One of the things I go back to all the time is transformation in a person. That's sort of the point: transformation is one of the great subjects for plays and movies. I think what I would like for the audience to get out of this is for them to be reminded that you can make a difference, that people do make a difference. It's not over. The possibility of what we call making a difference still exists." And Hanks tells Winfrey, "Charlie Wilson is a fascinating example of how things get done from the oddest quarters. That you would jump to a conclusion, that you would adhere to a stereotype about a no-good do-nothing guy from a little section of Texas that doesn't mean anything, and in fact a guy like that can change the world, which is an example to all of us, quite frankly."

The vacuity of this clichéd emphasis on "change" does not lessen its ideological power and ongoing resilience in US political discourse, where in 2007, the year of the film's release, it surfaced repeatedly in the speeches of democratic presidential candidates Barack Obama and Hillary Clinton during the primaries and then general election. Images of Obama's visage emblazoned with the word "Change" and photographs of him speaking at podiums displaying phrases such as "We are the change we have been waiting for," "Change we can believe in," "Change that works for you" resonated with the deeply ingrained American belief in individual agency. Midway through the primary season, Clinton too began to brand herself as the change candidate using the slogan,

"Countdown to change." Not only did candidate Obama construct himself as the agent of change, but he also successfully convinced voters of their individual agency and their ability to affect change through participation in the electoral process, harnessing their activism for his campaign. "The innovation and the brilliance of the 2008 Obama campaign was to offer the left-liberal electorate a simulacral alternative, steeped in the affect and iconicity of mass social movement, but absent the political referent," Eva Cherniavsky astutely observes, "The campaign was *not* the *representative* organ for a set of actually existing political possibilities for progressive change, which were at that point effectively foreclosed by the privatization of public office."[27] So too has the potential for a progressive shift in foreign policy been thwarted by the expansion of executive power and covert operations, particularly drone warfare, which are two legacies of the Obama presidency that are corrosive of democracy.

In noting the coincidence of this rhetoric of change in *Charlie Wilson's War* and the buildup to the 2008 presidential election, I do not intend to suggest that the film advocates support for a Democratic candidate in the 2008 election, though some reviewers take this position. Posted on one fan website is this observation: "*Charlie Wilson's War* comes on the eve of a presidential election year, this time involving Bill Clinton's wife Hillary as a candidate. Is it only a coincidence then that actor and producer Tom Hanks, a supporter of Hillary Clinton's (he has contributed $2,300 to her presidential campaign) has made an effort to focus on the film's ability to see past Charlie Wilson's moral flaws?"[28] Too many layers of mediation stand between Wilson and Hillary Clinton to make this particular interpretation of the film as an endorsement for Clinton's campaign convincing. It seems more likely that the film's pointed reference to Rudolph Giuliani's unsuccessful attempt to convict Wilson of drug use satirizes the former prosecutor with the aim of ridiculing Giuliani's presidential aspirations in the 2008 Republican primaries. My point in emphasizing the temporal coincidence and the presence of the rhetoric of change in *Charlie Wilson's War* and in speeches of the Democratic presidential candidates is to draw attention to the ways in which the film's representation of the liberal humanist subject mirrors dominant ideological strands in the American political imaginary and hails liberal Democrats into having an investment in the US imperial project.

The film contains a less subtle appeal to Democrats in its effacement of the larger institutional and governmental contexts that informed aid to the Mujahideen. Its promotion of Wilson, Herring, and Avrakotos as makers of history writes off the role of three other notable people who exerted a far greater influence in Afghanistan's affairs by virtue of their institutional and governmental authority: CIA Director William Casey, President Ronald Reagan, and General Secretary of the Politburo Mikhail Gorbachev. While Gorbachev's absence is symptomatic of an American nationalist myopia that is ignorant of his pivotal role in ending the Cold War, I want to reflect on the film's failure to reference either Casey's or Reagan's part in covert operations.

As Coll explains in his magisterial study *Ghost Wars*, Casey's fervent anti-communism was underwritten by an obsession with the view of the Soviet Union as expansionist, a deep Catholic piety, and a belief in Christianity's "moral mission to defeat communism."[29] Coll speculates that Casey's Catholicism led him to identify with the Afghan resistance, which shared a similar structure of feeling rooted in religion. "More than any other American, it was Casey who welded the alliance among the CIA, Saudi intelligence, and Zia's army," he writes. "As his Muslim allies did, Casey saw the Afghan jihad not merely as statecraft, but as an important front in a worldwide struggle between communist atheism and God's community of believers."[30] Significantly, Casey was one of Reagan's most influential advisors, earning full membership in the President's Cabinet, which was unprecedented for the Director of the CIA at the time. As a trusted advisor, Casey unilaterally altered the course of the secret war in Afghanistan and its objective from engaging in a Vietnam-type harassment of Soviet forces to securing an outright Afghan victory; he managed to increase funding for the Mujahideen exponentially and to take the Jihad—illegally as it turned out—against the Russians into the Soviet Central Republics.[31]

In addition to the film's failure to reference Casey's role in covert operations, it also neglects to acknowledge that covert operations in Afghanistan were very much tied to Ronald Reagan's crusade against the Soviet Union and were of a piece with his support for covert operations in other countries deemed to be at risk of contracting the communist contagion. The doctrine that bears his name builds on the containment policies of previous Presidents Truman, Eisenhower, Kennedy, Johnson, Nixon, and Carter, but where his predecessors sought to primarily limit the spread of communism through defensive measures, Reagan went on the offensive, acting in ways, particularly in Central America, that often appalled European allies.[32] In his February 1985 State of the Union Address, he avowed, "Our mission is to nourish and defend freedom and democracy and to communicate these ideals everywhere we can. We must stand by all our democratic allies. And we must not break faith with those who are risking their lives on every continent, from Afghanistan to Nicaragua, to defy Soviet-supported aggression and secure rights which have been ours by birth."[33] Notwithstanding Reagan's pious invocations of "freedom and democracy," in practice, the doctrine translated into support for anti-communist insurgencies in Nicaragua, Angola, Cambodia, and Afghanistan, along with brutal right-wing regimes in El Salvador, Indonesia, Panama, and the Philippines, to name a few.

A month after his State of the Union speech, Reagan signed the classified National Security Decision Directive 166, "Expanded US Aid to Afghan Guerrillas," which endorsed Casey's redefinition of the Afghan mission, approved the use of satellite images to plan Mujahideen attacks on Soviet targets, expanded efforts to train them in the use of explosives and sabotage techniques, and, most significantly, increased the quality and quantity of weapons supplied to the insurgents.[34] *Charlie Wilson's War* refuses to mention the President's pivotal part in escalating the US's secret war against the Soviets. By creating a movie in which Reagan and Casey do not even exist, the filmmakers excised Republicans from their own history.[35] One effect of the de-Republicanization of covert operations is to suggest that the Cold War victory belongs solely to the Democrats, who the film implies played an important, but unacknowledged, role in the defeat of the Soviet Union and its eventual demise.

The Premature-Withdrawal Narrative and Historical Causality

George Crile's book ends on a somber note, concluding with an epilogue, starkly titled "Unintended Consequences," in which he describes Wilson watching the 9/11 attacks on television and having the "sickening realization" that "the killers were Muslims" (507).

Retired from Congress, Wilson at the time was working as a lobbyist for the Pakistani government and was rumored to be earning an annual income of about $300,000. First comforted by the fact that the nineteen hijackers were Arabs and not Afghans, he admits that "[i]t didn't register with me for a week or two that this thing was all based in my mountains" (Qtd. in Crile 508). Wilson's formulation of 9/11 as a "thing" that was "based" in his mountains seemingly acknowledges a connection between the attacks and the earlier Islamic insurgency that he abetted. Yet Crile reveals that "[n]one of the sponsors of the campaign, least of all Charlie Wilson, has ever felt responsible for the path the CIA-sponsored jihad has taken; perhaps because their intentions were so pure and because the specific objectives they sought were initially so overwhelmingly successful" (509). Wilson, in other words, took ownership of the Mujahideen insurgency against the Soviet Union without taking responsibility for one of its long-term consequences, the globalization of jihad.

Crile himself emphatically links the September 11, 2001, attacks to Wilson's actions and the CIA's covert operations in Afghanistan during the 1980s. "For anyone trying to make sense of this new enemy, it would seem relevant that for over a decade in the 1980s and early 1990s, the U.S. government sponsored the largest and most successful jihad in modern history; that the CIA secretly armed and trained several hundred thousand fundamentalist warriors to fight against our common Soviet enemy; and that many of those who now targeted America were veterans of that earlier CIA-sponsored jihad" (508). Lamenting the lack of knowledge that Americans have of the CIA's role in what was their "largest and most successful covert operation," he worries that they cannot appreciate "that such secret undertakings inevitably have unforeseen and unintended consequences" (508-509). Crile ends his book with a somber proclamation: "To call these final pages an epilogue is probably a misnomer. Epilogues indicate that the story has been wrapped up, the chapter finished. This one, sadly, is far from over" (523).

Aaron Sorkin's screenplay initially translated onto the big screen Crile's analysis of the 9/11 attacks as directly linked to Wilson and the CIA's covert operations in Afghanistan. The original screenplay included footage of Avrakotos warning Wilson, "Remember I said this: There's going to be a day when we're gonna look back and say 'I'd give anything if [Afghanistan] were overrun with Godless communists.'" As Chalmers Johnson points out, this line does not appear in the final film.[36] Sorkin also concluded his original screenplay with a shot of the Pentagon in flames, which so upset the real Joanne Herring when she read the script that she assembled a legal team to pressure Hanks and his crew to alter the ending. According to her memoir *Diplomacy and Diamonds*, the legal team included Dick DeGuerin, who represented Tom DeLay against charges brought by the Texas District Attorney.[37] The ending was altered and met with both Herring's and Wilson's satisfaction. Herring disavows any connection between her and Wilson's support for the Mujahideen and the emergence of Islamic terrorism directed at the United States. "Can you ever predict a war?" she asks. "The shelf life of a Stinger missile is five years. There's no weapon we got them that can be used today."[38]

Charlie Wilson's War represents the back story of 9/11 and the origins of Al Qaeda, though it pointedly muffles the force of its criticism of covert operations in two ways. First, it proposes that the problem of Islamic terrorism is not the result of its incubation in the US covert security apparatuses and of the massive transfer of lethal weaponry to the Mujahideen—along with the emergence of a globalized iteration of militant Islam—but the consequence of the United States' premature withdrawal of its involvement with the region. Wilson, who had increased the CIA appropriations for covert operations in Afghanistan from $5 million to $1 billion, is pictured at the end of the film ineffectually pleading with Congress to allocate $1 million for the construction of a school in the region, a request that his colleagues flatly deny. We infer that the illiterate fourteen-year old boys invoked by Wilson in his requests for educational funding will metastasize into the Taliban. The film prepares us for this reading through the preceding scene in which Avrakotos warns him that the long-term stability of Afghanistan is contingent on US efforts to create commerce and civil society among a destitute population; he instructs Wilson to "Send them [Afghans] money. You can start with the roads. Move on to the schools, factories. . . Restock the sheep herds. . . Give them jobs, give them hope." Communicating the urgency of the situation, he reports to Wilson "that the crazies have started rolling into Kandahar like it's a fucking bathtub drain." The net effect of these scenes is to construct contemporary forms of terrorism as emanating from a too brief American engagement with Afghanistan and the complete failure to create the institutions of civil society and seed capitalist modes-of-production. This bleak prophecy of post-Soviet Afghanistan effaces the clandestine activities of the US and its role in militarizing the region.

The second way the film disrupts the historical causality of Islamic extremism is to claim the Russian withdrawal from Afghanistan as the first domino to fall in the demise of the Soviet Union, thus making Afghanistan into a metonym for the end of the Cold War. Crile quotes Representative Wilson as attributing the eventual collapse of communism to the achievement of the Mujahideen,

> I truly believe that this caused the Berlin Wall to come down a good five, maybe ten, years before it would have otherwise. Over a million Jews got their freedom and left for Israel; God knows how many were freed from the gulags. At least a hundred million Eastern Europeans are breathing free today, to say nothing of the Russian people. It's the truth, and all those people who are enjoying those freedoms have no idea of the part played by a million Afghan ghosts. To this day no one has ever thanked them.
>
> They removed the threat we all went to sleep with every night, of World War III breaking out. The countries that used to be in the Warsaw Pact are now in NATO. These were truly changes of biblical proportion, and the effect the jihad had in accelerating these events is nothing short of miraculous. (523)

Wilson's references to "freedom," "changes of biblical proportion," and miracles is symptomatic of the religious fervor of the Americans involved in covert operations, who generally perceived the battle against the Soviets as their Christian imperative to defeat the godless Communists.

Whatever misgivings the film raises about the potential consequences of the US's premature withdrawal from Afghanistan are tempered by American triumphalism at the Soviet Union's collapse. The film begins and ends with scenes of Wilson receiving a CIA award never before bestowed on a civilian. Standing on stage against a backdrop of a massive American flag and with a large banner that displays a quotation from Zia ("Charlie Did It.—President Zia ul-Haq of Pakistan, explaining the defeat of the Russians in Afghanistan"), Wilson sports an enigmatic expression as a CIA official honors him: "The defeat and breakup of the Soviet empire, culminating in the crumbling of the Berlin Wall, is one of the great events of world history. There were many heroes in this battle, but to Charlie Wilson must go this special recognition. Just 13 years ago, the Soviet Army appeared to be invincible. But Charlie, undeterred, engineered a lethal body blow that weakened the Communist empire. Without Charlie, history would be hugely and sadly different." Sketching a teleology that traces the dissolution of the Soviet Union back to Wilson's actions, the

CIA official succinctly reproduces the liberal humanist narrative of history in which the individual subject plays a monumental part in dismantling an empire.

The debate regarding the reasons for the collapse of the Soviet Union and the end of the Cold War continues among historians and commentators, who generally contend that a number of factors contributed to this outcome: a command economy committed to full employment, which impeded initiatives to improve productivity; a corresponding decline in scientific and technological innovation; an inefficient agricultural system that led to chronic food shortages; the widespread scarcity of housing and consumer goods; Soviet military overstretch in Afghanistan, Yemen, Mozambique, Angola, and Ethiopia, requiring a defense budget that sucked up twenty-five percent of the GNP; a breakdown in the social contract resulting in rampant corruption and bribery; challenges from nationalist movements in the Ukraine, Baltic, Eastern European states, and the Central Asian republics; and Gorbachev's idealism and rejection of the Brezhnev Doctrine in response to the 1989 Solidarity victory in the Polish elections—all of these are cited as factors that led to the decline of the Soviet Union.[39]

In the US national imaginary, however, the dissolution of the Soviet Union is a singularly American achievement generally accorded to Ronald Reagan. Although *Charlie Wilson's War* substitutes the Congressman for the President, it too rests on a tidy logic of individual agency whereby history is created by a few good men rather than the messy interactions of Afghan and Arab insurgents, multiple states (Afghanistan, Pakistan, the US, Saudi Arabia, Egypt, Israel, and China), and different divisions within those states (secret services, armed forces, legislative and executive branches). Rugged individualism and hegemonic masculinity, not collective agency, become the engine of history, grinding the gears of Soviet imperialism to a halt.

Afghanistan—The Bear Trap: "The Afghan Character" and Martial Race Theory

Brigadier Mohammad Yousaf does not grant a major role in bringing down the Soviet Union to Charlie Wilson in his account of Pakistani covert operations, *Afghanistan—The Bear Trap*. Instead, Wilson is represented with amused condescension. Although Yousaf acknowledges that Wilson "had been an energetic and persuasive spokesman for the Mujahideen cause inside the House of Representatives for a number of years," he also expresses wonder at Wilson's need for female companionship on congressional trips and describes staging highly choreographed visits for Wilson, who wanted to see a Mujahideen camp (62). Had the Congressman been injured, killed, or captured by the Soviets while touring an insurgent camp, the political and public relations fallout would have been a nightmare and possibly ignited an overt superpower conflict. Rather than take this risk, the ISI "concocted a plan whereby Wilson be allowed to approach the border, and then be stopped by Mujahideen on the pretext of inter-tribal fighting in the vicinity" and sent back to Pakistan (62). When the ISI eventually obliged Wilson's desire to visit the insurgents, they took him to a camp within five kilometers of the Afghan-Pakistan border, where he was able to pose for photographs "on a white pony dressed as a Mujahideen, with a bandolier of bullets across his chest" (62). Such photo-ops were of a piece with the routinely staged footage of the insurgency by US journalists, many of whom avoided venturing into Afghanistan because of the hardships of travel in remote areas and the dangers of war (Yousaf 5). In Yousaf's account, Wilson emerges as a peripheral figure, who must be placated with the simulacra of playing a major role in the fight against occupation and "documented" in an Orientalist tableau that has him costumed as a native, when his part was relatively minor.

Not surprisingly, given that he was in the ISI, Yousef's memoir grants hegemonic masculinity to covert Pakistani agents to whom he attributes the defeat of the USSR instead of American politicians. In 1983, the ISI tapped Yousaf, who was a Pakistani infantry brigade commander at the time, to head its Afghan Bureau; he served in this capacity till 1987, when he resigned and retired as a result of being denied a promotion to major-general. His imperative "to tell," in the parlance of life writing, emanates from his conviction that his "book may serve a useful purpose for posterity and for historians, if only to highlight lessons for political and military leaders" (3). Those lessons pertain specifically to "the conduct of guerrilla warfare" (40). If, as Gillian Whitlock has described, the genre of memoir is "a vehicle for haunted and fragmented accounts of the professional self in a specific historical context," then, in Yousaf's case, this leads to a narrative dilemma insofar as his job was to coordinate operations among rival Mujahideen factions over which he had no command authority.[40] Nor did he generally participate in political decision-making. His responsibilities cohered around managing a staff of "60 officers, 100 Junior Commissioned Officers, and 300 NCOs," organizing training camps for the Mujahideen, and distributing arms and ammunition to the leaders of the seven Mujahideen Parties that constituted an alliance (29). As represented in the memoir, Yousaf's duties, in other words, were bureaucratic rather than directly engaged in the rough-and-tumble of battle, activities that do not lend themselves to dramatic narration.

The Bear Trap repeatedly emphasizes Yousaf's belief that a military defeat of the Soviets and Mohammad Najibullah's regime was preferable to a negotiated, political settlement to the conflict, and he faults the US for the civil war that erupted after the Soviet withdrawal. Buttressed between conspiracy theories that open and close the book with assigning an outsize role to the US in the cover-up of Zia's assassination and the chaos that engulfed Afghanistan following the Soviet withdrawal, the memoir differentiates its construction of masculinity and historical agency on the basis of nationality. Yousaf creates unified actors out of groups such as the ISI and CIA that are too difficult to disaggregate, and he essentializes other subjects into archetypes of the "Afghan warrior" and the "modern Soviet soldier," rendering them as subordinate forms of masculinity. Together, these characterizations of agency indict the Soviets for expansionism and human rights violations, credit the Pakistanis for their role in forcing the USSR to retreat, and blame the US for the chaos that followed the Soviet withdrawal; in sum, these characterizations make Afghans peripheral to their own history.

Without any irony, Yousaf declares his intention to assemble "some clues" to the Afghan "character" for the edification of his readers. He devotes an entire chapter to an exegesis of this monolithic construction of subordinated masculinity, which has three notable features: extraordinary physical capabilities, near innate martial skills motivated by religious fervor, and a quarrelsome temperament. The "Afghan's hardy physique" enables him "to endure privations" and "walk for days, even weeks, on the minimum of food" because, like a "camel," he will "stuff [himself] with huge quantities" to stock up "for the next journey" (34-35). His "ability to suffer pain stoically, without fuss, and silently," combined with his "physical courage" (32), make him "a first-class guerrilla soldier" (34). Able "to withstand the extremes of terrain and climate," the Afghan's "most valued possession" is a rifle, "which is a part of his body" (35). "To be able to shoot straight is of far greater practical value" for him, Yousaf opines, "than to be able to write" (35). We are also told that the Afghan's "virtues are tempered with the vices of obstinacy, and an apparently insatiable appetite for feuding" (35). Yousaf's references to animal imagery, devaluation of literacy, and general prickliness render "the Afghan" as highly suited to the physical labor of warfare without having the intellectual mettle to resolve conflicts. He is, in Yousaf's characterization, instinctual rather than rational, a better foot soldier than commander, a follower rather than a leader.

The construction of "the Afghan" in the vocabulary of stoicism, courage, and physical endurance echoes the nineteenth-century British colonial discourse of the martial races. Following the 1857 Sepoy Mutiny, the colonial state categorized Indians as either martial or non-martial races under the belief that some groups were predisposed to be better warriors than the majority of the native population, a trait the British thought these groups had inherited.[41] As the astonishingly prolific Lieutenant-General Sir George MacMunn pontificates in his 1933 tome, *The Martial Races of India*, "the mass of the [Indian] people have neither martial aptitude nor physical courage. . . the courage that we should talk of colloquially as 'guts.'"[42] Informed by a mishmash of pseudoscience of eugenics and climate theories of race popular in Europe and the US in the late nineteenth and early twentieth centuries, Orientalist cultural attitudes, as well as imperial political considerations, the concept of the martial races became a central aspect of the colonial state's recruitment of native soldiers for the Indian Army. The British Raj recruited from those ethno-religious groups that had been loyal to the empire during the mutiny and marginalized those who had revolted in 1857 from the imperial military apparatus. Political exigencies of recruitment were mapped onto prevailing articulations of climate and health, as Kaushik Roy explains, in which "hilly regions with a temperate climate produced tall, robust and well proportioned humans whereas malarial tropical regions with swamps and marshes, such as Bengal Terai and Arakan, produced unhealthy races."[43] The martial races primarily hailed from mountainous areas and agricultural communities and included Dogras, Gurkhas, Pathans, Rajputs, and Sikhs. Bengalis and Maharatas (e.g., Maharasthrians), two groups that had rebelled against the British in 1857 and whose elite tended to be high caste and educated, were deemed non-martial races.[44] Both categories were overdetermined by gender insofar as the martial races were associated with hypermasculinity and the non-martial ones with femininity, a denigrated subjectivity.[45]

Significantly, "Pathans," the Hindi/Urdu term for ethnic Pushtuns, were designated a martial race by the British. After independence, Pakistan's Army adopted the structure of the colonial Indian Army and, because of a shortage of Pakistani officers, initially filled the ranks of commanders-in-chief and other senior military positions with British personnel.[46] These British officers helped establish the major military training and educational facilities.[47] The colonial inheritance of this ideology, in combination with the internalization of such attitudes among the Pakistan military classes, resulted in the ubiquity of martial race theory. In 1979, at the height of Brigadier Mohammad Yousaf's career, the Army consisted of majority Punjabi (70%) and Pushtun (14%) soldiers and officers, two groups that were categorized as martial during the colonial period.[48] Bengalis and Sindhis, two groups that were considered non-martial races, were underrepresented in the Pakistani Army. Stephen Philip Cohen largely attributes the resilience of the colonial martial race theory in the post-colonial period to Pakistan's desire to project strength in the face of a numerically and technologically superior Indian Army. The prevailing sentiment was that "one Pakistani soldier equaled ten or more Indians" such that "Pakistan could overcome the disadvantages of its apparent size and resources" relative to India in any conflict.[49] The absurdity of this view became evident when India handily defeated Pakistani forces in the 1971 war, which cost Pakistan its eastern wing, now Bangladesh.

In addition to containing echoes of martial race theory, Yousaf's characterization of Afghans reverberates with ahistorical, Orientalist constructions of natives. He asserts confidently, "The Afghans who annihilated the British during their winter retreat from Kabul in 1842 were virtually identical to those indestructible fighters who killed over 13,000 Soviet soldiers and wounded some 35,000, and sent its army scurrying home after nine years of bitter fighting. The people have not changed much over the centuries; even Alexander's Macedonian pikemen who marched up the Panjsher valley 2300 years ago would easily recognize the jagged, barren, rocky skyline today. Time does not change much in Afghanistan" (6). Here a century bleeds into millennia, rendering history in the larger scheme of things irrelevant. Afghans meld with the physical landscape in an ontological stasis which resists change and modernity. Elsewhere, Yousaf declares the Afghan to be "infinitely patient, there is seldom a rush, time is of little consequence to him" (43). Edward Said has analyzed the discursive mechanisms that western colonial powers employ to posit absolute difference between themselves and natives in order to legitimize their rule. Such maneuvers include abstracting natives and positing them outside of time. Yousaf's memoir, which neither emanates from the west nor is part of a formal imperial project, nonetheless provides a Cold War instantiation of Orientalism which contributes to the ideological justification of geostrategic intrigue and proxy wars by Pakistan and the US. The construction of the Afghan as essentially unchanged over time becomes both a negation of Afghan identity and an affirmation of Pakistani identity, specifically contributing to the "common sense" idea that Afghans are at an arrested stage of development and require the guidance of more modern handlers such as the ISI. Indeed, in the note to *Afghanistan—The Bear Trap*, the publisher pronounces the book to be the best account of Mujahideen operations in "the World's most primitive and hostile environments," calling Brigadier Mohammad Yousaf "their puppet-master" and, hence, implying that he animates the resistance by pulling the strings of his Mujahideen marionettes.[50]

The "Modern Soviet Soldier"

While Yousaf characterizes the Afghan warrior as a singular figure who exists outside of time, he inserts the "modern Soviet soldier" into history by noting differences in the quality of Soviet soldiers during World War II and the counterinsurgency campaign in Afghanistan. Expressing admiration for the Soviet soldier's "fighting qualities," Yousaf is initially "somewhat sceptical of the ability of the Mujahideen to defeat [the Soviet soldier] in the field" (54). He bases his skepticism, ironically, on the assessment of Major-General Friedrich Wilhelm von Mellenthin, a World War II German general, who wrote a quasi-Orientalist memoir, *Panzer Battles*, from which Yousaf quotes.[51] In a similar vein to Yousaf's representation of the Afghan warrior, von Mellenthin's text also presents the Soviet soldier as a monolithic entity, claiming he has an intimate connection to the landscape; for example, von Mellenthin asserts, "Natural obstacles simply do not exist for [the Soviet soldier]; he is at home in the desert, forest, in swamps and marshes, as much as the roadless steppes" (qtd. by Yousaf 54). The excellence of the Soviets' soldiering derives from the apparently inexhaustible numbers of recruits, according to the passages that Yousaf quotes. Von Mellenthin's *Panzer Battles* is infused with a version of Orientalism of the kind Michael Cherniavsky attributes to German generals of that era, who tend to blame their defeat on Russian soldiers' "characteristics."[52] In German accounts, according to Michael Cherniavsky, the Russian soldier remains "insensitive to bombardment and similar pressures," and is able "to live like an animal without the normal needs of the civilized soldier."[53] He is able to fight "with the soulless indifference of Asiatic man," enabling the Red Army to come "on like an Asiatic horde."[54]

Yousaf is oblivious to these Orientalist undertones, which is hardly surprising given his own propensity to reproduce martial race theory. Mellenthin's text serves as his means to contextualize the World War II-era Soviet soldier from the one battling the Mujahideen insurgency. Whereas the former fought for "personal and national survival," the latter waged war on behalf of an unpopular occupying regime (54). The extremely different motivations in these eras, along with the material conditions facing Soviet conscripts in Afghanistan, have resulted in the decline in the Soviet soldier's military skills, in Yousaf's opinion. The Red Army's reliance on young conscripts, forced to serve for two years when they turned eighteen, translated into a high turnover in the military; no sooner had soldiers acquired experience in the field then their tour had finished and they were replaced with raw recruits. These aspects of the conscription system, he points out, prevented the Army from becoming a professional force and from building on their technological advantage over the Mujahideen. In addition to this structural constraint, Yousaf puzzles over the lack of basic training Russian recruits were given, amounting to a mere three weeks, before their Afghanistan posting. It is worth noting that the Russian General Staff also blamed the conscript system, the lack of training (specifically in guerrilla warfare), and the desire to minimize Soviet casualties as factors that led to their defeat.[55]

Compounding the truncated training, conditions on the ground were abysmal: inadequate shelter (generally in tents in the middle of winter), poor sanitation, a "vitamin-deficient diet" and "insufficient rations," and low pay, "roughly the equivalent of five dollars a month" (55). According to other sources, these first four conditions, along with the breakdown of the Soviet military health care system in Afghanistan, resulted in a high percentage of hospitalizations among troops. Three quarters of the 40th Army did a hospital tour in Afghanistan, with the majority of these soldiers suffering not from combat injuries but from serious illness, including infectious hepatitis, typhoid, cholera, dysentery, and malaria, among other diseases.[56] Magnifying the physical challenges of counterinsurgency in Afghanistan, a Soviet military culture that encouraged hazing as a rite of passage for new recruits made for miserable working conditions.[57]

The chronic hunger, low pay, and general boredom, Yousaf believes, had several consequences. First, some Russian conscripts sold their weapons to Afghan peasants for food, participating in the illegal trade in small arms that I discuss in chapter 3. As one Soviet soldier from Estonia explains in a passage quoted by Yousaf, "because in the chaos of war to explain the loss of a weapon is easy. . . . We used to buy all kinds of food and drink, and even bread in exchange for our weapons. . ." (56). Second, to relieve the boredom, troops turned to alcohol and drugs, which could also be procured through weapons sales. Hashish and marijuana were the drugs of choice. The expense of vodka generally limited its consumption to Soviet officers while the conscripts made a home brew of *braga*, which they hid in the linings of their tents or between the external and water tanks of their armored vehicles.[58]

Yousaf maintains that together these material conditions rendered Soviet conscripts into "reluctant warriors" "loath to quit the comparative security of their bases, or to dismount from behind armour plate in the field" (56). Later he offers this assessment of the Soviet soldier: "By and large the Soviet soldier fought poorly, as he lacked motivation. He was frightened by night operations, he seldom pressed home attacks, he was casualty shy and kept behind his armour plate on the roads instead of deploying into the hills" (216). In contrast to the ahistoric construction of "the Afghan" as unchanging and pathologically prone to infighting, his pronouncements on "the Soviet soldier" are grounded in an enumeration of the deprivations suffered by conscripts. The implication is that under more auspicious circumstances, the 40th Army could have done much better militarily. One wonders whether Yousaf's more sympathetic representation of Soviet soldiers than Afghan Mujahideen and, in particular, the willingness to insert them into modernity derives from racial difference and their association, in his mind, with whiteness.[59] Yet both Afghan fighters and Soviet soldiers represent, for Yousaf, subordinated versions of masculinity.

The Soviets did not intend to spend a decade in Afghanistan when they first intervened as a response to political chaos in a buffer state along their southern border, believing they would leave in a few months after installing a pliant leader and shoring up an unpopular Marxist regime. It is perhaps this optimism that led the Soviets to call their forces in Afghanistan, "Limited Contingent of Soviet Forces" [LCSF]. Militarily, the USSR had technological superiority over the Mujahideen, and they fully expected to prosecute the type of war for which they had trained: conventional warfare suited to a European or Chinese theater. Instead, the Soviets were confronted with a guerrilla insurgency based in the mountains, where their tanks, infantry fighting vehicles, and self-propelled artillery could not be easily maneuvered and where high-precision jet aircraft could not provide support for ground forces.[60] Most of the Soviet troops were posted in cities and in areas along the eastern and northern borders of Afghanistan, strategically important because Mujahideen supply lines ran through Pakistan, and the Salang Highway was a crucial conduit for Soviet provisions. While both the ISI and the CIA hoped to draw the Soviets into a

Vietnam-type quagmire, the LCSF never reached the level of troop commitment as the US forces in Vietnam (numbering over 500,000 soldiers) in spite of the fact that Afghanistan is nearly five times the size of Vietnam—troop levels varied from 90,000 to 120,000, the majority of whom came from rural and working class backgrounds, from households too poor to bribe officials for military exemptions for their family members.[61] Of these troops, 13,833 died, according to official figures released by the Gorbachev Administration, but other sources estimate casualties at closer to 26,000.[62]

Corporate Agency: The ISI and CIA

In a cast of characters that includes quarrelsome but heroic Mujahideen, lazy and cowardly Soviet soldiers, and bumbling, clueless CIA agents, about whom I will say more shortly, the ISI emerges in Yousaf's memoir as a competent and formidable opponent to the USSR, and the paradigm of hegemonic masculinity. As head of the ISI Afghan Bureau, Yousaf oversaw the training of 80,000 Mujahideen, distribution of "hundreds of thousands of tons of arms and ammunition," expenditure of several billion dollars in logistical operations, and command of ISI teams in Afghanistan during the course of his tenure (4). Unlike the monolithic archetypes he creates of Afghans and Soviets, his representation of the ISI is of a corporate body, which he animates as being beyond corruption and sensitive to the value of civilian life.

The ISI wielded a great deal of power in determining which factions would become prominent in the resistance, given that it was charged by President Mohammad Zia-ul-Haq with distributing Saudi and US money, arms, and ammunition to the insurgents. The Pakistanis resolved that all aid would be delivered not directly to individual Mujahideen commanders but through the intermediary of the seven political parties that were headquartered in Pakistan, four of whom were fundamentalist groups and three of whom were moderate. Even though he was coordinating the overall guerrilla campaign, Yousaf was not permitted to issue direct orders to the Mujahideen commanders and had to rely on "cajoling and convincing" to push through his operational initiatives (3). While he avers that he allocated military supplies to the seven parties based on their "combat effectiveness"—which was verified through radio intercepts, satellite images provided by the CIA, and periodic inspections of their warehouses—the fundamentalist groups received a greater portion than the moderate ones, with an eye to installing an Islamist regime in Kabul that was sympathetic to Pakistan (103).[63]

Absent his impatience with the Mujahideen and scorn for the Soviets, Yousaf casts the ISI as a moral agent, highlighting, in particular, two characteristics, even as his memoir hints at evidence to the contrary. The ISI, unlike the Mujahideen, he maintains, is incorruptible, and it is respectful of civilian life in its operations. The money pipeline flowed from the US and Saudi Arabia to the CIA, which purchased arms from Britain, China, Egypt, Israel, and the US. These arms were then transferred to the ISI, along with money for "software" (food, clothing, building supplies, transport vehicles and pack animals, and other provisions), distributed, in turn, by the Pakistanis to the seven parties (82). At several points, Yousaf claims that possibilities for corruption in these transfers occur upstream when the CIA is handling the clandestine transactions and not downstream with the ISI. Yet his protestations contain equivocations that indicate the ISI has engaged in nefarious activities such as fraud. "Despite the allegations of corruption levelled at those involved with the arms pipeline, I remain totally convinced that as far as my organization was concerned nothing much went astray," he writes, "The middle section of the pipe was virtually corruption-free. The beginning section under the CIA was riddled with opportunities for fraud" (102). Here we get an admission that such charges *have been made* against the ISI and language that minimizes the wrongdoing. That "nothing much went astray" acknowledges that *something* did go astray and "virtually corruption-free" suggests *some* level of corruption existed. In fact, Mujahideen commander Abdul Haq had complained about ISI corruption to visiting US members of Congress.[64] Yousaf himself first attained his post as head of the ISI Afghan Bureau after the "Quetta Incident," in 1983, when several ISI officers accepted bribes from Mujahideen commanders to issue them extra weapons (20-21). He also reveals that the ISI "diverted" about two hundred 14.5 mm machine guns, RPG-7s, and SA-7s meant for the insurgents to the Pakistani Army without getting prior approval from the CIA (102). These details belie Yousaf's construction of the intelligence agency as principled and above bribery.

Just as the memoir undercuts the claim to incorruptibility, so too does it undermine Yousaf's profession that the ISI prioritized the minimization of civilian casualties; he maintains that the ISI "never deliberately fired indiscriminately" at targets in densely populated Kabul. "Our targets were always military, or associated with the Communist government in some way" (147). However, he also divulges the fact that "tens of thousands" of long-range rockets were fired on Kabul over the course of his tenure and that the majority of attacks occurred during the night. It is difficult to reconcile these realities with the concern for civilian well-being. Moreover, the revelation that he recommended sabotaging power lines and the dams that supplied the city with water evidences a strategy designed precisely to increase civilian misery. Such casualties are excused as accidental and "unintentional." And Yousaf chillingly remarks that in order to achieve victory, which he defines as the military defeat of the USSR and the ejection of Afghan communists from the capital, "Kabul had to burn" and later notes Kabul had to "be cut off, starved of food," neither tactic of which augured well for civilians (145 and 224).

In contrast to the accolades he heaps on the ISI, Yousaf has little praise for the CIA (apart from his high regard for CIA Director William Casey), which he casts as incompetent and prone to internal disagreements among techno-crats, agents in the field, and those on loan from the US Army. The agency's role was limited to purchasing and transporting arms and equipment to Pakistan, buying vehicles and arranging pack animals inside Pakistan and Afghanistan, training Pakistani instructors on weapons and equipment, providing satellite and radio intelligence, and doling out advice on technical matters as needed (95-96). Most of Yousaf's criticism involves the CIA's buying of weapons and ammunition, which was not synchronized, such that the right ammunition was not always purchased for the correct weapons, leaving the Mujahideen chronically short of anti-aircraft ammunition. Nor did the CIA take into account existing stockpiles of weapons, on occasion buying large numbers of rifles from India without having the storage capacity to warehouse them (85).[65] Most damaging are his charges that the CIA spent considerable sums of money purchasing logistically inappropriate, inaccurate, faulty, or outdated weapons for the insurgency. Indeed, the majority of the chapter on the CIA consists of a litany of such weapons purchases including cumbersome Swiss Oerlikon anti-aircraft guns; ineffectual British blowpipe surface-to-air missiles; badly corroded, World War II-era Turkish rifles, pistols, and guns; and unserviceable Egyptian rifles, along with damp, unusable ammunition.

Yousaf attributes these purchasing missteps to three factors. First, he suspects that the Mujahideen, in the CIA's view, does "not deserve or would not be able to use, modern weapons" (86). Though not explicitly stated, the implication is that the CIA has internalized Orientalist racial attitudes toward Afghans, an irony given Yousaf's own embrace of martial race theory and his construction of "the Afghan soldier" as premodern. Second, he imputes a greed motive to arms dealers who saw the insurgency "as a splendid opportunity to sell off arms that nobody else wanted, weapons that were obsolete or obsolescent, even ones that were dangerous to fire" (86). US congressmen are vaguely alluded to as the culprit pushing particular weapon sales, and one infers that the allusion is to Charlie Wilson, who championed the purchase of the cumbersome Oerlikon cannons, which were too heavy to be carted into the mountains on the backs of mules. Third, Yousaf indicts the CIA for assigning weapons procurement to agents who had no battle experience and, consequently, "could not begin to comprehend the Mujahideen's needs" (87).

Yousaf also explains how the CIA's inability to comprehend conditions on the ground meant that its officers did not understand the seasonal nature of the insurgency, which was fought during the spring, summer, and fall, and not during the winter when the Mujahideen returned to their homes. The agency was also unable to appreciate the advance planning necessary for oper-ations, typically requiring a nine-month lead. And in its cultural ignorance, it sometimes devised harebrained schemes to foment unrest along the Uzbek region of the Soviet Union, for example, proposing to produce and distribute "atrocity novels" to encourage the locals to rebel against the USSR, apparently without any knowledge of the reading practices or aesthetic tastes of the people whom the CIA hoped to reach. It was left to the ISI to recommend that Korans translated into Uzbek would garner a larger readership and be more relevant for the jihad.

Such gaps in knowledge—both cultural and operational—are symptomatic of the CIA's inability to read the larger geopolitical landscape of the Cold War. According to Coll, the agency was ill-informed about local conditions in Afghanistan from the get-go; it "failed to predict Afghanistan's initial 1978 communist coup," perhaps because its Kabul-based agents were more concerned with acquiring intelligence on Soviet weapons systems than on developing Afghan sources or analyzing Afghan politics.[66] More astonishing than this intelligence lapse is the revelation that Mikhail Gorbachev's decision to withdraw from Afghanistan blindsided the CIA. As early as 1986, Gorbachev had started to call the war a "bleeding wound" because of its humanitarian and economic toll.[67] While the agency had an inkling that the Soviet economy was underperforming, it did not realize to what extent or that Gorbachev was serious about reforming the system. "At the same time that Gorbachev was deciding secretly to initiate a withdrawal of his battered forces from Afghanistan," Coll divulges, "the CIA's Directorate of Intelligence circulated a report that the Afghan war 'has not been a substantial drain on the Soviet economy' and that Moscow 'shows continued willingness to incur whatever burden is necessary.'"[68] Apparently, the CIA did not realize that the Soviet Union "was so decayed as to be near collapse."[69]

Against a backdrop of Cold War intrigue, then, Yousaf presents four different versions of subordinated and hegemonic masculinities that are either individualized or corporatized, as well as differentiated on the basis of national identity. By rendering the "Afghan warrior" in essentialist terms as instinctual rather than deliberative and the corporate body of the CIA as colossally incompetent, he sets the scene for crediting the ISI for the defeat of the Red Army and the withdrawal of the Soviets. Unlike the liberal humanist subject celebrated as the locus of agency in *Charlie Wilson's War*, Yousaf proffers the corporate body of the ISI as the driver of world-historical events. Contemporary forms of liberal humanism in the US presuppose the ability and freedom of the individual to determine destiny regardless of the structural impediments and distributional inequality that might constrain the subject's action. The operative assumption is that all individuals are equal before the law, in both senses of the word, as in the will of the state and of the divine sovereign. Such a concept of the subject is incompatible with military dictatorship, where individuals are interpellated precisely according to their position in hierarchies determined by the state. Under such regimes, those individuals who are part of the armed services, police forces, and intelligence branches—Althusserian repressive state apparatuses, in other words—can only actualize their agency as a corporate body because of the monopoly of power held by the dictator, the sole individual and ultimate authority who is *officially* allowed to exercise agency qua his or her individual self. I do not mean to deny the obvious reality that individuals within these institutions do exert their agency but to point out that under a dictatorship, such actions must always appear to be those of the corporate body for the regime to shore up its authority. In its casting of the ISI as a corporate body, Brigadier Mohammad Yousaf's memoir reflects this structural understanding of agency under President General Zia ul-Haq.

The Black Tulip: Cold War Masculinity in the Twilight of Soviet Empire

Hegemonic masculinity and the liberal humanist subject are very much alive and well in Milt Bearden's espionage novel, *The Black Tulip: A Novel of Afghanistan,* which covers the last four years of the Soviet occupation of Afghanistan. Bearden, a consultant for the film *Charlie Wilson's War,* was a thirty-year veteran of the CIA, serving in Nigeria, Sudan, and Moscow, and as the CIA station chief in Pakistan from 1986-1989. Reviews of *The Black Tulip* reference these biographical details as evidence for the tale's veracity. Written in the third-person limited point of view, the novel follows its dual protagonists, Alexander Fannin and his KGB counterpart Anatoly Viktorovich Klimenko, as they wage the Cold War in spite of the impediments placed in their way by their respective security establishments. Neither the CIA nor the KGB is presented as a corporate body, as in Yousaf's treatment of security agencies. Bearden instead constructs the CIA as riven with internal petty feuds and the KGB as embroiled in an internecine conflict with the Red Army; in the novel, both agencies are collections of people who can barely tolerate each other. Notwithstanding the dysfunctional intra-agency intrigue, or maybe because of it, Fannin and Klimenko act in ways that have world-significant consequences, demonstrating that the liberal humanist subject will triumph at the end of history.

Perhaps because *The Black Tulip* had to receive clearance from the CIA censors, who probably felt compelled to sustain the fiction of a limited CIA role in the Afghan insurgency, Fannin is an ex-CIA agent rather than an active field operator, having left the agency out of disgust over the rumors over his loyalty following his engagement to a Ukrainian woman, the lovely Katerina Martynova. The son of a Russian father and Ukrainian mother who were refugees from Stalin, Alexander speaks fluent Russian and Ukrainian, and slightly accented Polish and German. Before becoming a CIA agent, Alexander did a stint as a helicopter pilot in Vietnam. His "unconventional origins" offend the "squeamish Ivy League sensibilities" of his immediate CIA superior, a reference to the actual class tensions that characterized the agency, pitting Ivy League graduates who were given management positions against their working class colleagues who were more often assigned to the field (5). While Bearden hints at Alexander's working class origins, however, his protagonist has ascended the social ladder through his engagement to the daughter of Martynov Trading Corporation, one of the largest trading houses in Hong Kong. We are meant to like this man and to be impressed with his accomplishments, his good looks, and his ability to go it alone professionally, all rendering him the paradigm of hegemonic masculinity. Even Zia expresses his admiration for Alexander, applauding CIA Director William Casey on his choice for the Afghanistan mission, "the name Alexander has a romantic ring for this region. I will wager that in no time our Afghan brothers are calling Mr. Fannin Sikander, the first Alexander to come to the Khyber over two thousand years ago" (29). "Sikander" is the South Asian version of "Alexander," and Zia clearly perceives Fannin to be a modern-day Alexander the Great.[70]

The fictional Alexander has been summoned by Casey to oversee the delivery of Stinger missiles to the Mujahideen and training on their use within Afghanistan, outside the official weapons pipeline that runs through Pakistan—all on the orders of Zia, who wants to avoid a retaliatory attack by the Soviets on Pakistan that the addition of Stingers is bound to provoke.

This basic plot is layered over several subplots, including the Aldrich Ames spy scandal and a noticeably contrived and mawkishly sentimental plot device that establishes a familial connection between Alexander and Anatoly. While a peripheral character, Ames provides the narrative framework that creates a justification for Anatoly, by the end of the novel, to become a double agent. CIA agents in the Russian security apparatuses are being picked up and executed by the KGB, alerting the CIA that there may be a mole in their midst. It is not quite clear why Bearden includes Ames, one of the few "historical" characters in his tale, given the minor appearances he makes and the fact that his narrative function could be delegated to a fictional character.

Shortly before his retirement in 1994, Bearden had received an official reprimand from the CIA for "failing to oversee" Ames in Bearden's capacity as the deputy chief of the CIA's Soviet-East European office in 1985. That year, Ames headed the division's Soviet counterintelligence branch and would begin a nine-year career spying for the USSR in which ten double agents working on behalf of the US would die and dozens of covert operations would be compromised. Later, from 1989–1990, Bearden again supervised Ames and was slow to respond to the mounting evidence that his subordinate was profiting from trafficking intelligence.[71] As a demonstration of what the *New York Times* characterized then as the CIA's "incompetence, malaise, back-biting, misdirected machismo and managerial failures," an anonymous "Snitch Fax" had been sent to the Senate Intelligence Committee in April 1994, which, among other revelations, accused Bearden of warning Ames that he was under suspicion, a charge against Bearden that seems highly unlikely.[72] What does seem likely is that Bearden used the Ames scandal as a framing device to shame the CIA for the indignities that he faced in the final year of his otherwise distinguished career.

Ames's appearance in the novel is not as jarring as the artificial plot device that Bearden invents to create a familial connection between Alexander and Anatoly. Early in *The Black Tulip*, we learn that Alexander's mother-in-law and Anatoly's mother are identical twin sisters, matching birthmarks and all. While Katerina's mother is able to escape from the USSR during Stalin's purges, Anatoly's mother is not. At some point, the two sisters re-establish contact, communicating over fifteen years the details of their lives through an allegory, "The Tale of the Maidens of Kiev." Written on parchment in stilted, baroque prose with references to "evil Tsars," "khans," and even "the Macedonian [who] had suffered serious wounds and near defeat in a great battle so long ago," Alexander learns from its pages that Anatoly has become a KGB agent (31). He immediately recognizes his cousin-in-law as the Soviet officer who goes by the name Major Andrey Belov, with whom he has been negotiating the transfer of a high-value Soviet hostage captured by the Mujahideen. By pairing the CIA agent to his KGB counterpart, Bearden unintentionally exposes the macro Cold War dialectic at an individual level in that just as the US and USSR are bound in a relationship of reciprocal need and self-validation, each agent requires the other as his self-justification. The family connection additionally hints that the peculiar intimacy of kinship relations and sibling rivalry characterizes such mutual interdependence in covert operations.

After establishing their shared distaste for Soviet totalitarianism and arranging for his wife's maternal aunt to flee the USSR, Alexander asks Anatoly to defect, which the KGB agent refuses to do. Throughout *The Black Tulip*, various KGB and CIA officers allude to the promise of earthly delights, which the CIA volunteers as an incentive to potential Soviet defectors: in the agency's stock phrase, defectors will get "a blonde with long legs and big tits" (71). It is difficult to judge which group the CIA expresses more contempt for with this promise: American women who are the sum of their body parts or Soviet men who are so feeble-minded that they can be tempted to forsake their families and country for sex. Along with the conflation of sexual conquest and the acquisition of US nationality, implicit in this promise too are the assumptions that blondes represent the apex of American womanhood and that Soviet women do not put out.

Although Anatoly categorically refuses to defect, Alexander persuades him to become a double agent on behalf of the Americans. This decision is not prompted by greed, as with the real-life Aldrich Ames who was paid over $2 million for the information he passed on to the Soviets, but out of a deep concern for his countrymen.[73] After many years in the KGB, along with his disgust with the regime's response to the Chernobyl disaster, Anatoly has concluded that the system is irredeemably corrupt. The "tripod" holding up the USSR, consisting of the Army, KGB, and Communist Party, faces a challenge from Gorbachev's policies, and Anatoly and Alexander believe that once initiated, the General Secretary's "attempts at reform will spin out of control," eventually destroying the system (208). A Soviet withdrawal from Afghanistan, they feel, will be a catalyst for the unraveling of the state. To this end, Anatoly agrees to be a conduit for Soviet military secrets. When his cousin Katerina attempts to convince him one final time to forsake his homeland, he piously responds, "You know my answer. I told you back in Paktia about a hundred years ago that I wasn't anybody's spy. That I wasn't working for anyone but the people of my Ukraine, and possibly for the Russian people as well. No, Katerina. I do not want to be exfiltrated" (259). Here, Anatoly's disavowal of the subject position of the spy, even as he is engaged in clandestine work on behalf of the US government, is also a simultaneous affirmation of individualism that is wrapped up in the guise of humanitarianism. The liberal humanist subject to the rescue once again.

But lest such high-minded principles posit a moral parity between the CIA operative and KGB agent, Bearden makes a clear distinction between the two. While Alexander takes considerable trouble and personal risk to rescue two severely injured Mujahideen fighters who have been ambushed during a successful Stinger attack on Soviet Mi-24 Hind helicopters, Anatoly time and again betrays a callousness to human life, ranging from collusion in the ruthless elimination of a KGB rival who threatens to reveal him to the deliberate sabotage of a Mujahideen weapons depot in a densely populated, civilian area. The latter incident is a fictionalized account of the massive explosion at the Ojhri Camp, located between Rawalpindi and Islamabad, on April 10, 1988, which set off rockets in both cities, killing over 100 people. About "30,000 rockets, millions of rounds of ammunition, vast number of mines, anti-aircraft Stinger missiles, anti-tank missiles, multiple-barrel rocket launchers and mortars worth $100 million" were reputedly stockpiled at Ojhri (the destruction of all records during the attack renders verification impossible). The cause of the explosion, which was officially deemed an "accident," continues to be debated in the Pakistani press with some laying the blame on the ISI, who was in charge of the camp.[74] In his memoir, Brigadier Mohammad Yousaf, however, speculates that the explosion could have been masterminded by the Americans, whose policy had changed at that point "to prevent fundamentalists winning the war"; "Mujahideen without ammunition at this critical junction coincided nicely with their objectives" (203). Why the Americans would choose to sabotage the camp on the very day that they had scheduled a team to inspect the facility remains unexplained by Yousaf.

To the rumors of ISI and American culpability, Bearden advances another theory: the Russians did it! *The Black Tulip* attributes the explosion to a plan hatched by Anatoly in a bid to hasten the end of the war by eliminating the Mujahideen's weapons stockpile. When asked by General Titov whether the attack "can. . . be done without killing a lot of civilians?" Anatoly chillingly replies, "Not really. But I don't think we need worry about the civilian casualties. They will be blamed on the people who stacked all the ordnance in the middle of a populated area in the first place, not on whoever blew it up. Besides, it will be ambiguous" (234). The operative logic is of a piece with American justifications for unleashing violence on civilians in the past, for example, during the nuclear attacks on Hiroshima and Nagasaki: the killing of many people is a preventive measure against killing many more people because it accelerates the conflict's end. For Anatoly, the problem of civilian casualties reduces to evading blame rather than inflicting death and destruction on innocent bystanders. His humanitarianism is of the nationalist variety, extending to fellow Ukrainians and Russians, but not to the Pakistani civilians and Afghan refugees who live in the neighborhoods surrounding Ojhri Camp.

Alexander successfully delivers Stingers to the Mujahideen, exposes Aldrich Ames as a KGB agent, and plots the demise of the Soviet Union by recruiting Anatoly to the US cause, but not without supporting help from an all too predictable repertoire of racist caricatures. From the Mujahideen Salahuddin who sports the "familiar look of something close to sexual arousal" during ambushes (35) to the unnamed Mujahideen fighters who mutilate and "torture" Arab fighters "simply for entertainment" (104) to the "Mad Mullah" commander who provides a feast for unsuspecting Algerians in a rival Mujahideen group only to blow them up with a bomb hidden inside a roasted goat (172), Afghans are generally represented as having a lust for extreme violence. Such crude Orientalism is supplemented with a more genteel variety in the novel's description of the "seventy-year-old houseboy," the Chinese servant to Katerina's family for forty years (146), and cringe-inducing dialogue that has her speaking in the patois of Chinese prostitutes. References to "little Chinese girls" also appear periodically in the text (165-167).

Barbaric Afghan fighters, servile elderly Chinese men, and cute Asian hookers create a colorful (pun intended) backdrop to better showcase white, Cold War masculinity. The last scene of *The Black Tulip* features Anatoly and his close friend, Sasha, a fellow KGB officer, watching the highly choreographed tableau of General Boris Gromov jumping from a lone tank and striding the last hundred yards of the Friendship Bridge on the Soviet-Afghan border to awkwardly embrace his teenage son. As the boy hands his father a bouquet of red carnations, Sasha remarks with some bitterness that "a single black tulip would have been just right for our hero," a reference to the novel's title which takes its name from the transport planes used to ferry dead Soviet soldiers home

(132). Black tulips grow in Afghanistan and had become a symbol of death in the Soviet Union. We are to infer that from the Soviet perspective at least, the decades-long occupation was a bust, and that without Alexander's and Anatoly's covert operations, it would have continued indefinitely with more loss of life. Such are the achievements of the liberal humanist subject: lives saved, a superpower humbled, and an empire teetering on the verge of collapse.

Conclusion

Throughout this chapter, I have focused on how instantiations of the premature-withdrawal narrative, depending on their national origin, differentially construct historical agency in terms of masculinity as either manifested in the liberal humanist subject or the corporatized body of intelligence services. But both *Charlie Wilson's War* and *Afghanistan—The Bear Trap* also end on a note of anxiety, expressing concern for the premature withdrawal of US assistance from Afghanistan, civilian in the case of the film and military in the case of the memoir. While not a feature of *The Black Tulip*, this anxiety also surfaces in interviews with its author, Milton Bearden, who comments in a *Frontline* episode,

> [A]fter 1989 and the withdrawal of the Soviet Union, the United States and the West dropped Afghanistan like a hot potato. Not because we are uncaring and cynical. But because the events beginning with the Hungarians cutting the wire with Austria and the Poles bringing in that electrician from [Gdansk] and throwing out all those old Communist bosses and the people of East Germany going out on the streets . . . [in] a few tens of thousands and then in the million, until November 9 of that same very year the Soviets pulled out of Afghanistan, the Berlin wall is breached and 329 days later, Germany is reunified, the Warsaw pact is dead. It's over. That's a very big event for the Bush administration. And nobody turned back. Somebody caught up with the senior administration official at that time and said something about Afghanistan and the word was, "Is that thing still going on?" Afghanistan by 1990 is going through its own tribal resolution and the Arabs are still over there. It's a totally failed state.[75]

Whether the motivations for US disengagement are attributed to a deliberate policy to prevent Islamists from taking power in Kabul, as Yousaf believes, or the result of benign neglect in the face of larger geopolitical developments such as the dissolution of the Soviet Bloc, as Bearden proposes, there is broad consensus that the current conflict is partly the result of the US abandoning Afghanistan and abruptly cutting off aid following the end of the Soviet occupation in 1989.

Guardian journalist Jonathan Steele points out, however, that the perception the US deserted Afghanistan is a myth; on the contrary, the US continued its involvement with the Mujahideen, funneling weapons their way to facilitate the overthrow of President Mohammad Najibullah's regime and "blocking moves toward negotiations," with the end results that the conflict was prolonged and the devastation of Afghanistan near complete.[76] Even Charles Cogan, the CIA Director of Operations for the Middle East and South Asia from 1979–1984, admitted in an interview that "aiding the mujahedin after the Soviets had left. . . was probably in retrospect a mistake."[77] Yet the premature-withdrawal narrative has become so engrained that it obliquely surfaced in the speeches of politicians justifying punitive action against Afghanistan following the 9/11 attacks. "One of the commonest promises Western politicians made after they toppled the Taliban in 2001 was that 'this time' the West would not walk away, as it had done after the Russians pulled out," Steele writes.[78] This theme was the subtext of President George W. Bush's November 10, 2001, "Address to the United Nations General Assembly" in which he pledged that "America will join the world in helping the people of Afghanistan rebuild their country. . . . The United States will work closely with the United Nations and development banks to reconstruct Afghanistan once the hostilities have ceased and the Taliban are no longer in control."[79]

The premature-withdrawal narrative became the basis for policy pre-scriptions in the Global War on Terror that consisted of throwing money at ill-conceived projects to spark economic development and seed civil society. Between 2001 and October 2014, the US and its forty-nine international coalition partners invested close to $900 billion "trying to establish Afghan security forces, build government ministries, and promote economic development" under the assumption that "a government that can provide essential services, foster economic development, and protect its citizens from organized violence, will be an inhospitable locale for terrorists."[80] "And yet," as Abdulkader Sinno observes, "the U.S.-led coalition produced generally dysfunctional Afghan state institutions" without having made much of a dent in the militant groups opposing it.[81] Sinno attributes the failure of state-building efforts to the reorganization of the Taliban after 2005 into a decentralized operation that created a loose network of support among diverse sectors of Pakistani society, including religious parties, ISI, businessmen, and the criminal element, among others; the incoherence of US military forces because of the privatization of the military and its reliance on contractors; and a basic lack of cultural knowledge among coalition partners. As the Taliban transformed into an insurgency movement, he explains, the coalition increasingly adopted "the tools of counter insurgency," resulting in a number of "inherent contradictions."[82] To name just three of those, he enumerates: the US has to secure the support of those groups they undermined by virtue of their initial intervention; they have to promote the rule of law in spite of the eventuality that coalition forces will themselves commit atrocities; and they must encourage support for the regime they have propped up in the name of "national unity" after themselves aggravating divisions through their intervention in the face of insurgents "who frame their resistance, much more convincingly, in nationalist terms."[83] The simulacra of premature withdrawal from Afghanistan inspire US aid, which create the illusion of progress in reconstruction and the creation of civil society with little to show for it in reality.

The contradictions flagged by Sinno vastly exceed the imaginative scope of the premature-withdrawal narrative, which can only assimilate the most clichéd conception of masculinity and historical agency as located in the liberal humanist subject. But what if we challenge the parameters of this narrative? Instead of positing the problem of Afghanistan to be the premature disengagement of the US in the region following the Soviet withdrawal, as this intervention narrative posits, what if we consider that the problem in the first place is itself the result of US covert operations during the 1980s? And that we mull the possibility that the decision to render aid to the Mujahideen did not correspond to any verifiable threat to US interests by the Soviet Union, but rather emanated from the delusions of Cold Warriors, including President Carter, who were so entranced by and entrenched in their limited worldview that they were unable to weigh the evidence against covert interventions? Such a diagnosis presumes an entirely different cure from the current one that consists of injecting the region with troops and capital, much of which is dissipated through corruption or ill-conceived projects that do not respond to ground-level needs: namely, a remedy requires a complete withdrawal from Afghanistan, this time not premature so much as belated.

Chapter 2

The Capitalist-Rescue Narrative

• •

Afghan Women and Micro-Entrepreneurship

Introduction

Following the 9/11 attacks, some US feminists have turned their attention to representing the experiences of Afghan women before and during the US occupation of that beleaguered country.[1] Books such as Gayle Tzemach Lemmon's *The Dressmaker of Khair Khana* and Deborah Rodriguez's *Kabul Beauty School* recount the challenges facing Afghan girls and women in light of gender-specific, state-sponsored sanctions under the Taliban; their heroism in surviving the Taliban era; and their attempts to piece together their lives and livelihoods after the US invasion.[2] As numerous feminist scholars have noted, the veiled woman became the iconic figure around whom public sentiment was mobilized to drum up support for the US military offensive, inspiring even the generally reticent then First Lady, Laura Bush, to declare that this lethal excursion was to save the Afghan ladies. Post-colonial, feminist accounts have analyzed this public fixation on the veiled woman as an updated version of what Gayatri Spivak describes in her seminal essay, "Can the Subaltern Speak?"; British attempts to legislate against native practices such as *sati*, she explains, can be reduced to the formulation of "white men saving brown women from brown men."[3]

To be sure, US politicians did highlight the rescue of Afghan women as one ideological justification for the military intervention, along with claiming it was a form of retributive justice for September 11. Yet a more complicated version of the rescue narrative has emerged among mainstream American feminists such as Lemmon and Rodriguez, who seem to have absorbed the lesson of third-wave and post-colonial feminism that women marginalized on the basis of their subject position (including their geopolitical location) are not passive objects in need of saving. Sensitized mainstream feminists, on the contrary, recognize that Afghan women exert their own agency, an awareness that manifests itself in what I am calling "the capitalist-rescue narrative." This narrative renders Afghan women as actualizing their agency through the opportunities provided by capitalism. The capitalist-rescue narrative represents Afghan women in terms of entrepreneurship, attributing their empowerment and social uplift to starting small-scale businesses targeted at other female consumers. Rather than constructing the American military—or, by extension, its government—as the savior of Afghan women, the agent of rescue becomes US-style capitalism with its attendant production arrangements and consumer practices.

Several rhetorical strategies characterize the capitalist-rescue narrative. Perhaps not surprisingly, given that the authors self-identify as feminists, the vocabulary of global sisterhood permeates this genre. By projecting fictive kinship ties onto their relationships with Afghan women, these American authors suggest an intimacy and equality of status between both groups of women, belied by the fact of US military occupation. The glossing over of the American military presence is of a piece with the historical amnesia that constitutes a second key feature of the capitalist-rescue narrative insofar as this genre dates the origins of US involvement in Afghanistan to 9/11, ignoring over two decades of covert operations and the destabilization of the region.

A third rhetorical strategy that appears in the capitalist-rescue narrative is the description of Afghan women's economic activity in terms that evoke earlier moments of US-style capitalism or that equate modernity with current US consumer practices. Afghanistan, in either case, emerges as subject to a different experience of time, as inhabiting a kind of belated temporality in which it plays catch up to US capitalist development. Temporality functions as a neoliberal updating of Anne McClintock's formulation of "panoptical time" (temporality organized as teleology) and "anachronistic space" (Third World societies as offering a prehistory of modern ones) in the colonial era. She explains that in combination, these concepts result in the figuration of "Geographical difference across *space*. . . as a historical difference across *time*."[4] To travel the geographic distance between Afghanistan and the US today is to journey back in time.

The construction of Afghanistan as at an arrested stage of development is linked to the fourth rhetorical strategy of the capitalist rescue narrative that establishes a neoliberal teleology for reconstruction in which the country's integration into the global economy becomes evidence of its arrival into modernity. Afghan women become significant agents for economic integration through their absorption in the NGO sector, a move that often entails the shift from independent small-scale entrepreneurship to wage labor.

In this chapter, I analyze two variations of the capitalist-rescue narrative, Gayle Tzemach Lemmon's *The Dressmaker of Khair Khana* and Deborah Rodriguez's *Kabul Beauty School*. An account of Kamila Sidiqi's home tailoring enterprise, Lemmon's *The Dressmaker of Khair Khana* reproduces dominant American ideological assumptions about the power of capitalism to improve the conditions of life for Afghan women, rendering their existence less precarious by providing them with freedom from material scarcity within the extreme constraints of Taliban-version patriarchy. Beginning chronologically where Lemmon ends, Rodriguez's *Kabul Beauty School* treats Afghan women's entrepreneurship in the period following the fall of the Taliban and the US invasion by describing the efforts of one British-born and several US-based beauticians to establish an academy to train Afghan women in hairstyling techniques and makeup application. This training, the well-intentioned beauticians hope, will facilitate the creation of home beauty parlors by their students, which have the potential to dramatically augment their family income and elevate the Afghan women's status in their households.

Crucial distinctions inhere in how these two texts tell their tales of capitalist rescue. In extremely simple prose, Lemmon de-emphasizes herself and centers her narrative on the Afghan women who are its subject, whereas the more elegantly written, co-authored *Kabul Beauty School* foregrounds Rodriguez's role as entrepreneur pedagogue to the detriment of conveying the texture of her students' lives. Yet both narratives also have elements that ultimately challenge their ideological mission, narrative threads that, when pulled, threaten to unravel the feel-good warp and weave of capitalist uplift. For Lemmon, those threads consist of the possibility of an alternative form of capitalism that is articulated with Islam, conveyed by the seamstress protagonist, Kamila, who repeatedly explains her economic activity as a Muslim imperative to help her community. In Rodriguez's tale, the ubiquitous presence of the US military and international NGO aid workers make explicitly visible the dependence of this form of capitalism on military force, thus discrediting the neoliberal fiction of upward mobility as individual achievement.

I begin by parsing the limitations of post-colonial academic feminist interpretations of the US intervention in Afghanistan before considering the two instantiations of the capitalist-rescue narrative. In my reading of Lemmon's and Rodriguez's texts, I pay particular attention to the rhetorical strategies each employs, the "capital fictions" that underwrite these strategies, and the contradictions that undermine the theme of feminist capitalist triumphalism. Revealing less about the lives of Afghan women than they do about the perceptions of mainstream American feminists, these texts become a metaphor for the US intervention in Afghanistan: well-intentioned and naïve in their assumptions that the introduction of the American way of life and US-style capitalism can be the foundation for the building of a stable nation-state. Lemmon and Rodriguez illustrate how benevolent understandings of US imperialism have become fixated on the figure of the Third World woman as micro-entrepreneur, who both creates avenues and becomes the site for capital investment in the periphery. But if it is the Third World woman who offers opportunities for feminist solidarities and capitalist identifications, it is the First World woman as the author of such accounts, who provides "a global conscience, and transforms the distance of gender and race into a liberal intimacy with the world's" aspiring middle classes, a subject I return to at the end of this chapter.[5]

The Academic Feminist Narrative: Brown Women as Objects of White Male Rescue

Two essays, Lila Abu-Lughod's "Do Muslim Women Really Need Saving" and Miriam Cooke's "Saving Brown Women," set the terms of the academic feminist response to the Bush administration's invocation of humanitarian intervention targeted at Afghan women; numerous feminist scholars cite these essays and accept their formulation of US foreign policy rationales as constructing brown women as objects of white male rescue.[6] Both Abu-Lughod and Cooke invoke Gayatri Spivak's seminal essay "Can the Subaltern Speak?" as a tool to analyze the rhetoric of humanitarian intervention. In her 1988 essay, a foundational text in post-colonial studies, Spivak analyzes the difficulties of locating the gendered subaltern's voice in the colonial archive. Examining nineteenth-century debates about the abolition of *sati* (widow immolation), she observes that the British campaign "has been generally understood as a case of 'White men saving brown women from brown men.'"[7] Abu-Lughod's and Cooke's reworkings of Spivak signal important continuities in the gender dynamics of colonial rhetoric in the nineteenth and twenty-first centuries, between British imperialism in South Asia and US interference in Afghanistan. In both cases, women have been perceived as an index of the natives' civilizational maturity. There are certainly compelling reasons for understanding the gender politics of the US invasion of Afghanistan through Spivak's paradigm. As an explanatory model, however, this paradigm suffers from three major limitations.

Cooke succinctly delineates stages in the "gendered logic of empire" as manifest in the colonial rescue narrative: "(1) women have inalienable rights within universal civilization, (2) civilized men recognize and respect these rights, (3) uncivilized men systematically abrogate these rights, and (4) such men (the Taliban) thus belong to an alien (Islamic) system."[8] While Spivak's original formulation of the colonial rescue narrative identifies it with British attempts to legislate against *sati*, this narrative would gain currency in the early twentieth century with the 1927 publication of Katherine Mayo's *Mother India*. An American, Mayo was a pro-imperialist feminist who had written in strong support of the US imperial mission in the Philippines in her book *Isles of Fear*. In *Mother India*, which was reprinted five times by the end of August 1927, Mayo attributed all of India's "material and spiritual" problems—such as "poverty, sickness, ignorance, political minority, melancholy, ineffectiveness [and] a subconscious sense of inferiority"—on the Indian male's "manner of getting into the world and his sex-life thenceforward."[9] Her book caused a sensation in Britain where conservatives mustered it as evidence to argue against Indian self-rule; editorials in the *New Statesman* and *Nation* alluded to the degraded status of Indian women and, hence, deemed the impulse to grant independence criminal.[10] These debates figured colonialism as a form of gender uplift, as an intervention by British men which was necessary to save Indian women from hyper-sexualized Indian men.

In their invocation of Spivak's paradigm, Abu-Lughod and Cooke usefully foreground the remarkable resilience of colonial discourse vis-à-vis the ways in which the status of native women continues to serve as a justification for the civilizing mission. Yet the power of Spivak's formulation in this context also might well be its most important limitation: by emphasizing *discursive* continuities between the two periods, we risk collapsing significant *material* differences between the two imperial regimes. Although both forms of imperialism rely on what David Harvey calls "accumulation by dispossession," the two are discontinuous in terms of their economic and territorial objectives, and the military means by which they secure their dominance.[11] Whereas the old imperialism was partially motivated by the economic impulse to extract natural resources from the periphery in order to industrialize the metropole and to create captive markets in the colonies, the new imperialism seeks to control access to oil in order to direct the global economy in the near future and to integrate national economies into the neoliberal world order.[12] Whereas colonial powers directly ruled large swaths of territory in the old imperialism, the territorial dimension in the new imperialism is restricted to the exercise of control over small pockets of land that house military bases. Whereas in the old imperialism, naval supremacy was an important aspect of materializing geopolitical power, in the new imperialism aerial force is a necessary part of realizing geopolitical dominance.[13]

Recognizing the differences between the old and new imperialisms enables us to explore the US's geostrategic and economic aims in Afghanistan and the Global War on Terror. As I explained in the introduction of this book, the Bush administration appears to have been motivated by three objectives: containing Islamic militancy in the region, namely in Afghanistan, Iran and Pakistan; establishing military bases as a pre-emptive warning to nearby peer competitors such as China and Russia; and to secure access to energy reserves in Central Asia, giving the US leverage over Pacific Rim and Pacific Basin countries whose growing economies are dependent on such imports.

The use of Spivak's paradigm in the context of Afghanistan has a second limitation insofar as it constructs the United States in racially monolithic terms and the US military as a masculine institution under the sign of "white men." Although "whites" constitute the majority population of the US, comprising about 61.72% of the total population, the other 38.28% of the population consists of categories delineated by the US Census Bureau as "Black and African American," "American Indian and Alaska Native," "Asian," "Native Hawaiian and Other Pacific Islander," and biracial individuals. (The US Census, along with the US Department of Defense asks respondents a separate question regarding their "Hispanic" identity; according to the Census, 17.66% of the general population identifies as Hispanic).[14] People of color constitute 30.57% of active-duty enlisted men and 47.62% of active-duty enlisted women in the military.[15] Spivak's formulation, in this instance, obscures the racial complexity of the US general population and the US military, which also includes non-citizen enlistees from the Philippines, Mexico, Nigeria, India, and Germany, among other countries.[16] Moreover, it figures the military subject as male and elides women's participation in the US armed forces where they constitute about 20% of the services.[17]

A third limitation of the use of Spivak's paradigm is that it homogenizes important ethnic differences in Afghanistan under the signifier of the "brown subject," differences that are crucial to understanding gender in the region. In Afghanistan, "ethnicity itself," as Elaheh Rostami-Povey cautions, "is complex and variously defined by language, religion, descent, region and profession."[18] Because Afghanistan has not had a systematic census in decades, precise demographic figures are unavailable; the Afghan constitution recognizes fourteen ethnicities including, "Pashtun, Tajik, Hazara, Uzbek, Aimak, Turkmen, Baloch, along with other ethnicities such as Kirghiz, Wakhi, Farsiwan, Nuristani, Brahui, Qizilbash, Kabuli, and Jat.[19] Although Afghan women shoulder the burden of maintaining the family's respectability and social standing by adhering to gender codes associated with shame and honor, the standards for acceptable female conduct and male attitudes toward the correct treatment of women vary widely among different ethnic groups. Some ethnic groups, such as the majority Pushtun, conform to customary practices such as *purdah* (female seclusion) and veiling more strictly than other groups, though it is important to acknowledge that there are regional differences among them, with those in the southern provinces adhering to more conservative gender norms than the Pushtun in the eastern provinces of Afghanistan, who tend to value female education.[20] Other ethnic groups have functioning canons that espouse equality, justice, and education, and encourage both men and women to engage in community service. The Hazara, for example, have tended to encourage girls to gain an education and women to pursue professional careers in teaching, healthcare, and the civil services.[21] Differences regarding attitudes toward women among ethnic groups are further complicated by the diverse interpretation of women's rights among reformists, Islamists, and ultraconservatives.

The Bush administration's cynical exploitation of the condition of Afghan women as a justification for military intervention also implicitly promoted a gendered version of American exceptionalism that posits American women as the paradigm of rights-possessing subjects who enjoy a high social status unprecedented in the world. Yet in a 2018 study by the Thomson Reuters Foundation that ranks the ten most dangerous countries for women, the US placed tenth behind India, Afghanistan, Syria, Somalia, Saudi Arabia, Pakistan, Democratic Republic of Congo, Yemen, and Nigeria. The study assessed the status of women based on healthcare, discrimination, cultural traditions, sexual violence, non-sexual violence, and human trafficking. The US's high marks in sexual violence (number 3) and non-sexual violence (number 6) seem to have earned it a spot in this hall of shame.[22] Even in 2017, women in the US only earn eighty and a half cents to the dollar paid to men.[23]

While the academic feminist narrative of US intervention in Afghanistan provides a valuable heuristic to criticize this form of American exceptionalism and to focus attention on the discursive continuities between different imperial regimes, it elides important material distinctions between the two imperial formations, constructs the U.S. as unambiguously "white" and male, and too easily racializes ethnicity in Afghanistan as "brown."

Capitalist Fictions of *The Dressmaker of Khair Khana*

Gayle Tzemach Lemmon has been shaped by elite institutions of US and global finance, where the dominant ethos has been to confuse democratization with the spread of US-style capitalism. As is apparent from her webpage, she has been embedded in some of the most influential and powerful media, educational, financial, and political institutions of our day, and it is not startling that she perceives capitalist enterprise as the means for women to improve their material conditions in conflict-ridden societies. A former ABC News producer, Lemmon had become fascinated with women's economic activities in conflict zones, an interest that developed into a research topic when she earned an MBA from Harvard Business School. Since receiving an MBA, she has had an unusual career, working as a one-time vice president for the global investment management firm PIMCO; writing articles on women and entrepreneurship for influential publications such as *The New York Times, The Financial Times, Fast Company, The Christian Science Monitor,* and *Newsweek Daily Beast*; consulting for the World Bank; and serving as a senior fellow at the Council for Foreign Relations. On her web-page, she explains that women often "make the difference between survival and starvation for their family during conflict. . . through business." These entrepreneurs, Lemmon maintains, "create jobs and hope." Regardless of con-text, the values girding capitalist enterprise are constant in her view: "The backdrop may be different than entrepreneurs in the US and elsewhere face, but the principle of entrepreneurship remains the same: find an opportunity and make the most of it, not just for yourself, but for all those who depend on you."[24] Lemmon's description of entrepreneurs as job creators who are motivated by altruistic concerns for their communities echoes a common refrain of conservative American politicians since former President Ronald Reagan popularized the idea that the rich would create wealth for the deserv-ing, impecunious segments of society rather than hoarding it for themselves, provided that their capital was unfettered by restrictions.

The coupling of job creation and entrepreneurship constitutes what Ericka Beckman calls a "capital fiction," those seemingly commonsensical formula-tions that masquerade "as impeccable economic logic today."[25] Invoking Karl Polanyi (himself drawing from Marx), Beckman emphasizes "the centrality of ideology and imagination in governing economic life" and "argues that mod-ern capitalism can function only once certain fictions come to be accepted as real."[26] While her concern is to delineate the capital fictions specific to Latin America in the late nineteenth century, her conceptualization of this category can be productively applied to the twenty-first century. In addition to the capital fiction that entrepreneurship means job creation, the contemporary US cultural dominant equates democracy with capitalism.[27] Partly a remnant of the Cold War ideological conflation of modes-of-production with political systems and the correlation of a more equitable distribution of wealth with Soviet-style authoritarianism, present-day American capital fictions have also been shaped by the increasing power of corporations and the tendency to anthropomorphize capital. Elsewhere, Laura E. Lyons and I have written about current forms of corporate embodiment, including in advertising icons such as Uncle Ben's and Betty Crocker, the identification of corporations with their celebrity CEOs (for example, Apple, Inc. and Steve Jobs), and, more perniciously, the granting of personhood status, and thus legal rights, to cor-porations under the US Constitution.[28] This tendency to embody capital as the corporate form facilitates the conflation between economic and political systems, where the freedom of capital from regulations gets coded as a signifier for individual liberty. Such capital fictions underwrite foreign policy and what has come to be known as the Washington Consensus, the 90s-era drive to export the specific class interests of American elites and project them as being in the collective interests of everyone. This capital fiction enables the type of conceptual confusion evident in *The Dressmaker of Khair Khana*: business enterprise gets figured as community uplift, which in turn contributes to the overall US mission in Afghanistan of gunboat democracy.

Given the fictional nature of such ideas—they originate as explanations for the conditions of real life, which then acquire a power of their own and "become the ground for actual transformations of material life" —it is perhaps not surprising that Lemmon's text draws on the stylistic conventions of fiction, appropriating formal techniques associated with the novel that are combined with journalism to produce a hybrid form of life writing.[29] Framed by a first-person introduction in Lemmon's voice, the account of Kamila Sidiqi's tailoring business is told from the third-person omniscient point of view and very much reads like a work of literature. The blurring of fact and fiction is not uncommon in colonial travel narratives, and indeed Lemmon's frame narrative relies on familiar tropes of the First World traveler in an exotic Third World setting. Cringe-inducing revelations such as her description of her first encounter with a head scarf ("No one had prepared me for how hard it was to stay covered while in motion, let alone when lugging heavy baggage." [xiii]); confusion over the rendezvous with her "fixer," Mohamad (the twenty-first century version of the proverbial native informant); admissions of her ignorance about Afghanistan ("as soon as I arrived I realized just how little I actually knew about the country" [xviii]); and the description of Kabul as "an urban Wild West" (a leitmotif shared with Deborah Rodriguez's *Kabul Beauty School* [xvi]) are reminiscent of colonial travel account clichés. But instead of the crude racism of the colonial narrative, we get an updated, more politically correct version of that familiar story where the second-wave feminism of universal sisterhood replaces the positing of absolute difference between Western and native subjects. Transnational female solidarity is articulated in kinship metaphors: "over time Kamila's family became part of" Lemmon's own (xxv). "What I found in Kabul," she confides in the frame narrative, "was a sisterhood unlike any I had seen before, marked by empathy, laughter, courage, curiosity about the world, and above all a passion for work" (xxv).

Lemmon's feminist sensibilities counter the racism of colonial travel narratives that is generally visible in degrading representations of natives or in their relegation to serving as props for the actions of a metropolitan protagonist. She does not reproduce either of these representational patterns, and she is acutely aware of the tendency for Westerners to perceive Third World women as objects of sentimental pity. "We're far more accustomed to—and comfortable with—seeing women portrayed as victims of war who deserve our sympathy rather than as resilient survivors who demand our respect," she writes. "I was determined to change this" (xviii). Her explicit agenda is to represent Afghan women as subjects of history, not its objects, and to recount the laudatory role of capitalism in enabling their entry onto the national and global stages. Lemmon's introduction repeatedly states her desire to transmit the "story" of women's entrepreneurship, that of "a burqa-clad breadwinner starting a business," and often refers to Afghan women as "heroines" and "protagonists" (xx). The "story" she "set[s] out to tell" is of "a young woman who believed with all her heart that by starting her own business and helping other women to do the same, she could help save her long-troubled country" (xxv-xxvi). The story, in other words, is that of capitalism to the rescue.

The terminology of fiction that Lemmon uses in her introduction—of stories, heroines, and protagonists—is telling. In contrast to the first-person voice of the introduction, the embedded narrative of Kamila Sidiqi's tailoring business is written in the third-person omniscient point of view, lending it the aura of literary fiction, an aura that is magnified by the author's failure to explain the creative process and the relationship between Sidiqi's narrative and the interviews that Lemmon conducted over several years. This raises a number of questions: Are the direct quotations that appear in the embedded narrative of entrepreneurship drawn from her interviews? On what basis did Lemmon determine the content of passages that reveal the unspoken thoughts of the Afghan women? And did her interviewees approve the final copy of the text? Just how much mimetic accuracy are we to attribute to this moving tale of women's ingenuity? At one level, the omniscient point of view replicates, in narrative form, US foreign policy insofar as the American narrator assumes the right to divine the thoughts and feelings of Afghan women in ways that resonate with the American state's assumption of such powers in relation to Afghan governance. On another level, it reproduces the tired tendency, as Srimati Basu explicates, of First World women arrogantly serving as ventriloquists for women in the Third World.[30]

Rhetorical Strategies of Lemmon's Capitalist-Rescue Narrative

Just as the embedded narrative of capitalist uplift contains significant gaps regarding its creative process, so too is it marked by significant lacunae in the historical record, which are part of the text's overall ideological mission to equate Afghan women's empowerment with entrepreneurship. I turn now to the rhetorical strategies in the embedded story of Sidiqi that inform this version of the capitalist-rescue narrative, beginning with Lemmon's omission of the role of the US in destabilizing the region since the early 1980s. To subscribe to the version of history advanced by *The Dressmaker of Khair Khana* is to believe that US involvement in Afghanistan began in October 2001 with the commencement of the aerial bombardment of the country in the name of retributive justice for the September 11 attacks and as punishment against the Taliban for harboring Osama bin Laden. Nowhere in the text does Lemmon indicate any prior US activity in the region. While space constraints do not allow me to fully rehearse the complex history of Afghanistan that involves

Iran, Pakistan, the USSR, and the US, the 1979 Iranian Revolution alarmed both Cold War belligerents for different reasons. With the fall of the Shah of Iran, the Carter Administration worried about the loss of its geostrategic advantages in the Persian Gulf region, including access to intelligence, military bases, and, ultimately, oil. A Marxist regime in Kabul compounded the danger of an Islamic one in Tehran in terms of curtailing US influence in the Middle East. Carter began to funnel aid, in July 1979, to the Islamic insurgency in Afghanistan months before the Soviet invasion.[31] Shortly after the Soviet invasion of Afghanistan (which occurred in December 1979), Carter issued what is now the doctrine that bears his name, asserting the right of the US to safeguard its access to oil through the use of "any means necessary, including military force."[32]

From the Soviet perspective, three factors served as evidence of the worrisome spread of fundamentalism across the region: the Iranian revolution and Ayatollah Khomeini's ascendance to power, the emergence of an Islamic insurgency against the Khalqi regime in Afghanistan—which had itself declared a commitment to Islam within the contours of a secular state—and Zia ul-Haq's Islamization of Pakistan. The Soviets feared that Islamic fundamentalism could spill into the Central Asian republics and challenge the integrity of the Soviet Union by giving rise to sectarian movements.[33] Afghanistan provided a buffer between the Soviet Union, Iran, and Pakistan, and thus could not be allowed to succumb to religious fundamentalism. Military intervention in Afghanistan, in the Soviet calculus, became the means to secure its status as a buffer state.[34] Initially planning to provide support services to the Afghan army in response to Islamic insurgency and to limit their own occupation to several months, the Soviets stayed for nearly a decade. They waged a brutal counterinsurgency campaign in the rural areas that included firing on villages from Mi-24 Hind helicopters, planting numerous landmines that children mistook for toys, and committing other atrocities against civilians; estimates of Afghan casualties vary from 876,000 to 1.5 million, and by 1987, some 5 million Afghans had fled the country.[35]

The Soviet invasion of Afghanistan caused Pakistan serious concerns about being encircled by hostile states: to its east was its nemesis India and to its west was Afghanistan, now occupied by the USSR, the ally of its historic enemy India. In addition, Pakistan had to contend with the influx of Afghan refugees within its borders, estimated at 3 million by the UNHCR, which it feared would create a situation analogous to that of Palestinian refugees in Arab countries.[36] Not wanting to provoke a retaliatory attack on themselves, the Pakistanis determined that the Soviets could be drawn into a Vietnam-type quagmire in their attempts to put down the Islamic insurgency. To this end, they covertly supplied the Afghan resistance with aid, intelligence, operational training, and arms.[37]

The United States also perceived the invasion as an opportunity to inflict a Vietnam-style humiliation on the Soviets by entangling the USSR in a protracted conflict. It initially channeled outdated weapons and a modest appropriation to Afghan rebels through Pakistan's Inter-Services Intelligence. Over time, the US's strategic aims in Afghanistan changed to the outright defeat of the Soviet forces, albeit through a proxy war fought by the Mujahideen, Muslim holy warriors, as the insurgents were called. Largely because of then CIA-Director William Casey's influence over Ronald Reagan, the appropriation for covert operations increased to a billion dollars annually (totaling between $4–5 billion), which Saudi Arabia matched for a combined total of approximately $10 billion.[38] The massive increase in appropriations and influx of sophisticated weapons resulted in the Mujahideen's defeat of the 40th Army.

Never a unified force, the Mujahideen were splintered not only by ethnic and regional factors, but also by nationality and, as a result, sectarian differences between Saudi Arabian Wahhabi-style Islam and Afghan traditions, which at that time were inflected with Sufism.[39] The Afghan insurgency had been augmented by a recruitment drive in parts of the Muslim world (primarily Algeria, Egypt, Palestine, Sudan, and Yemen) in the name of waging jihad against communism and the Soviet Union. These recruits received arms and training from the CIA.[40] Following the Soviet withdrawal, civil war erupted between the different Mujahideen factions, plunging Afghanistan into chaos.[41] When the Taliban consolidated power at the end of 1994, they were initially welcomed by Afghans who had tired of the anarchy of civil war and who believed that the Taliban would disarm the population and restore peace. Civil war was replaced by a form of state terrorism, as the Taliban moved to recreate their interpretation of an ideal Islamic society, which they associated with the one in which the Prophet Mohammed lived 1,400 years ago. Draconian restrictions on the population, including prohibitions on almost all forms of pleasure (e.g., playing games such as cards or flying kites, arts and entertainment, and even laughing in public) along with brutal forms of punishment (e.g., beating, amputation, stoning, and other execution methods) for violations of the law, made life under the Taliban extremely difficult to bear.

The Dressmaker of Khair Khanna makes no references to this historical context and the US's considerable part in destabilizing the region during the 1980s by underwriting the Mujahideen and creating the conditions for the emergence of the Taliban. A curious imperial amnesia permeates the text whereby Soviet atrocities in the countryside are recounted, but not the expansion of education and professional opportunities for women in urban areas under their occupation. That women in Kabul had a much higher status in the decade preceding the civil war is acknowledged in one off-hand observation about the founding of the Kabul Pedagogical Institute during the Soviet occupation, "which saw the expansion of state institutions," but not much more information is given (4–5). Even here, Lemmon's use of the passive voice obscures the agency of the Soviets in establishing educational and civic institutions.

Nor does Lemmon contextualize the civil war as a logical outcome of covert operations and the failure of the US to transform its military operations into reconstruction efforts after the Soviet withdrawal. Rather, the civil war is presented as a historical non sequitur, as erupting spontaneously in the aftermath of the Soviet occupation. In order for the capitalist-rescue narrative to have any legitimacy, the US—as the paradigmatic capitalist democracy—must be disarticulated from illiberal movements such as those represented by the Mujahideen and Taliban. This necessary evasion constitutes an important rhetorical strategy of the capitalist-rescue narrative. If the Cold War is understood as the US government's attempt to enact a foreign policy meant to advance capitalism around the globe, the diagnosis of the origins of the current status of Afghanistan as a failed state—as *being of* the Cold War, in a narrative that proposes the curative powers of capitalism—would be to advocate for the disease to be the treatment for the illness: entrepreneurship as a means to remedy the harmful consequences of a foreign policy aimed at spreading capitalism.

A second rhetorical strategy of the capitalist-rescue narrative consists of projecting Fordist modes-of-production onto cottage industries. The Taliban imposed severe restrictions on women, banning them from most workplaces (apart from women's clinics, which were woefully underfunded), discouraging cosmetic use and prescribing a strict dress code, and prohibiting women's presence in public places without the accompaniment of a husband or *mahram* (unmarriageable kin).[42] Barred from employment and most market transactions without the mediation of "a responsible male guardian," women's economic situations became desperate, as did those of their families who depended on their incomes. With few to no options for wage labor, women turned to the informal sector, producing goods or providing services in their homes; such activities were permitted by the Taliban as long as the women did not mingle with men.

Mulling over the options to augment the family income, Kamila Sidiqi hits on the idea of becoming a seamstress. This occupation, she thinks, has many advantages: "she could do the work in her living room, her sisters could help, and most important of all, she had seen for herself. . . that the market for clothing remained strong. Even with the Taliban in power and the economy collapsing, women would still need simple dresses" (52). The market opportunity for ready-made clothing that Sidiqi intuits has been partly created by the Taliban edict forbidding tailors from "sewing ladies cloth and taking female body measures [sic]."[43] The fact that Kamila does not know how to sew is no impediment, as she feels confident that she can learn this skill from her elder sister, Malika, a talented seamstress.

In the embedded narrative of Sidiqi's business venture, Lemmon emphasizes the capitalist thematic of growth even though she is depicting a fledgling
home-based business. She describes Kamila's first experience going to the market with a clothing sample, with her younger brother Rahim as her *mahram*,
and landing an order from a shopkeeper. Kamila, her four sisters, and a neighborhood friend set up their sartorial operation in the Sidiqi home, establishing
a regular routine organized around the timely production of their orders. In
spite of its small scale, from the start, Kamila focuses on expanding the business
by seeking new markets for their garments. On acquiring a second customer,
the third-person omniscient narrator attributes the following thoughts to her:
"This is how it starts. . . Now we just have to keep it growing. And we have to
make sure nothing goes wrong" (98). Marx's observation about capitalism's
voracious appetite for growth is evident in Kamila's hunger for more orders, a
craving that becomes more pronounced as the business gets established and is
only satiated when her enterprise assumes a pedagogical mission, about which
I will say more shortly.

The larger number of orders for dresses and *salwaar kameezes* (South Asian
tunic and trouser sets) necessitates a regularization of production and more
seamstresses; Lemmon's rendering of this change primarily relies on dialogue
that projects Fordist modes of production onto this home-based system of
production. Kamila realizes that "they needed a better, more streamlined process" and "more hands" (98). Brainstorming about how to respond to market
demand, the Sidiqi sisters devise ways to increase their efficiency:

> "What if we divide up the cutting and beading—make it something like an
> assembly line, so that one person is responsible for each," Saaman said. "Who-
> ever is best at cutting can do it for all of us. That would help the dresses look a
> little more professional too."
>
> Nasrin nodded. "I agree. I also think we should clear out this room to make
> more space to sew. Mother isn't here in her usual place, and Father doesn't need
> his seat in front of the radio anymore. We might as well turn this into a real
> workshop. . . .
>
> "Nasrin, you are going to have us turn the entire house into a little factory!"
> Kamila said, breaking out into a giggle. "Our own parents wouldn't recognize
> their own home!" (99)

Nasrin's comment that their father "doesn't need his seat in front of the radio
anymore" as a partial rationale for transforming their living quarters to facilitate expedited production is telling. This literal unseating of kinship relations hints that the daughters' economic activity augurs a future change in the
structure of the patriarchal family. References to assembly lines, workshops,
and factories in this passage, along with the specialization of labor and the

reorganization of the family's physical space, evoke a production model loosely based on Fordism, yet without its crucial reliance on a mechanized moving production line and its typical associations with an economy of scale at the national level and an accumulation regime based on mass production and mass consumption. The overall effect of describing the family tailoring business as a small-scale factory is to naturalize industrial capitalism as the next stage of economic activity, implicitly proposing capitalist development as the telos for Afghanistan.

The transformation of home to factory, domesticity to production, recalls the nineteenth-century origins of the industrial revolution in the textile industry. As if anticipating this development, Kamila introduces a managerial level of oversight, hiring Sara, a widow, who the text identifies as "their first official employee." A "division of labor between the two women" evolves organically; Sara is "a good manager—in fact she was a natural," and her presence liberates "Kamila to focus on the part of the operation she was coming to love most, despite all the risks: the marketing and the planning" (112). The enterprise has grown sufficiently to result in the differentiation of managerial functions, not atypical of more complex capitalist institutions.

The seamstresses have carved out a market niche by designing women's garments that combine the elegance of French styles that were fashionable in Kabul during the 1970s–1980s and the sartorial modesty mandated by the Taliban. Neither the reorganization of the production process in the Sidiqi home nor the women's fourteen-hour workdays are sufficient to keep up with the demand for their clothes. But Kamila has a plan to respond to both the labor shortage and her desire for more growth: she determines to start a school for young women to teach them sewing and embroidery, imparting the skills that they would need to establish their own tailoring businesses. The idea, then, is to begin a vocational school for small-scale garment operations that resemble her own. Laura E. Lyons and I have noted how the biographies and autobiographies of celebrity CEOs not only purport to tell the tale of singular achievement, but also to sell a particular way of doing business.[44] In Kamila's pedagogical designs, as in the life writing of CEOs, we also see the desire to stitch and sell a *product*, clothing, along with the urge to popularize a particular *method* of stitching and selling clothing. The tailoring operation expands to a seamstress-vocational program, organized in two shifts comprised of twelve students each, taught by two of the Sidiqi sisters; this activity occurs as a supplement to the ongoing tailoring project and the coordination of the women who have elected to sew in their own homes, who are picking up fabric and thread from and dropping off finished garments at the Sidiqi domicile.

The establishment of the school for tailoring-entrepreneurship aids the growth of Kamila's business by expanding her labor force but not in ways that resemble the familiar mechanisms of wage labor. Lemmon describes Kamila's rationale for making the venture tuition-free:

> Though some schools in the neighborhood were charging a small fee, Kamila had decided it was better not to; the girls would pay nothing while they were learning, and in exchange they wouldn't earn a salary until their training period ended. During their apprenticeship they would help make garments that Kamila could take to the market, so their work would contribute to the business almost immediately. How soon a girl completed her training depended on both her skills and her commitment to her work. Only Kamila and Sara would have the final say on that question, with input from their teachers, Saaman and Laila. (125–126)

Michael Denning has asserted the necessity of rethinking the centrality of wage labor in "conception[s] of life under capitalism."[45] "For capitalism begins not with the offer of work, but with the imperative to earn a living," he observes.[46] Through the implementation of a barter system, Kamila replaces the employment contract with the educational contract, and the promise of imparting skills that will yield future profit to the women in exchange for their immediate labor. Denning's astute conclusion that "wageless life, not wage labour, is the starting point in understanding the free market" seems particularly apt here.

Yet it is difficult to make definitive pronouncements on labor arrangements in Kamila's various enterprises because *The Dressmaker of Khair Khanna* carefully avoids giving even the barest details of either financial transactions or the economics of the business as a whole, the third rhetorical strategy of this version of the capitalist-rescue narrative. Apart from learning that Kamila's first order nets "an envelope filled with afghani, enough to buy the family flour and groceries for a week" (90) and that Sara's "small income was now contributing to her brother-in-law's kitchen and paying for the books and pencils her sons needed for school" (135), little other information on finances is disclosed. Nor does Lemmon enumerate the costs of doing business, such as inputs for supplies and labor and outputs in profits. These are strange omissions for a journalist who covers these issues for major Western business publications. One consequence of these omissions is to make it impossible to judge the efficacy of capitalism as the means of rescuing Afghan women from their dire circumstances. If the wages are low, then Sidiqi can be accused of exploiting a vulnerable workforce and reproducing the worse features of the capitalist system, rendering questionable the capital fiction of job creation. If wages are high or equitably distributed among all the women, then the tailoring venture risks being more akin to a cooperative or socialist venture in Kamila's deliberate decision to forgo a significant profit margin for herself and family.

A third possibility exists insofar as there are innumerable ways that capitalism does not stand on its own, but is supported, enabled, and strengthened through cultural mores and institutions such as the extended family that can and often does come to its "rescue." In such cases, it becomes difficult to ascertain the degree to which capitalism or its support services are responsible for financial success. In any of these scenarios, capitalism as a mode of rescue would be discredited, albeit for different reasons, explaining perhaps Lemmon's silence on these topics.

Unraveling the Capitalist-Rescue Narrative

The third rhetorical strategy of the capitalist-rescue narrative, the withholding of details of financial transactions, is partly obscured by Lemmon's description of Kamila's motivations to expand her business as a product of her faith. The representation of Afghan Muslims in Lemmon's text is structured by a now familiar binary opposition between bad Muslims and good Muslims elaborated by Mahmood Mamdani.[47] Bad Muslims are intolerant, oppose modernity, adhere to an extremist form of patriarchy, and have a literalist interpretation of Islam, e.g., the Taliban, and they are also hypocrites insofar as their wives number among the Sidiqis' direct customers. Good Muslims, in contrast, believe in educational and professional opportunities for women and are community-minded, being guided by an Islamic sense of obligation and collective responsibility to their families and neighbors.

Early in the embedded narrative of the tailoring business, Lemmon makes it clear that the Sidiqis belong to the category of good, civic-minded Muslims. Of Kamila's father, she writes, "To him it was his highest obligation and a duty of his faith to educate his children so that they could share their knowledge and serve their communities" (17). Kamila too feels a responsibility to her family: "Her work would help her family, which was a sacred obligation of Islam" (65). As the embedded narrative progresses and more women, some of whom are strangers, entreat her to employ them, this sense of religious obligation increases. On hearing Sara's backstory of pain and hardship, Kamila reflects, "Her father had told her, and her religion had taught her, that she had a duty to support as many as she was able. Right now that meant she must quickly build upon the modest successes they had achieved so far. This business was her best—and right now her only—hope for helping her community" (111). Kamila interprets the divine imperative to help her community as an injunction to build her business or in the book's preferred parlance "to grow" her enterprise, implying that capital is an organic being in yet another example of a capital fiction.[48]

The relationship between capitalism and Islam has been up for debate at least since Max Weber pronounced their incompatibility, with some scholars asserting that "Muslim legal practice places institutional constraints on economic growth" and others claiming that the values of "hard work, self-discipline, and individual accountability" associated with the ideal concept of the Islamic self are also aligned with Weber's gloss on "the spirit of capitalism."[49] Yet other scholars have explored Islamic alternatives to capitalism and the development of faith-centered socialism, banking, and financial practices. Rather than view Islam as categorically hostile or sympathetic to capitalism, Amira Mittermaier makes a persuasive case for "approaching Islam (or religion more broadly) as heteroglossic," an approach that "draws attention to instabilities and ambiguities and allows us to consider how Islamic discourse and practice might be inflected by modern modes of calculative reason while at the same time destabilizing capitalism, neoliberalism, and market logic as 'the only games in town.'"[50] Following her lead, I believe it is worth considering that Kamila's spirit of religiosity and stated commitment to rendering aid to her community can potentially unravel the logic of Lemmon's capitalist-rescue narrative. I qualify this observation with the word "potentially" because in the absence of information about the actual wages and profit margin of Kamila's tailoring business, it is impossible to judge.

While the first three quarters of *The Dressmaker of Khair Khana* treat the period from 1996–2001, the years the Taliban were in power, describing the establishment and expansion of Kamila's tailoring business, the last quarter of the narrative presents a compressed account of her activities leading up to and following the US invasion in October 2001. Lemmon does not shy away from acknowledging the violence of the US bombing campaign or the distortion of the Afghan economy as a result of the influx of well-meaning foreign aid workers. Out of a sense of Islamic obligation, Kamila decides to work for an NGO, the UN's Community Forum, teaching women about income-generating projects; the fate of her tailoring business remains unclear.

Kamila's NGO appointment—which positions her differently in the capitalist economy as a wage worker, even though she admittedly earns a pittance of $10 a month, instead of as a business owner—is followed by a series of jobs with NGOS: the UN's International Organization for Migration and then Mercy Corps. Of the ubiquitous presence of aid workers and development programs in Kabul, Lemmon reports that "Kamila welcomed the world back with open arms" (219): "'This is a golden chance for Afghanistan,' she said. An opportunity to help her fellow Afghans rebuild what war had destroyed: the roads, the economy, the country's educational system—all the vital infrastructure that had collapsed—and to give her generation and the next one the first chance they had ever had to live in peace. For the past four years, Kamila had been doing her part, working with the foreigners on behalf of her countrymen. . . .

Women like her who had experience with the international community were in short supply and high demand." (220)

In Kamila's optimism regarding reconstruction and the opportunities it affords Afghans, as conveyed by Lemmon, we hear echoes of another capital fiction: that capitalism is a force of creative destruction in which the destruction of the old enables the birth of creative, new forms of production in sync with modernity. After a few years, Kamila becomes restless with the NGO sector, and the final pages of the book describe her founding of another business, Kaweyan, whose goal it is to teach entrepreneurship to aspiring Afghans. "Afghanistan needs business," Kamila believes, "if it is going to keep growing once the foreigners leave" (225). The concept of a business begetting other businesses perfectly expresses confidence in capitalism's capacity to save people and nations.

I do not mean to minimize Kamila's heroism and creativity in devising a survival strategy to circumvent the severe restrictions imposed on women by the Taliban. Her ingenuity not only enables her family to survive but it also allows her neighbors and community to withstand Taliban-era deprivations. My intent rather has been to flag the limitations of Lemmon's account of the Sidiqi sisters' agency, which she can only represent through its translation into the idiom of US-style capitalism. The end result is to assimilate Kamila's story of women's self-empowerment into post-9/11 justifications for US military intervention that seemingly expanded economic opportunities for women by opening the door to NGO projects and facilitating their entry into wage labor. Given the complex nature of the socioeconomic formation in contemporary Afghanistan, along with the military occupation, Kamila's experiences, as well as those of her compatriots, exceed the terms of their representation in Lemmon's narrative.

Kabul Beauty School and the Beautifying Mission

The Dressmaker of Khair Khana's representation of capitalist pedagogy—which is embodied in the school Kamila and her sisters start to inculcate business skills in aspiring seamstresses—has an analog in the Kabul Beauty Academy, a venture of US and British beauticians to teach Afghan women about American beauty techniques in order to help them either to establish their own home beauty salons or to increase their clientele by offering superior services to those provided by local women. *Kabul Beauty School* shares with Lemmon's text the rhetorical strategies of invoking global sisterhood, of historical amnesia and the forgetting of the US's decades-long involvement in the region, and of reproducing a belated temporality of capitalist development. Capitalist modernity, in this venture, becomes equated with the Afghan women's embrace of US beauty practices and consumer products, which is couched in the language of feminism.

To understand why beauty practices became powerful signifiers for Afghan women's emancipation and how the beauty salon acquired its iconic status as a site of resistance to the Taliban, we need to recall the US media landscape prior to the invasion of Afghanistan on October 7, 2001. In the month leading up to the invasion, the mainstream media began to highlight the condition of Afghan women under the Taliban. Capitalizing on the sudden interest in Afghan women, the White House paraded the heretofore reticent Laura Bush to deliver a national radio address on November 17, 2001. In her remarks, Mrs. Bush emphatically named misogyny to be a crucial aspect of the structure of terrorism, declaring that "The brutal oppression of women is a central goal of the terrorists."[51] And she credited the United States with helping to free Afghan women: "Because of our recent military gains in much of Afghanistan, women are no longer imprisoned in their homes. They can listen to music and teach their daughters without fear of punishment. Yet the terrorists who helped rule that country now plot and plan in many countries. And they must be stopped. The fight against terrorism is also a fight for the rights and dignity of women."[52] Significantly, Mrs. Bush's interpretation of terrorism's gendered contours included women's right to wear cosmetics, along with more fundamental rights such as access to education and healthcare. "Only the terrorists and the Taliban forbid education to women," she announced. "Only the terrorists and the Taliban threaten to pull out women's fingernails for wearing nail polish."[53]

Mrs. Bush's articulation of beauty consumer practices with resistance to a brutal form of patriarchy would become a leitmotif in mainstream American narratives about the condition of Afghan women. Ellen McLarney persuasively argues that Afghanistan provided "a fertile ground for the capitalist imagination: emancipation from the stranglehold of communist ideology on local and regional markets, emancipation from an oppressive religious regime, emancipation from 'backward' social and cultural practices, emancipation of the Muslim woman."[54] Together, McLarney notes, these "discourses of repression" coalesced around the figure of the Afghan woman, whose body functioned as a signifier of emancipation through the consumption of cosmetic and sartorial commodities associated with the new capitalist economy.[55] Such a construction is not unique to the Afghan context, appearing before in media coverage of women and market reforms in Eastern Europe, the former Soviet Union, and China during the 1980s and 1990s.[56] "Identified in socialist ideology as a corrupt bourgeois practice oppressive to women," Kathy Peiss observes, "cosmetics-use then marked a turn away from totalitarianism to Western-style individualism and autonomy."[57]

On the same day that the First Lady aired her radio address, the State Department released its "Report on the Taliban's War Against Women" and CNN televised Saira Shah's Channel 4 documentary, *Beneath the Veil*, an undercover investigation of life for Afghan women under the Taliban, which the network had first broadcast in August 26, 2001, without much reaction.[58] CNN's subsequent airing of the film shortly following 9/11 attracted five and a half million viewers, earning it the distinction of being CNN's most-viewed documentary.[59] The network replayed *Beneath the Veil* at least ten times that autumn, and Shah's documentary helped establish beauty parlors as iconic sites of gendered resistance to Taliban rule.

A British journalist of Afghan origin, Shah journeys to the region to discover what life is like under the Taliban. The title of the documentary "Beneath the Veil" both references Shah's literal donning of a burkha to gain an insider's knowledge of the Taliban and acts as a metaphor for "Afghanistan's veil of terror" against women. Her journey is at once "personal and perilous": framed as a quest for paternal origins, Shah describes growing up hearing stories of her father's homeland, "a place called Paghman," comprised of "gardens and fountains, a kind of Eden," only to discover rubble and ruin where pleasure gardens once bloomed. In contrast to her father's memories of a pre-lapsarian paradise, she finds destitute women and children, scenes of Taliban massacres and executions, girls traumatized by rape, derelict hospitals, and clandestine girls' schools and beauty parlors.[60]

To her credit, Shah tries to present a complex view of Afghan women that acknowledges the extreme oppression of their circumstances by a theocratic state even as it emphasizes their agency. The documentary depicts women's agency in collective terms, centered on the Revolutionary Association of the Women of Afghanistan (RAWA), whose members transform the veil into a weapon against the Taliban by hiding cameras under their *burkhas* to shoot secret footage of executions and of women forced to beg for their livelihoods.[61] Other scenes in the documentary picture Afghan women in other activities: marching in RAWA-organized demonstrations, teaching in underground schools, and operating secret beauty parlors.

In spite of the range of resistance represented in the documentary, the beauty parlor clearly impresses Shah as the most radical form of defiance. Even though she identifies studying and teaching as the "riskiest activity" for women and girls, she proclaims the clandestine beauty parlor as "the most subversive place of all": "Excluded from every part of society, but some women are still holding on to their dignity. I was led past overflowing sewers, through what were once luxury apartment blocks. My destination: the most subversive place of all. I have been invited to a secret beauty parlor. If they are caught, these women will be imprisoned, but they still paint the faces they can never show in public."[62] Shah's designation of the beauty parlor as "the most subversive place" seems overblown for two reasons: first, beauty parlors enabled the economic empowerment of women at the individual rather than collective level; second, the major focus of resistance efforts by women's groups and organizations such as the Women's Association of Afghanistan in this period centered on operating underground schools for girls and women.[63] Rostami-Povey reveals that in Kabul itself, 2,000 girls and women "were awarded certificates for the skills they had acquired under the Taliban years in women's secret schools."[64] Immediately after Shah's astonishing claim, the film cuts to a beautician explaining, "This is a form of resistance. We are defying the Taliban." As footage of women's blurred faces applying nail polish and lipstick is projected on the screen, Shah editorializes, "Women trying to keep life normal in a world gone completely mad. That was the image RAWA left me with."[65] The comparatively longer footage as well as the amount of commentary devoted in the documentary to the beauty parlor relative to the clandestine school renders it as *the* iconic site of feminist resistance to the Taliban. The visual image of women applying cosmetics together with Shah's pronouncements on normative women's activities in an insane world and her reference to RAWA reinforce the link between consuming beauty products and challenging the Taliban.

I do not wish to be dismissive of the beauty parlor as an actual site for feminist resistance, but merely want to remark on the inordinate importance Shah assigns to it in comparison to other forms of collective and less class-based resistance, such as the demonstration and the clandestine school represented in the film. As Paula Black notes, "The practices and discourses which intersect in the [beauty] salon are varied and complex."[66] In Afghanistan where many beauty salons are located in homes, they occupy a liminal area between the private and public spheres. Closed off from men and providing an intimate space for women to gather in the private sphere, the beauty parlor is shaped nevertheless by public forces in the wider world around it.

Cynthia Enloe cautions against the assumption that feminized spaces such as beauty parlors are not political. "For many women, especially in a time of foreign military occupation, governmental flux, masculinized rivalries, and increasing sexual violence," she writes, "a feminized space may be the most secure political place for them to trade analyses and strategies."[67] For instance, in the Nimo Beauty Salon in Iraq, women discuss the electoral strength and weakness of male clerics, the intentions of US armed forces, abductions and assaults against women, and the escalation of lawlessness following the fall of Saddam Hussein.[68] While it is a truism that beauty standards and practices encode attitudes related to gender, race and ethnicity, social identities, class, and citizenship, beauty parlors also provide the occasion for conversations about these topics among women, rendering such spaces into de facto political forums.

CNN's frequent broadcasts of *Beneath the Veil* in the six-week period leading up to the US invasion helped suture international terrorism against the US with national domestic terrorism against Afghan women, thereby enabling a conflation in the public sphere of two separate entities, Al Qaeda and the Taliban. The documentary's exposure of the deplorable status of women under the Taliban created a receptive environment for the Bush administration's rationales for the US intervention against Al Qaeda, which could then be coded as a gendered form of humanitarianism. The film's inclusion of clandestine beauty parlors as iconic sites of resistance, in turn, inspired American women to conceive of the beauty school as the means of self-empowerment and salvation for Afghan women.

Beauty Without Borders

The idea to open a beauty academy in Kabul originated in 2002 with Mary MacMakin, a longtime resident of Afghanistan and founder of PARSA, a vocational training program in cottage industries for Afghan war widows. MacMakin consulted with Terri Grauel, a beautician who had been hired by *Vogue* to style MacMakin's hair for a photo shoot, and together they approached beauty industry officials for contributions to jumpstart the enterprise.[69] Paul Mitchell, *Vogue,* and Estée Lauder responded generously, giving beauty products and cash donations. Commenting on *Vogue's* $25,000 donation to the project, editor-in-chief Anna Wintour identifies the goals of this venture: "The beauty industry is incredibly philanthropic. But here we could be helpful not only with financial support, but through teaching and with product. Through the school, we could not only help women in Afghanistan to look and feel better but also to give them employment."[70] The pedagogical mission of the beauty academy exports US beauty practices and Western commodities, thus cultivating a new market for beauty products, and also capitalist ideology that conjoins female appearance and economic uplift as empowerment for Afghan women.

These efforts are given a humanitarian makeover in the venture's name, Beauty Without Borders, which trades on the public's awareness of the heroic efforts of Doctors Without Borders to provide medical aid in conflict zones and organizations such as Reporters Without Borders and Architects Without Borders that contribute their professional expertise to social justice efforts around the world. The mission statement of Beauty Without Borders foregrounds the commercial aspects of the enterprise:

> Our mission is to provide women in Afghanistan with access to a comprehensive educational program that teaches both the Art and Commerce of beauty. The program teaches women the skills needed to work in an array of beauty-related businesses: salons, distributorships, bookkeeping, and beauty education. Graduates of our program will learn the skills they need to create a brighter, self-reliant future for themselves and their families. We believe in helping Afghan women build a bridge from where they are not to where they want to go. The beauty industry provides an income for millions of people throughout the world and Afghanistan is no exception.[71]

Beauty Without Borders' mission statement draws on a neoliberal vocabulary of "self-reliance" in its description of the commercial side of the venture in terms of production, distribution, and accounting. Yet elsewhere, cosmetic industry executives emphasize the consumption angle of the enterprise, suggesting that "the beauty school could not be judged a success if it did not create a demand for American cosmetics before too long."[72] Such an assessment is underwritten by the assumption that US beauty standards have a universal appeal and need not be adjusted or jettisoned for existing cosmetic tastes in other national contexts, an assumption that some of the instructors of the Kabul beauty school project initially share.

Passage to Kabul

The convictions that women's entrepreneurship and particular forms of consumption signify feminist modernity are leitmotifs in the second variant of the capitalist-rescue narrative, appearing in Deborah Rodriguez's *Kabul Beauty School*. (The memoir appears to be ghost written by Kristin Ohlson, an award-winning science writer, who gets credit on the title page inside the text but not on its cover.[73] The nature of the writing collaboration is nowhere explained.) Unlike Tzemach Lemmon's account, however, Rodriguez's tale tends to self-aggrandizement and downplays MacMakin and Grauel's role in the conception and founding of the academy. She magnifies her own part—a part that is presented as a parallel and independent effort to theirs—hatched in Holland, Michigan, her hometown, and that includes hoarding nearly half a million dollars of cosmetics donated by Paul Mitchell and other companies to take to Afghanistan.

Rodriguez's first-person memoir begins in medias res with her dramatic intervention in her young Afghan friend Roshanna's wedding night. Sexually assaulted by an ex-fiancé who later abandoned her, Roshanna is in danger of being exposed as an "immoral woman" on her wedding night without the blood-stain evidence attesting to her virginity. After several futile attempts at consummation between husband and wife, Debbie is summoned by Roshanna's mother to the marital chamber for a consultation. Banishing the groom from the room, Debbie deliberately cuts herself with nail clippers and smears her blood over a handkerchief, which she instructs Roshanna to brandish as proof of her virginity following penetration. This opening vignette constructs Debbie as a savior of Roshanna in this most patriarchal rite. Debbie's North American nationality and feminist sensibility imbue her with greater knowledge and appreciation of sexual pleasure than her Afghan friend. Advising Roshanna to relax during intercourse, Debbie explains, "Then I give her the advice that so many women who don't really like sex cling to—just lean back, open your legs, and try to think of something else. I tell her that it won't hurt after the first few times, that you might even find it as pleasurable as I do. She looks at me as if I'm trying to convince her that she will enjoy chewing broken glass someday" (29). The handkerchief trick works and Roshanna's virtue remains intact. (While the truth status of autobiographies and memoirs is never certain, if we willingly suspend our disbelief at this anecdote, we must wonder about the wisdom of revealing this information given that it could put Roshanna at risk.) Debbie's self-presentation as a savior serves to establish the theme of feminist solidarity that permeates the text: benevolent American women are able to game Afghan patriarchy in aid of Afghan women, who are often described in kinship terms as "sisters" and "daughters."

These events, we find out in the next chapter, occur in 2006, the narrative present of the memoir, which then flashes to 2001 to detail Debbie's back story and how she made her way to Afghanistan. A hairdresser and single mother in Michigan with a penchant for partying and attending church, Debbie makes a disastrous marriage to a "traveling preacher," who eventually becomes abusive. To escape her domestic situation, she volunteers for disaster relief training with the Care for All Foundation [CFAF], a Christian aid organization, in August 2001, during which time she first learns "where Afghanistan was" (63). That September sees her offering her services, e.g., "massage therapy and trauma counseling," to the firemen clearing the rubble of the World Trade Center (64). Back in Michigan after this stint, Debbie becomes obsessed with the status of Afghan women and, judging from her reference to the executions in the stadium, most likely views Shah's *Beneath the Veil*: "At home again, I sank back into dread. I couldn't stop watching television coverage of Afghanistan and the Taliban. I was especially struck by the footage of the Taliban executing women in Kabul's Ghazi sports stadium. I read book after book about Afghanistan, and I felt like I was leading a life that was nearly as contained as those of the women there" (64-65). Debbie's experiences of intimate partner violence that include living with an abusive husband who monitors her movements and activities, make her see parallels between her life and those of Afghan women, resulting in a form of feminist solidarity.

Improbably selected to be part of a CFAF medical contingent to Kabul, Debbie finds herself at loose ends during the mission and occupies herself with doing the other aid workers' laundry. Because she never leaves home without her scissors, combs, a salon cape, and "some product" and out of boredom, she is soon styling the hair of her fellow mission compatriots along with the Afghans who work in their housing compound. Word trickles out to the NGO community that an American hairdresser is in town. Before long, Debbie is inundated with requests for haircutting appointments from Western expatriates. About this time, she realizes that she has become smitten with Afghans ("I had fallen in love with the Afghan people as a whole—with their friendliness, their humor, their hospitality, and their courage." [48]) and has become infused with humanitarian zeal ("I wanted to think of some way I could come back and actually do something that would help them. And I was starting to get an idea." [48]). A trip to her first Afghan home beauty salon and an up-close view of the limitations of local perming practices convince her that she has a unique contribution to make: "I had discovered the one thing I could do to help the Afghans—and only I, out of all the talented and dedicated Westerners I'd met here, could do it," she excitedly explains. "I knew that I could help the Afghan women run better salons and make more money. I knew from my own experience as a hairdresser back home that a salon is good business for a woman—especially if she has a bad husband" (54-55).

Debbie's epiphany regarding the rescue potential of this kind of gendered capitalist enterprise has several elements, including her assessment of the scarcity of Western makeup and beauty products; her sense that Afghan women possess only "rudimentary hairdressing skills" (in other words, they give "frizzy perms" and do not know how to do "highlights"); her alarm at unhygienic beauty practices such as the application of kohl, an indigenous eyeliner, from an unsterilized stick; and, perhaps most importantly, her certainty that Afghan women could make a decent salary from such work. Indeed, she notes that even without American training, Afghan beauticians earned about "eighty dollars a month, at least twice as much as the average salary in Afghanistan" (53). These insights crystallize in her decision to "come back to Afghanistan with several suitcases of good hair care products and supplies, then hang around in the salons for a couple of weeks." She announces, "I could teach the women whatever I knew and show them how to expand their services and make more money. I could also teach them the sanitation principles I'd learned in beauty school" (55).

An NGO friend convinces Debbie to think bigger and to consider opening a beauty school. Back in Holland, Michigan, she contacts beauty industry CEOs in search of donations of their products, getting pledges of cosmetics, along with "salon stations and chairs, combs, blow dryers, hand mirrors," and "perm rods" (69). During a phone solicitation with one cosmetic company representative, Debbie hears of the parallel and better-organized efforts of MacMakin and Grauel to open a beauty school in the Afghan Ministry of Women's Affairs compound and decides to join forces with them. Set to open in July 2003, the women plan on selecting their first class of students based on interviews and on limiting admission to Afghan beauticians who have been operating home salons. The six Kabul Beauty Academy instructors are divided into three teams of beauticians that pair an Anglo-American teacher with an Afghan-American one, who also acts as a translator and teaches beauty techniques. Overseen by Patricia O'Connor, a British-born marketing consultant, each pair teaches a month of the three-month course, and then returns to the United States, with the apparent exception of Debbie, who while committed to staying for longer periods of time, doesn't bother to learn either Dari or Pushto.

Makeup and Modernity

As is apparent from several scenes in Liz Mermin's documentary about the beauty academy, which includes footage of Debbie but under the last name of "Turner" rather than "Rodriguez," the Anglo-American women universalize their own experiences as applicable to Afghan women and, consequently, sometimes express varying degrees of cultural insensitivity and general cluelessness toward the lives of their students.[74] Sheila McGurk, for example, whom the film represents as having an overbearing personality and evangelical zeal for meditation, tends to abstract the students from their social contexts. We first see her as she enters the school and announces, "I hope they're ready for me. It's going to be a little different!"[75] After arranging the students in a circle, she begins imparting meditation techniques:

> We all have so many things in our mind. We are so busy in our lives. It's good to try to rest the mind for a few minutes so we can be very focused on the work we have today. So please breathe here, the center of the woman. In. Out. Simple. Close eyes. No talking. When you find your life very busy, very troubled, take two minutes and practice the breathing and you will find that you will be more calm. And more important, you'll be at peace with yourself because we are touching women all day. We are not just cutting their hair. We're not just perming their hair. We are healing them. We're making themselves feel better about themselves inside. You are going to play a very important role in healing this city.[76]

In this soliloquy, humanitarian intervention *becomes* the beautifying mission. By increasing the self-esteem of individual Afghan women, McGurk maintains, beauticians provide an important form of spiritual aid that will eventually "heal" Kabul. With eyes closed and her breathing deliberate, she models the technique while most of the students keep their eyes open, stifle their laughter, and sport ironic smiles at her instruction and example. That McGurk fails to comprehend the domestic challenges facing her students becomes apparent through Mermin's skillful editing in a later scene when one Afghan woman complains about her overly aggressive husband and children and the inordinate amount of cooking and cleaning demanded of her at home. McGurk blithely advises that "she should do a meditation before she goes in the door of her house."[77] How meditation will alleviate domestic abuse and exploitation she does not explain.

In the same documentary, Debbie most explicitly connects modernity to cosmetic consumption. With her short, spiky, bright red hair and colorful makeup, she literally embodies artifice and cosmetic consumption, practices that she urges on her Afghan students, telling them,

> I want to say something to you guys about being a hairdresser, ok. There needs to be something special about you that makes you different than the woman who is the secretary or, you know, office worker. You can't have fuzzy perms and bad hair color and bad haircuts. It is your job as hairdressers, the most progressive hairdressers in Afghanistan, to set the new trend for new hairstyles, new hair color. It is your responsibility. You're the first class. If you guys don't do it, how can Afghanistan change and get into a more modern-type look? How will Afghanistan change if you guys don't change?[78]

Cosmetic consumption, according to Debbie, helps individualize the women by making them "different" from other women in the public sphere. Skillful perms and good haircuts not only advertise the beautician's professional talents, but they become harbingers of modernity and progress by heralding a New Look for Afghan women. Significantly, Debbie establishes a connection between individual cosmetic consumption, agency, and the national good by asserting that Afghanistan's national progress rests on the consumer behavior of individual Afghan women and their willingness to embrace hairstyling and cosmetic novelty. A constitutive contradiction underwrites her injunction to her students: they are urged to establish the individuality of their appearance by following US widespread norms of understated cosmetic usage; the "artifice" of makeup and hair styling are employed to achieve a "natural" look that is part of the US cultural dominant. Whether the students accept Debbie's construction of progress and modernity seems doubtful. Several students spiritedly challenge her advice, pointing out that makeup can ruin skin, "mascara looks funny," and they face familial prohibitions against using cosmetics.[79]

Though she describes herself in Mermin's documentary in the settler colonial language of a "pioneer," Debbie, unlike her white American cohorts, voices enchantment with Afghanistan and gains more cultural sensitivity to her students as the documentary progresses. The only one of the three Anglo instructors to appreciate that the Afghan women do not like being gawked at by curious men through the large windows of the academy, she orders curtains to afford them privacy. Her instructions are countermanded by O'Connor, who seems irritated at Debbie's initiative, and who elsewhere in the documentary likens Afghanistan to "hell," mentioning that after a week in the country she is "losing [her] mind."[80] In her memoir as well, Debbie periodically admits to her lack of knowledge about Afghanistan and her occasional social bungling;

for example, she realizes that certain topics related to hairdressing practices are better broached individually than in a collective setting where women might feel shamed by having their actions scrutinized (86), and she realizes that her ignorance regarding the complex ethnic landscape of the region has inadvertently led to an initial selection of prospective students who are primarily Hazara (243).

While such moments of awareness punctuate Debbie's memoir, *Kabul Beauty School* also shares with *The Dressmaker of Khair Khana* the rhetorical feature of historical amnesia insofar as history proper begins for Debbie with the US defeat of the Taliban. (In fairness to her, she acknowledges that "we had bombed the bejesus out of their capital and countryside to do it" [22]). Periodic references to "graveyard[s] of tanks and planes" and live landmines hint at the brutality of the Soviet Occupation, but Debbie doesn't appear to recognize the role of the US in destabilizing the region during that era. Indeed, she identifies the golden age of Afghan history as the early 1970s in the last days of King Mohammad Zahir Shah when "there were dozens of beauty salons in the city" and "they did a thriving business" (49). A historical naïveté inheres in her decision to marry a former Mujahideen fighter, Samer Mohammad Abdul Khan, on less than three weeks' acquaintance, despite the fact that neither speaks the other's language or that he has a wife and seven children in Saudi Arabia.[81] Abdul Khan had served under the Uzbek Mujahideen leader, General Abdul Rashid Dostum, who himself was on the CIA payroll and has been accused of suffocating nearly 2,000 Taliban prisoners to death in 2001. Dostum served as vice president under Ashraf Ghani's administration until 2017, when he had to flee the country for Turkey to avoid charges of having a rival politician raped with an assault rifle.[82] Previously he had twice been denied a visa by the State Department to visit the US, most recently in April 2016, for his complicity in human rights violations. Debbie describes being introduced to Dostum as an "honor," and the former warlord/vice president's fighters make cameos in the raucous parties thrown by the couple (262).

It eventually occurs to Debbie that "Western ideas about makeup didn't make any sense in Afghanistan," given that Afghan women favor a more pronounced use of cosmetics. "Sure, all the brides would still want to look like drag queens," she observes breezily, "but I figured that they could at least be more attractive and unique drag queens" (161). Her observation implies that Afghan women aspire to a femininity that they can only perform as an exaggerated identity rather than as authentic females. Debbie indigenizes the curriculum to better meet the local tastes of the Afghan clientele by teaching her students how to enhance the natural beauty of their clients with cosmetics: "How to contour a chubby face and enhance the cheekbones, or how to make a big nose look smaller. How to lighten someone's skin without making it look as if she had fallen into a bucket of flour" (161). Indeed, by the end of Liz Mermin's documentary, Debbie ignores her own earlier prescriptions for adopting "modern" hairstyles and being part of the Afghan beauty vanguard. Either through feminist solidarity, some kind of Orientalist fantasy of going native, or both, she undergoes an Afghan makeover. Acquiring an elaborate coiffure worthy of the Bollywood starlets who are so popular in the country, Debbie attends the graduation ceremony of the academy in a dazzling gown that would not be out of place at a Kabul wedding.

Capitalism and ISAF to the Rescue?

Debbie's decision to indigenize the curriculum speaks to her ability to differentiate among several markets: local Afghan brides, expatriate Afghan brides, and NGO workers, all of whom are willing to pay higher prices for beauty services. At Debbie's salon, the Oasis, which helps underwrite the costs of the beauty school, she charges expatriate brides double or triple the going rate of $100 to $160 for a whopping bill of $300 per bride and $10 per member of the bridal party (180). (The desire to avoid competition with her students' salons is her stated motivation for setting such high prices.) In addition to feeling a humanitarian impulse toward male NGO and embassy workers, she knows "they could provide a good income stream" ("I felt sorry for these men who needed a little luxury in their lives" in the way of haircuts and manicures.) (180). The consummate entrepreneur, Debbie also hits on the idea of making house calls to NGO workers when Kabul is under a "White City" security alert; not only are these clients grateful for the "diversion," but they are also big tippers, much to the delight of her students (182). She wants her students to become "accustomed to the foreigners' odd ways" because "if they learned to cater to the foreign crowd, they'd really be able to make good money" (178).

More than once in the memoir, Debbie claims that Afghan beauticians, when trained properly, can significantly increase their incomes. According to her, Bahar, one of her graduates, has her monthly income multiply from "forty to nearly four hundred dollars" (237). Toward the end of the book, Debbie declares that "I could show anyone who was interested in a survey demonstrating that our students' family incomes rose 400 percent after graduation" (266). One of the students, who is profiled in Mermin's documentary, reports that while her husband earns 1,700 Afghanis a month, she can make 3,000 Afghanis from a single bridal client alone. The dramatic increase in the Afghan beauticians' salaries, according to Debbie, has a transformative effect on social relations in general and on the status of working wives in their families in particular. She notes that as Bahar's income grows, Bahar is less willing to be on call (literally) for her husband: "[A]s she made more money, Bahar became stronger and more independent. There were several times when I heard her speak sharply to her husband when he called and tell him not to bother her. Finally, she stopped answering the phone if he called too many times" (237).

Toward the end of the memoir, Debbie is explicit about her belief that capitalism, whether materialized in entrepreneurship and the running of home salons or in wage labor and being employed in the Oasis, has resulted in much better domestic lives for her students. The "Kabul Beauty School's part" in rebuilding Afghanistan "seems small in comparison with many of the other efforts, but it is nevertheless huge," she writes.

> I know how the lives of the women who have come to the school have changed. Whereas they were once dependent on men for money, they are now earning and sharing their wages. Whereas they were once household slaves, they are now respected decision makers. Not all of them, not all of the time. But enough to give them and so many other women here hope. (267)

The assumption here is that Afghan women's status has markedly improved as their earnings have increased, transforming "household slaves" into "respected decision makers" (267). Such an assertion posits a binary opposition between two identities: the exploited domestic-worker wife and the quasi-companionate wife. In reality, many women assume a triple burden of earning a wage, bearing the responsibility for housework, and being the primary caretaker of their children. As women's earning power increases, they often do gain a higher status in the family, though this might not translate into any reduction in women's household responsibilities and domestic workload. But whatever advantages accrue to the overall improvement of the condition of Afghan women in society at large through this venture, they are dependent on individual entrepreneurs. While it is difficult to press against the claim that women's economic empowerment benefits society as a whole, the social value which accumulates from women taking up other professions such as those in healthcare, engineering, the civil services, and teaching is much greater insofar as these professions aid people and contribute to Afghanistan's civic and material infrastructure. Debbie's views of female entrepreneurship, in addition, rely on gender-segregated labor sectors that eventually result in a lower income than men.

The financial success of the beauty academy's graduates seemingly depends on their integration into the circuit of capital supplied by NGOs. From the earliest affiliation with PARSA to the German NGO that provides funding once the initial money for the beauty school runs out, to Clairol's and Vogue's emergency bailout of the enterprise, to the foreign NGO-worker clientele who can be charged higher rates for services, the Afghan beauticians have been absorbed into the global economy and not on terms advantageous to them compared to others. At the local level, the integration of economic life in a neoliberal regime of capitalism has meant the skewing of the pre-existing wage scale, as well as rents and real estate being rendered astronomical in cost.

Moreover, the NGO sector in Afghanistan is itself dependent on the presence of the International Security Assistance Force [ISAF], now the Resolute Support Mission [RSM], to guarantee the peace.[83] As Lara Olson and Andrea Charron explain, the boundaries between international civil society and military forces in Afghanistan have become fuzzy because of a number of factors such as "the early use of civilian dress by US special forces, Colin Powell's infamous remark about NGOs as 'force multipliers,' and the widespread use of aid [by the military] for intelligence, force protection, and hearts-and-minds efforts."[84] The beauty academy relies on the security forces to create a climate that enables its functioning and commerce. When Debbie's neighbors, who occupy the next compound and are suspected of being involved in the kidnapping of aid worker Clementina Cantoni, begin to harass her students and rough up her *chowkidor* [watchman], she appeals to the Afghan police to intervene. After the police prove ineffective, she informally petitions some ISAF troops who are "leaning against their tank" for their assistance. "Next time you're out patrolling," she asks, "can you come down my street and stop in front of their house? Maybe point that big gun at them?" (232) Her request meets with success:

> A few days later, five tanks from the international peacekeeping force rumbled down our street and groaned to a halt in front of my compound. I ran to the bad neighbors' house and banged on the gate until one of the brothers stuck his head out. I pointed to the tanks and told him that if his family bullied anyone on the street again, I'd have their house blown up. Of course, I didn't really have that power, but they didn't know it. To my knowledge, no one in my neighborhood has had any trouble with them since. They became as cordial and well-mannered as my old neighbors back in Michigan. (234)

This anecdote reveals the dependence of the beauty academy—and, by extension, US capitalist-style enterprise—on ISAF, demonstrating how fragile such well-intentioned efforts actually are. Without the international forces' presence to guarantee some semblance of security, the implantation of capitalist initiatives like the beauty school would wither and die.

Debbie's admission that ISAF's display of force is a sham meant to scare the neighborhood thugs could serve as a trope for the military occupation of Afghanistan: ISAF's and RSM's presence allows for the simulacrum of security which does not in fact exist. The military occupation is based on a dialectical dependency: NGO projects require the services of security forces, and security forces, in part, justify their presence by creating an environment that allows NGOs to function. The co-dependent relationship between the two exposes the fiction of the capitalist-rescue narrative insofar as the triumph of upward mobility for a few enterprising women is not the result of individual achievement per se, but rather is a result of an uneasy equilibrium between repressive state apparatuses and civil society groups (so called non-governmental organizations which have close ties to states and the international community) that is always under threat of being disrupted.

Because of a dispute with the Afghan Ministry of Women's Affairs, Debbie moved the beauty school into her home compound. Since the publication of Debbie's memoir, the beauty academy has closed. Receiving an $80,000 advance from Random House for her book, which Columbia Pictures also optioned, she embarked on a publicity tour in the US.[85] The memoir has generated controversy among Debbie's fellow instructors, who accuse her of magnifying her role in the venture and sensationalizing her experiences.[86] More troubling are charges by her students that the book has endangered their lives. Though the book has not been published in Afghanistan, portions of interviews with Debbie have aired on Afghan television and pictures of the women in the salon without head scarves have circulated in the country. The beauty academy received threatening phone calls and a visit from two women in an unmarked car with armed guards who ominously admonished the women for "maligning Afghan culture."[87] Shortly after the end of her book tour, Debbie, to her students' and Afghan husband's bewilderment, abruptly left Afghanistan and announced her intention of not returning. Thousands of dollars in debt for rent, the school eventually closed and several of the women have left Afghanistan with their families out of fear for their safety.[88]

Conclusion: A Tale of Two Women

Since leaving Afghanistan, after a two-year stint in California, Debbie has landed in Mazatlan, Mexico, where she has opened another salon, Tippy Toes, and founded Project Mariposa, which channels funds to Mexican teenagers to attend beauty school.[89] As Liz Mermin points out, it is difficult to avoid reading Debbie's departure and the ignoble demise of the Kabul Beauty Academy as a metaphor for US foreign policy in Afghanistan.[90] With a great deal of fanfare, "good intentions, and very little [actual] knowledge" of the local culture in spite of decades of meddling in Afghanistan's internal affairs, American soldiers and experts descended on Afghan soil.[91] How long and deep the US commitment to rebuilding Afghanistan proves to be, and with what consequences for Afghans, remains to be seen.

Unlike Debbie's, Kamila Sidiqi's commitment to Afghanistan has not wavered. Kaweyan Business Development Services, which she founded after her home-tailoring business, offers short courses on different aspects of entrepreneurship, ranging from "business accounting" to "tax management" to "capacity development" among other topics.[92] The course line-up also includes "human rights awareness" and several classes that are certified by the International Labour Organization, suggesting that Kaweyan strives to foster some social consciousness in its clients.[93] Since its founding in 2004, Kaweyan has transformed into a group of companies that specializes in startup business development, research and consultancy, and creating a business infrastructure for Afghanistan's dried fruit industry. One of the initiatives, Kaweyan Cabs, not only consists of providing a taxi service in Kabul, but has also sought to increase Afghan women's mobility around the city by giving driving lessons to women.[94] In a brief online video about Kaweyan, Kamila stresses her belief that women need "the chance" to have opportunities for self-advancement through enterprise. Women's incomes contribute to the well-being of the family, she notes in the video, and their financial security can advance the nation-state by enabling women to earn degrees and eventually enter public service.[95] Proving by example, Kamila herself now serves as Deputy Chief of Staff to President Ashraf Ghani; her portfolio in the president's office encompasses "technology, finance, admin and hiring."[96]

Capitalist projects that percolate from the ground up, such as those mentored and supported by Kaweyan, which employ workers outside the immediate family, seem to have a bigger and longer-lasting social impact than the attempt to seed US-style beauty salons in Kabul. In the long run, however, one wonders at the capacity of such enterprises to provide upward mobility to a significant percentage of the population and to expand the size of the Afghan middle class for several reasons. First and foremost, Afghanistan's security situation is dismal; the foreign occupation has not guaranteed the safety of civilians. Indeed, a resurgent Taliban now shares a conflict landscape also populated with Islamic State offshoots characterized by intra-insurgency violence. Distrust of government security forces and the Afghan Local Police remains high because of their responsibility for human rights violations and extrajudicial killings.[97] Second, exacerbating the anarchic security situation, the lack of a physical infrastructure in the country impedes the transport of goods and mobility of workers and consumers, making the conducting of business on any scale larger than the local one difficult. Third, given the tendency for capitalism to increase inequality, particularly under neoliberal regimes of accumulation—as even the International Monetary Fund recently acknowledged—the absence of a functioning regulatory state does not augur well for the ability of the Afghan government to rein in the worst excesses of business.[98] And finally, widespread corruption and fraud present enormous challenges to the success of businesses, siphoning off capital that could be reinvested in the expansion of production and its efficiency. Whether capitalism in a form recognizable to those living in bourgeois democracies can be seeded, take root, and grow under such inauspicious conditions is still uncertain.

Seven years after the publication of Lemmon's text in 2011 and more than a decade after that of Rodriguez's memoir in 2007, we do know that the condition of Afghan women outside urban pockets of the country has not improved considerably. The 2018 United Nations' Human Development Index, which scores countries based on their literacy rates, life expectancy at birth, and standard of living, places Afghanistan at 168 out of 189 countries surveyed.[99] The Thomson Reuters Survey of the World's Most Dangerous Countries for Women, which I cited earlier, lists Afghanistan as number two. It ranked first in discrimination, health, and non-sexual violence against women; second in the category of "culture & religion"; and seventh in both sexual violence and human trafficking.[100] In the face of such ubiquitous physical insecurity and the lack of access to such basic necessities as nutritious food, healthcare, sanitation and clean water, and adequate housing for many Afghan women, as well as men, the dream of capitalism's rescue is more a chimera than a promise.

I opened this chapter by invoking the post-colonial feminist formulation of the US intervention in Afghanistan as a version of gender uplift that rehearses Spivak's gloss on nineteenth-century British imperialism. British debates about sati, she had asserted, could be succinctly summarized by the phrase "white men saving brown women from brown men." *The Dressmaker of Khair Khana* and *Kabul Beauty School* propose a revision of this formula: white women saving brown women by ushering them into entrepreneurial modernity. In this provocative rewriting of Spivak, brown men drop out of the formula altogether insofar as the capitalist-rescue narrative forecloses their entry into entrepreneurship. They function instead as representatives of archaic, patriarchal traditions, which must be shunted aside to enable brown women to come into their own as businesswomen. These empowered women, in turn, will save their men with the influx of their earnings, hopefully, refashioning more equitable gender relations in the family.

This representation of Afghan women resonates with recent ones of Third World women more generally. Ananya Roy has argued that Third World women have become iconic figures to signify global poverty. She coins the term "poverty capital" to describe how poor people have become both recipients of microfinance loans and a new "market" for credit, beneficiaries from the democratization of capital and candidates for further exploitation.[101] The impoverished micro-entrepreneur of Roy's study undergoes embourgeoisement, emerging as the upwardly mobile, middle-class businesswoman of Lemmon's and Rodriguez's accounts. In the revision of Spivak, white women play a crucial role, encouraging micro-entrepreneurship and advertising its successes through their writing. The capitalist-rescue narrative contributes to the ideological project of transforming the heretofore systematically underdeveloped periphery into an opportunity for investment within the contours of a global conflict economy in which NGOs and security industries play an outsize part. Brown women sutured to micro-entrepreneurship become exemplary subjects to define the horizons of an American liberal imaginary that perceives itself as benevolent, independent of its ability to create more just, equitable social relations in Afghanistan.

Chapter 3

The Canine-Rescue Narrative
and Post-Humanist Humanitarianism

●●●●●●●●●●●●●●●●●●●●●

Introduction

As a child shuttling back and forth between Indiana and India, I was always pleased to visit my paternal grandparents in Begusarai, Bihar.[1] For much of my childhood, my grandparents had a series of dogs, acquiring a new dog with the demise of the old one. The family dog was always named "Tommy." Curious about the origin of the name, I asked my father to tell me about Tommy the first. The story goes that a gentleman by the name of Satyabrata Singh Roy, an officer in the British Indian Army who later rose to a Major General in the Indian Army following independence, was sent in 1919 to present-day Iraq in order to suppress a Kurdish revolt. From Iraq, Major General Roy made his way to Egypt, where he acquired a dog, the first Tommy, whom he brought back to Dacca and gifted to my great grandfather, Rai Sahib Surendranath Bose.[2] In hearing about the origins of Tommy the first, I was struck by how geopolitical violence can shape canine itineraries, which, in turn, can provide maps of the imperial world: a colonized Indian subject traveled to the British Mandate of Mesopotamia, where he functioned as an agent of the colonial state—putting down an insurrection of people, who, like him, were also colonized subjects—and eventually arrived in Egypt, a British protectorate, before returning to British India with a canine in tow.

No record exists for Major General Roy's motivations for acquiring and transporting Tommy, but what has remained as part of the family lore is the affective, close relationship between this dog and my great grandfather. In this family account of the bond between a man and his dog, the violence of British colonial military intervention against Kurds—which provided the conditions of possibility for Tommy's emigration to Dacca—has largely been forgotten other than through the meaning of the dog's name, which is the colloquial expression for a British soldier. Tommy provides a palimpsest for this chapter insofar as the story of his origins, along with the four dogs who have shared my life over the years, piqued my interest in the recent spate of memoirs of US soldiers serving in Iraq and Afghanistan that foreground a softer side of military intervention. Sometimes co-written with professional writers, these memoirs take as their primary subject matter a soldier's or Marine's strong emotional attachment to a dog, either a stray dog or a military working dog [MWD], and the challenges of bringing this canine companion safely back to the United States. Sporting such titles as *From Baghdad, With Love: A Marine, the War, and a Dog Named Lava; Welcome Home, Mama and Boris: How a Sister's Love Saved a Fallen Soldier's Beloved Dogs; Saving Cinnamon: The Amazing True Story of a Missing Military Puppy and the Desperate Mission to Bring Her Home;* and *Top Dog: The Story of Marine Hero Lucca*, these memoirs represent a variant of the rescue narratives that have provided popular ideological justifications for the US interventions in Afghanistan and Iraq.[3]

In the last chapter, I explored how mainstream American feminists construct capitalism as an agent of rescue for Afghan women. Having absorbed some of the critiques articulated by feminists of color and post-colonial studies in the 1980s and 1990s, liberal feminists have become more sensitive to questions of representation and agency: stereotypes of passive veiled women are to be avoided, as are generalizations about the confinement of Afghan women to the home. Liberal American feminists have emphasized instead the agency of Afghan women vis-à-vis entrepreneurship. Accounts of Afghan women, like *The Dressmaker of Khair Khana* and *The Kabul Beauty School,* articulate women's empowerment through US-style capitalism and its attendant production arrangements and consumer practices, which enable Afghan women to enter into modernity. Rather than the bald assertions of nineteenth-century British colonial rulers that imperialism constituted a direct means of uplifting native women, the justification of the US intervention in Afghanistan, in part, rests on the claim that the introduction of a particular form of capitalism has facilitated the empowerment of Afghan women.

Insofar as Afghan women are figured as entrepreneurial subjects, they no longer function as abject natives who need to be rescued through imperialism. The fully wretched native subject under US imperialism has become the dog, who takes the place of women and must be brought back to the US to sustain the nostalgic myth of the family. The canine-rescue narrative renders dogs as highly visible tropes for objects of US humanitarianism while simultaneously making invisible Afghan civilians and the politics of this conflict. It provides a compensatory fantasy about the benign, indeed salutory, effects of US military intervention on noncombatants by supplying a happy ending in which stray dogs and MWDs are saved by virtue of their adoption by and incorporation into American families. Membership in American families, the conventional ending of the canine-rescue narrative, gives dogs the opportunity to fully actualize their dogginess in the land of opportunity and the home of the free. And yet the narrative simultaneously reveals the American family to be in a state of crisis riven with sibling tension and long-simmering resentments.

This chapter analyzes the narrative strategies in three very different texts whereby a canine protagonist displaces Afghan civilians as a sentimental figure for identification for the American public: a memoir about rescuing an Afghan stray dog, *Saving Cinnamon: The Amazing True Story of a Missing Military Puppy and the Desperate Mission to Bring her Home*; a biography of a MWD, *Top Dog: The Story of Marine Hero Lucca*; and a novel, *Max: Best Friend, Hero, Marine*, based on a film released in summer 2015 about an MWD who is adopted by the family of his Marine handler, a combat fatality in Afghanistan. All three texts interpellate canines as family members while evacuating Afghans from the narrative. A teleological plot structure that culminates in the successful rescue of the dogs and their migration to the US contains ideological echoes of the rhetoric of manifest destiny and an American form of exceptionalism that valorizes Americans as more compassionate pet owners than people in Central and South Asia. All three canine-rescue narratives demonstrate how the production and management of sentiment employs what Gillian Whitlock calls a "soft weapon" of the war in which a specific form of life writing, the canine-rescue narrative, functions as propaganda.[4]

I begin by historicizing larger cultural shifts toward pets in the United States, which involve the increasing anthropomorphism of canines—a trend that is visible in consumer practices, the medicalization of veterinary care, and the emergence of dogs as subjects in legal discourse—before providing a close reading of *Saving Cinnamon*. Not a soldier herself, Sullivan, in the memoir, recounts the challenges of bringing a stray puppy from Afghanistan to the United States, a puppy to which her brother became attached while serving in an Afghan army camp in his capacity as a navy reservist. Turning to *Top Dog*, I describe how military policies toward MWDs mirror the transformations in attitudes toward dogs in the larger culture; in this version of the canine-rescue narrative, dogs are paradoxically figured as both the rescuers of humans and themselves in need of rescue. Finally, I analyze *Max*, which, within a fairly conventional narrative that draws on clichéd American film and television representations of the family, provides a limited critique of the Afghanistan War. *Max* suggests that the violence of US military intervention cannot be contained in South Asia and that the chickens will eventually come home to roost in the trauma experienced by former combatants (human and canine), as well as the creation of a transnational illicit trade in drugs and stolen military weapons.

At the heart of the canine-rescue narrative resides a representational challenge, namely, the difficulty of conveying the subjectivity of a sentient being who exists outside of language and modes of self-representation. While canine subjectivity is ultimately unknowable, the illusion of our access to it persists in our receptiveness to the attributions of emotions and thoughts to dogs by their owners and handlers as indices of their consciousness.

While I trace the process through which Cinnamon, Lucca, and Max are incorporated into the family and conferred American natonality, I want to emphasize that my reading of these books is not grounded in post-humanist conceptions of species difference. I have neither the desire here to assert the complex subjectivity of canines and the nature of their relationships to humans, nor to advance a justification for their claims to the status of rights-bearing subjects. Contra Donna Haraway's injunction to understand dogs qua dogs in their "historical complexity" and not as alibis for "other themes," my interest is in what the conjuncture of nationalism and canine subjectivity, which Lisa Uddin dubs "canine citizenship," reveals about the ideological legitimization of US imperialism.[5] Understood less in conventional terms that define citizenship as a legal status with civic obligations to a larger polity, informed by ethical and moral dimensions, canine citizenship has more metaphoric resonances as elaborated by Uddin. For these memoirs, those resonances include the family, nation, and God, three abstractions that gird the American imperial imaginary.

Pets, American Style

That the soldier-canine memoir emerged in the first decade of the twenty-first century is not surprising, given profound changes in American attitudes toward pets in the twentieth century, particularly at the century's end.[6] In her thoughtful history *Pets in America*, Katherine C. Grier contextualizes shifts in cultural feelings toward animals in terms of the rise of the middle class in the nineteenth century and the "domestic ethic of kindness" attached to liberal evangelical Protestantism.[7] Prior to the Civil War, child-rearing was oriented toward "socializing children to be citizens of the American public," and "kindness to animals" became one element of a benevolent ethos directed at those designated incapable of independent living, such as "children, the elderly, the chronically ill, the enslaved," among others.[8] Bourgeois morality demanded that animals be treated well, and the tending of pets became a pedagogical tool in gentile homes for inculcating civic values.

These cultural attitudes simmered in the environment of US-style capitalism, as Grier notes, resulting in several major contradictions that arose in different periods but which are still present today. The first contradiction

occurred with the transformation of a farming economy to large-scale industrial production in the late nineteenth and twentieth centuries. Through the
1920s, chickens, pigs, cows, and horses were a ubiquitous part of the urban
landscape.[9] Grier explains that "American families relied for their comfort and
convenience on the direct labor of animal workers and on the products derived
from their bodies (simply put, they knew where meat came from)."[10] Entailing
the classification of animals into those that are loved (pets) and those that are
eaten (livestock), the first contradiction created a distinction between subjects
for nurture and objects for nourishment. Observing the "presence of a cultural
reason in our food habits," Marshall Sahlins notes that "categorical distinctions
of edibility among horses, dogs, pigs, and cattle" emanate from the incorporation of these animals in a symbolic system.[11] Since the late nineteenth century,
dogs (and to a lesser extent, horses) in the US have been taboo as a source of
meat primarily because of their symbolic integration into the family, a topic I
treat shortly.

During this period, birds such as parakeets and canaries were popular
household pets and were available for purchase in pet stores, the advent of
which Grier dates to the 1840s. The terms "pet store" and "pet industry," as
she astutely observes, captures "perfectly the tension between sentiment and
commodification that still resonates throughout the business" and constitutes a
second contradiction in American attitudes toward pets.[12] Aspects of pet ownership related to commodification not only entailed the actual sale of animals,
but also the marketing of a host of products perceived as necessary for their
well-being, including commercial pet food, toys, medicines, collars and leashes,
and beds. According to Grier, "trade literature and advertisements" for pet
supplies reveal "an ongoing conversation among manufacturers, store owners,
and consumers" that "demonstrate[s] how changing perceptions of the needs
of animals often paralleled a new understanding of human needs."[13] Various
reform movements targeted at improving human health and comfort often had
their corollaries in marketing campaigns for pet products. The development
and marketing of commercial pet food, for example, echoed the themes of
nutritional requirements and vitamin supplements that were a prominent part
of reform efforts to improve human diets.[14]

Modern dog food was inspired by the British military's attempts to combat widespread malnutrition among its soldiers during the Crimean War by
developing "meat biscuits" or "hardtack."[15] The first commercial dog food in
the US was manufactured, marketed, and sold across the country in the late
nineteenth century.[16] US households were reluctant to embrace the purchase of
what was felt to be a superfluous product insofar as most family dogs dined on
table scraps. The dog food industry had to invent a market where none existed
by emphasizing themes in its advertisements that would emotionally resonate
with pet owners such as the promotion of canine health, patented formulas

for different life stages of the dog, the need to minimize canine flatulence and obesity through specially formulated diets, and, of course, the ease and convenience of relying on kibbles, which liberated housewives from the tedium of additional food preparation for the family pet. These themes are still a staple of marketing dog food today.[17]

For my purposes, however, the key point here is that the development of products such as dog food presaged the anthromorphism of canines into sentient subjects of a special kind: family members, who, depending on the ethos of particular families, occupied a status slightly below that of children or on par with them. By the advent of the big box petstore in the late 1980s, household animals were increasingly figured as family members. Petsmart, the largest retail chain for pet products in the country, has as its slogan "Where pets are family." According to the Harris poll, in 2015, 95% of pet owners considered their pets to be family members."[18] The interpellation of domesticated dogs as members of the American family is legible in the vocabulary of dog ownership which relies heavily on kinship terminology and vocabulary related to parenting children. Dogs that are acquired from animal shelters, for instance, are "adopted" by their owners. An advertising mail circular from Petco in the spring of 2013 hails pet owners as "pet parents," advising that parental responsibilities entail "more than just play time, walk time, feeding time and all the other times in between"; rather, they are "about the daily commitment to helping your pet reach their full potential, and to having the best quality of life together." In advertising copy that could apply equally well to childraising, the circular identifies four areas for pet owners' attention: "It's important to keep your pet physically fit, mentally alert, socially engaged and emotionally happy." Petco, needless to say, has recommendations for products that can maximize the pets' well-being in all of these areas.

The projection of the parent-child relationship onto that of owner-pet, Heidi J. Nast convincingly argues, is characteristic of contemporary forms of what she calls "pet love" in post-industrial societies that are oriented toward hyper-consumerism. Noting the transformation of the meanings associated with children in Western societies from active contributors to the household (either through their domestic work or wages) to sentimental figures who do not add to the family income but rather drain it, she remarks on the "downward pressure on family formation and procreation" exerted by large-scale changes in the organization of the economy, as it has transitioned from industrialization in specific nation-states to neoliberalism. For the middle and upper classes in certain parts of the world, children are now an impediment to individual mobility and consumption, making pets desirable substitutes. Nast explains, "In post-industrial places pet animals (especially dogs and cats) are not merely ideal love-object substitutes for children: their anthropomorphic malleability and their insertion into an economy where mobility of labor and capital is an advantage, means that pets (especially dogs) today supersede children as ideal love objects; they are more easily mobilized, require less investment, and to some degree can be shaped into whatever you want them to be—a best friend, a lover, an occasional companion."[19] Unlike children, pets can be physically altered to change undesirable behavior and can be expendable should they become too much of a financial responsibility or obstacle to mobility. Pets also enable new avenues for consumption, which, on the whole, tend to be less expensive than those required for the maintenance of children. In addition to some of the products mentioned earlier, Nast describes new forms of pet consumption in post-industrial societies that mimic adult leisure activities such as "doga" (yoga for dogs) and formal dancing for canines.[20]

For such services and pet products, pet owners constitute a major market, which has expanded rapidly over the last two decades. In 1988, 56% of US households owned a pet, a percentage that increased to 68% in 2017.[21] Americans are only too willing to shell out money for the dizzying array of products and services now available on the market for their animals. Whereas in 1994 consumers spent $17 billion on their household animals, that amount jumped to $69.51 billion in 2017.[22] By far the biggest expenditure on American pets in 2017 was on food ($29.07 billion), followed by supplies and OTC medicine ($15.11 billion).[23] To put these figures in perspective, in 2017 the US spent approximately $42.4 billion in foreign aid to over 140 countries, of which $25.6 billion was for economic and development assistance and $16.8 billion for security assistance.[24] Perhaps recognizing that there is money to be made from pet owners, companies such as Paul Mitchell, Omaha Steaks, Origins, Harley Davidson, and Old Navy, which were traditionally oriented toward sales of commodities for human use, "are now offering lines of pet products ranging from dog shampoo, pet attire, and name-brand toys to gourmet treats and food."[25]

This trend toward increased consumption for goods and services for pets reveals a basic paradox which now characterizes American pet ownership. In the epilogue to her study, Grier identifies what she sees as an "unprecedented" attitude among American pet owners today, consisting of a fundamental contradiction between the desire to help the pet actualize herself/himself qua her/his animalness and the equally compelling wish to "civilize" the pet and make her/his behavior better conform to human aesthetic and behavioral norms through medical alterations. In addition to declawing and debarking, pet owners more and more rely on pharmaceuticals to alter the behavior of their animals "in part from a growing desire for more convenient, obedient household animals."[26] In 2005, pet owners spent at least $15 million on behavior-modifying drugs for their animals. In the previous year, for the first time, sales of drugs for pets exceeded those for farm animals.[27] And in 2013, Americans doled out approximately $7.6 billion on pills for their pets.[28] As one pharmaceutical company executive commented, "All of the behavioral issues that we have created in our-selves, we are now creating in our pets because they live in the same unhealthy environments that we do. That's why there is a market for these drugs."[29] The launching on the internet and DIRECTV of DogTV, a channel that screens nonstop images designed to appeal to dogs, suggests American dogs can become as sedentary as many of their owners. "The idea is that your dog can watch while you're at work, or while you're home but ignoring the poor beast, or whatever," quips Neil Genzlinger.[30]

Pet industry representatives view such anthropomorphism as a market opportunity, which they name "humanization."[31] Their marketing logic involves building on the current ethos of considering pets as family members in order to sell more products to the animals' owners. The larger ideological context of American–style capitalism, specifically a version of individualism, also constitutes an important part of the attitudinal mixture; as Grier astutely recognizes, pets, for Americans, "are distinctive individuals whose uniqueness should be celebrated."[32] (319). In a capitalist society where individual identity is constituted through consumption, it is not so much of a jump to perceive those sentient beings on whose behalf we consume as unique individuals.

The US iteration of capitalism also depends heavily on the concept of the ownership of private property, which is the subtext of debates about pet indi-vidualism and animal personhood.[33] Not only are pets unable to own prop-erty—with the rare exception of Leona Helmsley's pooch—under US and British law, household animals have been historically defined as the property of human individuals.[34] Animal ethicists and animal rights advocates, in recent years, have argued for a change in vocabulary to avoid characterizing pets as personal property. In the 2011 inaugural issue of *The Journal of Animal Ethics*, the editors write, "Despite its prevalence, 'pets' is surely a derogatory term both of the animals concerned and their human carers [sic]. Again the word 'owners', whilst technically correct in law, harks back to a previous age when animals were regarded as just that: property, machines or things to use without moral constraint."[35] The editors urge the elimination of terms such as "vermin" and "pests," and the substitution of "free living" or "free ranging animals" for the phrase "wild animals." The "derogatory" term "pets," the editors believe, should be replaced with "companion animals," and "pet owners" should be referred to as "animal caregivers" or "animal guardians."

The movement to alter the vocabulary of human-animal interactions does not have just semantic consequences, but also legal ones and has sufficiently alarmed the American Veterinary Medical Association [AVMA] to result in the authoring of a 2005 "issue paper" titled "Ownership versus Guardianship."[36] The AVMA issue paper warns against the use of "guardian" to describe pet ownership because the legal status of "guardianship" entails "a fiduciary rela-tionship (the highest legal civil duty owed by one person to another). The ward's interests are always to prevail over those of the guardian." Parsing out the potential legal ramifications of an embrace of the term "guardianship" for service providers, society, and animals, the AVMA emphasizes that such a semiotic change would grant legal status to animals and subject their relationships with their owners to outside intervention from third parties, who could bring civil lawsuits on behalf of the animals, and/or from the state. These interventions could include decisions regarding veterinary care and euthanasia for animals, the legality of keeping assistance animals, the bureaucratization of animal ownership through the imposition of onerous requirements for additional paperwork and registration, and the possibility of the state's seizure of private property defined here as pets, among other consequences.[37]

Current debates about the vocabulary of pet ownership simultaneously and contradictorily attest to changes in attitudes toward household animals that involve anthropomorphism of a specifically American consumer variety, on the one hand, and to the replaying of earlier nineteenth-century liberal, evangelical Protestant construction of animals as belonging to a group of sentient beings incapable of independent living, who require responsible guardians, on the other hand. What distinguishes the twenty-first-century attitude from its historical precursor, however, is the possibility of pets now acquiring a different legal status than their previous designation as private property.

This tension between perceiving dogs as property and granting them canine personhood of a familial kind permeates the canine-rescue narrative. Whether stray dog or WMD, the canine becomes the locus for sentimental attachment for the American public and displaces Afghan civilians as worthy subjects for concern and material support. In *Saving Cinnamon*, the puppy's successful rescue is a positive outcome of the Global War on Terror, a campaign infused with such humanitarianism that the US military and its supporters are committed to saving the most abject of native subjects: stray dogs.

Canine Rescue as Displaced Humanitarianism

Discussions about humanitarian intervention and the Responsibility to Protect often involve weighing the considerations of national sovereignty against the individual's claim to human rights. Humanitarianism also crucially depends on affective elements that can contribute to campaigns for mobilizing public sentiment in support of military intervention. For example, such sentiments were very much on display on October 10, 1990, during the buildup to the 1991 war against Iraq, in the tearful testimony of the Kuwaiti ambassador's daughter, Nayirah, to the Congressional Human Rights Caucus; she asserted that Iraqi soldiers had hauled incubators back to Iraq and left Kuwaiti babies to languish on bare hospital floors. Her testimony, which was replayed over and over on television in the following three months, turned American public sentiment in favor of war when before it had been tepid. It emerged later that the testimony was fabricated, made up by the US public relations firm Hill & Knowlton, hired by the Kuwaiti government to drum up support for the invasion.[38] According to John McArthur, "Of all the accusations made against the dictator, none had more impact on American public opinion than the one about Iraqi soldiers removing 312 babies from their incubators and leaving them to die on the cold hospital floors of Kuwait City."[39]

Arguably, justifications for humanitarian intervention that continue to resonate emotionally with metropolitan publics have their precursors in the nineteenth-century rhetoric of the civilizing mission, which called for a reinvigorated imperialism to intervene, by legislative fiat and through policing, in the debasement of women as manifested in native practices such as child marriage and *sati* (widow immolation). Whereas those earlier objects of imperial intervention (girls and women) were rational subjects, what is striking about the later objects of humanitarian intervention (babies) is their pre-linguistic status, which heightens their vulnerability and the pathos of their purported victimage.

The canine-rescue narrative, I want to argue, is a form of displaced humanitarianism that extends this logic of mute abjectness in which the figures of girls, women, and babies have been supplanted by the non-human canine subject who has been interpellated as a family member, an interpellation that is consistent with American changes in attitudes towards pets in the last few decades. Nast has called for "critical pet studies" to be attentive to geography and considerations of the location of "pet love," "how it is territorialized," and "where and how it has traveled." She urges the contextualization of "pet love" under "neoliberal regimes of accumulation" to gauge how pets are both "commodities themselves" and serve "as sites of intensely commodified investment tied to global inequities."[40] Within the larger neoliberal regime of accumulation, war is one means of restructuring national economies and forcing their integration into global circuits of capital: the destruction of infrastructure and the upending of civilians' lives and livelihoods enables the infiltration and imposition of transnational capital under the guise of reconstruction. Pre-modern modes-of-production and economic transactions based on local, subnational, and national scales can thus be replaced or transformed into economic arrangements more amenable to transnational exchanges and neoliberal accumulation.

Pet love can be territorialized through the larger military operations of imperialism. When juxtaposed with the extreme deprivation of civilians in Iraq and Afghanistan, the considerable funds that rescuing a stray dog from these two conflict zones entail reveal the very stark contours of global inequality. Yet the fact that stray dogs are not themselves commodities in the conventional sense also aids in the construction of this form of canine transnational mobility as a humanitarian form of intervention. While market transactions involving the transport of the dogs from Afghanistan and Iraq to the metropole are a necessary part of such missions, canine rescue largely traffics in the economy of sentiment rather than commodities. Indeed, missions of this kind often necessitate the assistance of military personnel and native professionals to facilitate the acquisition of requisite travel documents and to secure transport for the canine. This labor is often unremunerated and represented as motivated by the affection that the people rendering assistance feel for dogs and the sympathy they experience for the aspiring pet owners. Affect, thus, becomes a kind of currency that can be parlayed into canine companionship.

Christine Sullivan's *Saving Cinnamon: The Amazing True Story of a Missing Military Puppy and the Desperate Mission to Bring Her Home,* one of the few canine-rescue narratives to emerge from Afghanistan, baldly expresses this form of displaced humanitarianism. Sullivan reproduces several other characteristics of the canine-rescue narrative through the three themes that dominate her memoir: the power of Christian faith, what we might call "American pet exceptionalism," and family. Where her text departs from others in the genre is in the complete absence of individual Afghans from the tale, an absence whose ideological significance I probe later. At the center of this tale of canine rescue is not Cinnamon, who remains offstage and missing in Kyrgyzstan for much of the narrative, but Christine Sullivan and her frenetic activities directed at locating and retrieving the lost dog, whom her brother, navy reservist Lieutenant Commander Mark Feffer, had befriended in Afghanistan and decided to bring home. (Because the military prohibits its personnel from fraternizing with native dogs, the fate of strays on military bases is not pretty, generally involving their removal or elimination.) The point of view alternates between Christine's first-person voice and third-person limited (generally from the perspective of her brother Mark), interspersed with email messages (a common feature of canine-rescue narratives). The end result of suturing together Christian faith, American pet exceptionalism and family is that Cinnamon's successful rescue becomes the post-humanist version of manifest destiny.

From the get-go, Sullivan emphasizes the power of prayer and Christian faith. After the dog is abandoned in Bishek, Christine gets busy on the internet to locate Cinnamon, working her contacts to identify an animal activist in Kyrgyzstan, Yulia Ten, the founder of the Animal Welfare Society of Kyrgyzstan, who agrees to help Sullivan. Aside from the hectic cyber messages Sullivan fires off to various dog rescue activists, the requests for prayers she has received in the past through chain emails "inspire her" to compose one on behalf of Cinnamon.[41] Explaining the circumstances behind the request, she writes in this message, "All I am asking, is that you PLEASE, PLEASE, PLEASE say a prayer for Cinnamon. We do not know if she is safe and being taken care of. We are praying for a miracle that at least she is well taken care of and hopefully can be found and brought to the U.S. to be with her adoptive family. I sincerely believe that the more people who pray for Cinnamon's return the more likely that we will indeed be blessed by her homecoming" (120). The seventy to eighty recipients of this initial prayer plea, in turn, beam it out to their family and friends, and soon the well-wishes materialize on Christine's computer screen.

Within twenty-four hours of dashing off her request for prayer solidarity, Christine learns that Yulia has managed to locate Cinnamon and has established contact with the airport employee who had entrusted the dog to a "relative" for safekeeping. In Sullivan's mind, her chain email has wrought this "miracle": "I couldn't believe what had taken place . . . It had been . . . less than a day since I had asked friends and family for their prayers that we would find her. That email had been forwarded over and over, and had potentially gone out to hundreds of people. I was convinced that this support is what led us to find Cinnamon. There was no other way. She had been lost to us for good, and now we had found her. Although I had witnessed the whole thing, it was still hard to believe. Finding Cinnamon was truly a miracle" (137). The vocabulary of "belief," "witnessing," and "miracles" renders the successful discovery of the canine as an act of divine intervention. Buoyed by this success, Christine sends an update to her family and friends, crediting "the awesome power of prayer and the grace of God" for Cinnamon's discovery and asks for additional prayers (146). "It sounded corny, but that didn't concern me," she confides. "I felt certain that the first e-mail I sent asking for prayers was a key factor in our finding Cinnamon" (147).

Repeated references to the "success" of the prayer chain emails are sprinkled throughout the memoir. The power of faith and Christian belief also appear in other guises. On several occasions, Alice, Mark's wife, is depicted praying and beseeching God for a "sign" that the couple is meant to "adopt" the dog (76). Mixed in with the Christianity too is a bit of New Age Hinduism. Based on the expression in Cinnamon's eyes which she has seen through Skype, Alice is convinced that this dog is a reincarnation of the golden retriever, Jackson, that the couple has lost to cancer. Elsewhere, Mark refers to Cinnamon as a "blessing" and reads rainbows as a "sign" of divine grace (27). Religious faith even infuses Mike Thomsen, the defense contractor who agrees to escort Cinnamon to the US; fretting over the dog's safety during the long flights back to the States, he decides "to trust that if God intended for him to get this far with Cinnamon, he wouldn't allow him to get there and have things be all wrong" (215). Indeed, Christine explains the imperative to tell Cinnamon's story as emanating from the desire "to inspire others" through the tale of "miracles and unlikely coincidences" (235). One friend has already revealed that "her own faith had been renewed through Cinnamon's miracle," and the implication is that this memoir will also catalyze a faith revival in its readers (230).

Before the "miracle" of Cinnamon's homecoming can occur, however, numerous obstacles must be overcome, the chief among them being to convince the Kyrgyz family who has possession of the dog to relinquish her. The American dog handler charged with being Cinnamon's initial escort abandons her at the Bishkek airport. Having neglected to purchase a ticket for the dog and unable to buy one at the counter, he is abusive to Turkish Airline officials and threatens to kill Cinnamon to rid himself of the inconvenience of finding alternative transportation. A compassionate ticket agent, Anna, gives Cinnamon to a close co-worker/quasi relative, Katib, who takes her home, where she becomes an instant hit with his three children. This gentleman and "his family love the dog very much," according to Anna, and he requests that they be allowed to keep Cinnamon (134). Even Yulia, the head of the Animal Welfare Society in Kyrgyzstan, believes that Cinnamon's best interests are served by keeping her with Katib. After reminding Christine that she is "always on the animals' side," she gently suggests that "sometimes it is an act of love to leave a situation like it is" (165). Christine and her brother, however, refuse to entertain this possibility so convinced are they that the dog rightfully belongs to Mark, an assertion that seems odd given that the memoir describes Cinnamon as a camp dog beloved and cared for by multiple soldiers and officers.

Their rationales for denying Katib's request that they relinquish the dog are primarily couched in a rhetoric of American pet exceptionalism. My use of "American pet exceptionalism" seeks to capture the patronizing, sanctimonious, and imperial connotations of the term "American exceptionalism" in its late twentieth- and early twenty-first-century invocations in relation to attitudes towards pets. The canine-rescue narrative asserts the virtues of Americans and their institutions, particularly those geared toward dogs. A clear message of these narratives is that it is better to be an American dog than an Afghan or Kyrgyz one because Americans love dogs and Afghans and Kyrgyzes do not. Sullivan constructs the United States as being the doggy promised land of material abundance (in her words, "the land of Milk-Bone biscuits and honey" with streets "paved with doggie gold") and emotional plenitude, where dogs are "pampered and doted on with lots of yummy treats just for being adorable" (64 and 156). In contrast to the loving care they receive in the US, Sullivan claims without any evidence that "[p]ets in Kyrgyzstan were lucky to get a meal once a week. They were lucky to live from one day to the next" (156). While expressing gratitude to Katib and his family for "the compassion and the care they gave" to Cinnamon, she notes in an aside, "(This is not generally the case in their culture)" (190). She is similarly certain that Cinnamon would have been killed had she remained in Kandahar (231).

Given the absolute distinction the text draws between the status of dogs in the US, on the one hand, and Kyrgyzstan and Afghanistan, on the other, perhaps it is not surprising that Sullivan attributes to Cinnamon aspirations for achieving the "American dream." A life outside of the territorial US "wouldn't be the American dream" for the dog, and Christine is determined "to reunite

Cinnamon with her American dream" (94 and 173). The "American dream" typically signifies an utopian ideal: the opportunity for each individual to achieve success and prosperity through hard work and initiative. Over the twentieth century, it became associated with consumer culture and the acquisition of stuff and wealth. For Cinnamon, the American dream presumably represents the opportunity to actualize her dogginess and to be interpellated as a family member. Sullivan repeatedly expresses the belief that Cinnamon "was meant to have a new life in the United States" and that "she and her story were meant to enhance countless lives near and far" by serving as an exemplar (236). The teleological nature of these sentiments, with the invisible hand of providence at work, articulates a version of canine manifest destiny. Rather than the outward territorial expansion of the nineteenth century, however, here we have an inward territorialization where the "native" canine is imported into the US and bequeathed American citizenship. It is Cinnamon's destiny, in other words, to become incorporated into an American family.

The representation of family is not unambiguous, however, evidencing a contradiction between Christine's assertion of close ties between kin and descriptions of interactions that indicate some distance. In a number of places, she claims that "We are a close family," a statement that she supports by explaining that she converses with her mother on the phone on a weekly basis, a frequency that in today's era of copter parenting would not be considered often. Elsewhere, Sullivan's descriptions of family interactions—particularly, with her brother Mark and his wife Alice—belie the assertion of a close-knit family. Lamenting that "Mark was never one to stay in touch on a regular basis," she reveals that "[c]alls to him sometimes took weeks or even months to be returned, if they were returned at all. It was frustrating—maddening, at times. But there wasn't a whole lot I could do about it. There were times when almost a year would go by and I hadn't spoken with him" (14).

Other sections in the book hint that Sullivan's perception of familial closeness is not shared by her brother and sister-in-law. In addition to his lackadaisical telephone response times, Mark seems astonished at his sister's desire to see him before his deployment to Afghanistan. Here too, one gets the sense that husband and wife have ducked Christine's attempts to visit them in the past, as the following reference to "deterrence" indicates. "Mark and Alice were incredibly gracious that we'd decided to visit," Sullivan writes, "At any other time, I would know not to impose on their time, and they might even have tried to deter it. . . Mark, I believe, was a bit taken aback that we would drive all that way to see him before he left" (14). On another occasion, Sullivan seems surprised that Alice has answered the phone, giving the unflattering impression that the couple screens her calls. Later, Sullivan's suggestion that she accompany Alice on a long-distance drive from Maryland to Chicago to pick up Cinnamon elicits a "lukewarm" and noncommittal response from her sister-in-law.

But if the text codes the sibling relationship as ambivalent, it is unambiguous at representing Cinnamon as Mark and Alice's child. Numerous references to the "new baby" describe Mark's reunion with the dog. While sitting in the backseat of the car with Cinnamon on the way home from the airport, he feels "like he was caring for a new baby. He was overwhelmed with tenderness for her as she fell into a long, deep sleep" (223). Back in Maryland, Alice experiences relief at hearing of Cinnamon's arrival: "Her new baby was finally in safe hands. The emotions she felt overwhelmed her" (222). The reunion, for Christine, provokes both joy and sadness, as she must adjust to playing a distant role in the dog's life after intensely laboring to bring her "home." "During the time we searched for [Cinnamon]," she confesses, "it felt as if she were my baby, but now I had to let her go. She'd live with Mark and Alice in Maryland. I'd have to settle for being her aunt" (223). The vocabulary of parenthood and aunty-hood in these passages attests to how dogs have become "ideal love-object substitutes for children" in post-industrial societies today.[42] Indeed, Christine remarks on hearing "the pride of parenthood" in Mark and Alice's voices as they update her on Cinnamon's "latest antics" with her canine siblings, Pete and Elvis, who have been subsequently adopted and have augmented the nuclear family unit (238).

Dogs completely displace Afghans in *Saving Cinnamon*, which differs from other canine-rescue memoirs, particularly from Iraq, in its representation of civilians where they often play a sympathetic role in facilitating the emigration of the dog. Sullivan does not even appear cognizant of the fact that Afghanistan is peopled with individuals for whom life is precarious because they are targets of violence either by US military forces and drones or by various Islamic insurgencies such as the Taliban, remnants of Al Qaeda, or emergent factions of the Islamic State. Where one might expect her to be defensive about saving stray dogs rather than Afghan civilians from a conflict zone, she appears oblivious to this potential critique. Instead, her moral calculus consists of tallying the comparative worth of saving *foreign* dogs against the large numbers of *domestic* dogs in the US in need of rescue. "Mark, Alice, and I were and continue to be aware that millions of animals in the United States and worldwide wait in vain for their rescuers," Sullivan admits. "Whether they live hardened lives as strays on the streets or wait endlessly at shelters without love or a family to call their own, too many die alone or are euthanized by a rescue and adoption system that is too overwhelmed to save them all" (236–237). She continues,

> We have many critics who feel our exorbitant expenditure of time, effort, and money may have been better spent on saving multiple dogs here at home. I understand and can empathize with that position. I would save all the animals if I could. We all would. Tragically, however, we cannot. And leaving Cinnamon behind would not have changed that. Saving the world's homeless animals is a monumental undertaking, but I firmly believe that, just as in Cinnamon's search

and rescue, everyone must do their part, no matter how big or how small. And if each and every one of us follows his or her heart and takes action, then we can make a difference for animals everywhere, just as we did for Cinnamon. (237)

The refusal to prioritize the needs of "American" strays over "Afghan" ones bespeaks a kind of canine internationalism even as the absence of an acknowledgement of the tenuousness of Afghan *human* lives, as one result of the Global War on Terror, suggests that dogs' lives matter in a way that Afghan ones do not. In its concern to advocate for the welfare of dogs, Sullivan's iteration of post-humanism completely displaces Afghan civilians, police, soldiers, and insurgents from the scene of military intervention.

Military intervention becomes the means for stray dogs in conflict zones to acquire families and symbolic citizenship in the United States; in this sense, their incorporation into the national imaginary becomes one form of evidence for the success of the democratizing project. While the US failed to export democracy to Afghanistan, individual soldiers working in tandem with American civilians are able to markedly improve the lives of the most abject subjects in Afghanistan, stray dogs, by literally importing them into the democratic space of the American nation. The anonymous quotation that closes Sullivan's memoir suggests this much: "Saving one animal will not change the world, but surely the world will change for that one animal" (239).

Canines to the Rescue: Military Working Dogs

Sullivan's text represents a civilian variant of the canine-rescue narrative: a helpless and innocent stray dog is given a better life through the combined agency of American civilians and individual military personnel. Maria Goodavage's *Top Dog: The Story of Marine Hero Lucca*, is a military variant of the canine-rescue narrative—a subgenre that upends one of the basic premises of the civilian narrative genre. Focusing on the relationship between a MWD and his or her handler, it showcases canine combatants as saviors of soldiers and Marines through the use of their superior olfactory and auditory senses. Unlike native stray dogs such as Cinnamon, who are portrayed offstage and as helpless objects of sentimental attachment, MWDs take center stage in this narrative variant and are represented as heroic agents who prevent or minimize injury to their fellow soldiers. To put it bluntly, they rescue the humans rather than they themselves being objects of rescue by humans.

Written in third-person omniscient, *Top Dog* contains direct dialogue pieced together and created by Goodavage from the recollections of military personnel and family members of dog handlers whom she interviewed between 2013 and 2014; she supplemented the interviews with text messages and Facebook queries and by perusing photographs, videos, and online sources to better capture the experience of combat.[43] *Top Dog* is very much focused on the narrative present of the events it describes and the point of view of American soldiers and Marines—primarily Lucca's handlers, Marine Gunnery Sargeant Chris Willingham and Marine Corporal Juan Rodriguez. Like *Saving Cinnamon*, it never engages with the politics of these conflicts and the role of the US in destabilizing both regions over the last few decades. Nor does it historicize the changing attitudes toward MWDs in the military, which mirror the tensions in the greater public between perceiving pets as private property or family members.

These tensions are evident throughout the latter half of the twentieth century in military attitudes and policies toward MWDs. On the one hand, the Department of Defense classifies MWDs as a kind of property, as "equipment," and various nonfictional accounts of these canines refer to them as "force multipliers," "valuable assets," "outlays," and "weapons."[44] "'The working dog is a weapons system that is resilient, compact, easily deployable, and can move fast when needed. Nothing compares," observes Air Force Master Sergeant Antonio Rodriguez, who coordinates over one hundred military working dog teams for twelve air force bases.[45] The classification of these animals as equipment might have contributed to the fact that MWDs were considered expendable at the end of conflicts such as the Vietnam War (1954–1975) or their retirement from combat. The US military dramatically increased its dependence on MWDs during the Vietnam War, sending close to 4,900 dogs and about 10,000 handlers to that theater, where they were used to scout for ambushes and booby traps, to guard outposts and bases, to track lost soldiers and downed pilots, and to detect underwater North Vietnamese forces.[46] At the end of the war, to the anguish of their handlers, the majority of these dogs were euthanized or left behind (only 204 made it out of the country).[47] Fast forward to the end of the century: as recently as 2000, MWDs were euthanized after they were deemed too old for military service at around the age of ten.[48] The expendability of these dogs indicates their status as a form of property to be disposed of when their utility to the military had ceased.

On the other hand, reflecting larger cultural trends in the United States over the last few decades that have bestowed a type of "personhood" on canines, the policy of euthanizing post-combat MWDs has been replaced by "retiring" the dogs when they are around 8.3 years old to allow them some leisure years before the end of their lives.[49] Many are adopted out (the waiting lists are long), some are transferred to civilian law enforcement bodies, and a small number, who are determined to be too aggressive, are euthanized. Other evidence that the military brass considers canines to be more than "equipment" inheres in the high quality of veterinary care they provide to the dogs. When the Daniel E. Holland Military Working Dog Hospital at Lackland Air Force Base opened in 2008, some of its medical equipment (the CT scanner, for example) was better quality than was available at the hospital for humans. The Holland Hospital also boasts a physical therapy room, complete with "underwater treadmills designed just for dogs."[50] In combat, severely wounded MWDs are routinely airlifted to facilities equipped to amputate their limbs and to treat other serious injuries, as was the case with Lucca whose leg had be removed after an Improvised Explosive Device [IED] attack. Soldiers and Marines, in these situations, often risk their lives in order to get their dogs emergency medical care. In addition to treating physical injuries, since 2011, the military recognizes that canines can experience their own version of PTSD; those who receive this diagnosis are given therapy and anxiety medication or are reassigned to less stressful work or are retired.[51]

If the military considered MWDs to be solely equipment, it would not invest this kind of effort and labor—some of it quite dangerous—and incur considerable expenses to treat and rehabilitate wounded combat canines. Indeed, the senior veterinary surgeon in Afghanistan, Lieutenant-Colonel James Giles III, who amputated Lucca's leg, reflects that if she "had been injured at an earlier time" in his "veterinary career, she would not be going home"; "There would have been no surgery. Since she could no longer serve her country, he would have to euthanize her" (246-247).

MWD handlers and the military personnel who train them clearly perceive their dogs as sentient beings with whom they develop a strong and enduring attachment. Air Force Master Sergeant Antonio Rodriguez, who also operates a consultancy for police and military dogs, emphasizes to his clients and his military comrades "that a dog is not a piece of equipment, but a working, breathing animal that needs to be treated respectfully and kindly," reminding them that "[y]our dog is your partner and values meaningful interaction. You just don't think about equipment in the same way."[52] It is perhaps the affective relationship between canine and handler that has led to the tradition of considering MWDs to be non-commissioned officers who are one rank higher than their handlers, so the saying goes, "to prevent handlers from mistreating their dogs." Sergeant First Class Regina Johnson, the operations superintendent at the Military Working Dog School at Lackland, believes "the tradition grew out of a few handlers recognizing the dog as their partner."[53] In actuality, MWDs are not given *official* ranks, though the military classifies them on the basis of their skills.

A similar sentiment of canine personhood motivates attempts by nonprofit organizations such as the United States War Dogs Association to lobby the DoD to grant MWDs medals and awards that recognize their sacrifices, and to petition the United States Postal Service to issue commemmorative stamps that honor the dogs. To date, both campaigns have failed, partly out of the sense that such awards trivialize those given to soldiers. But that has not prevented individual soldiers and Marines from bestowing their own medals (Purple Hearts and Silver Stars) on their dogs and the creation of unofficial honors such as the Meritorius Service Medal, the Army Commendation Medal, and the United States Military Working Dog Service Award.[54] Moreover, the first official monument to MWDs was installed at Lackland Air Force Base in 2013, and numerous privately funded monuments and statues have been erected in cities and towns across the country, including Knoxville, Tennessee; Riverside, California; Holmdel, New Jersey; Mobile, Alabama; and Hanna City, Illinois, among other locations.

Maria Goodavage's *Top Dog: The Story of Marine Hero Lucca* leans toward the canine personhood end of the spectrum in its representation of a MWD. Colloquial for "boss or leader" or the projected winner of a competition, the book's title, "Top Dog," along with the subtitle's terms "Marine Hero," anthropomorphize the canine protagonist. The narrative, in effect, is a canine bildungsroman that charts Lucca's interpellation into a Specialized Search Dog [SSD], tracing her education through various training programs run by Oketz (the elite K-9 unit of the Israeli Defense Forces) and the DoD. By her first deployment to Iraq, Lucca has passed off-leash bomb detection courses at Tel Aviv, Lackland Air Force Base, and Yuma Proving Ground in Arizona, where the army has established simulacra of Iraqi and Afghan villages and towns to better prepare troops for combat conditions.[55] Goodavage describes this training in the terms of US higher education, noting, "If standard military working dogs have bachelor's degrees, specialized search dogs have PhDs" (20). The title alludes to the fact that Lucca is "the clear top dog of her class" in these courses (20).

Whereas in the civilian version of the canine-rescue narrative, the stray dog acquires symbolic American citizenship by virtue of its arrival in the United States, the MWD acquires figurative nationality through the combat tour on foreign soil. The DoD annually purchases hundreds of MWDs (mostly Belgian Malinois, German Shepherds, and Labrador Retrievers) from European breeders, primarily in Bulgaria, the Czech Republic, Germany, Poland, the Netherlands, and Slovakia. Because of cost controls, the government does not buy the best canines available, which would run from $7,000 to $14,000 each; rather, they settle for "dual purpose" dogs, capable of both patrol and detection, costing between $3,000 to $4,500 each.[56] Yet in spite of the "foreign" birth of these animals, references to "duty," "service," and "sacrifice" to their "country" saturate representations of MWDs.[57]

Service, in other words, trumps the country of origin in terms of bestowing national identity; MWDs acquire symbolic citizenship from being in combat on foreign soil. *Top Dog* opens with a chapter titled "Line of Duty" which describes the dramatic IED attack in Helmand Province, Afghanistan, that injures Lucca. From the narrative's beginning, Goodavage presents Lucca as a Marine and emphasizes her combat experience. "It was March 23, 2012, just one month shy of her sixth anniversary as a marine," Goodavage explains, "With two deployments behind her, she was an old pro at the business of sniffing improvised explosive devices while off leash" (4). The narrative continues, "She had led more than four hundred missions, and no one had gotten hurt by an IED when they were with her" (4). "More experienced than some of the soldiers," Lucca had been named "Mama Lucca" by the Green Berets on this detail (4). Once she is hit, they form a protective cordon around her, facing outward, while they await evacuation by Special Forces medics, who are also trained in veterinary care. Commenting on her success on an earlier tour in Iraq, when Lucca had tracked and caught a suspected insurgent in spite of the fact that she had not been trained as an attack dog, Willingham, her handler at the time, boasts, "Well, there's a reason for that. It's 'cause Lucca is a real marine" (137). The Green Berets also claim her, along with another MWD, Darko, as one of their own. According to Special Forces Sergeant Jake Parker, both dogs "seemed to embody most of the core attributes of the Special Forces, including adaptability, perseverance, a team-player mentality, courage, capability and professionalism" (212-213). Evidence of symbolic citizenship inheres in Lucca's moniker as a "Marine" and her linguistic induction into the Special Forces—subject positions that function as synecdoches of the nation.

Throughout *Top Dog*, soldiers and Marines anthropomorphize Lucca and the other MWDs who are on combat tour, projecting human relationships onto the interactions among the dogs. Thus, Cooper is called Lucca's "boyfriend," Posha is described as a bashful suitor who is "like a sixteen-year-old boy going on his first date," and Buddy is characterized as "just a friend" because Willingham doesn't want his "girl to get a bad reputation" (160–161). Such descriptions reveal several things: an uneasiness with women in combat insofar as the female dog's identity can only be assimilated through projecting heterosexual relationships and normative gender roles on the dogs—in Lucca's case, suggested by her nickname, "Mama Lucca"; a desire to normalize life in dangerous outposts by invoking the everyday mundane of teenage dating rituals; and the extent to which MWDs are implicitly figured in familial tropes as beloved children. MWDs, in other words, familiarize the unfamiliar, particularly in Forward Operating Bases, in contexts that are removed from the large American military bases such as Bagram Air Base, which resemble small American towns complete with bowling alleys and fast food franchises.

The domestic associations with MWDs appear at the rural Helmand Province combat outpost where Green Berets are training Afghan Local Police as part of General Petraeus' COIN strategy of winning hearts and minds. Goodavage dwells on Lucca's ability to soothe soldiers by her presence: "Lucca was a huge morale booster around the combat outpost. Despite the relatively nonviolent months leading up to the fighting season, being a Green Beret in Taliban country was still an intense job. And while Special Forces are among the toughest of the tough, that didn't stop them from missing home. As she had in Iraq, Lucca brought a piece of home with her. Soldiers petted her, talked to her, told her their troubles. 'She's really calming,' Parker told Rod while petting her one day. 'You can't say that for a mine sweeper.'" (212). The presence of MWDs helps make the foreign space of combat, which is marked by cultural and geographic alterity, familiar by enabling tactile interactions between soldiers and dogs that evoke the comforting ethos of home. Consistent with the transformation in attitudes toward pets in the US that I described earlier, dogs, in effect, become a signifier of home and family. In the fraught environment of the FOB, their presence makes combat more bearable. The mundane act of stroking and speaking to a dog renders the foreignness of the combat environment less strange and imaginatively transports soldiers to the reassuring scene of domestic life. (Apart from the psychological relief provided by MWDs, troops benefit physiologically as well, given recent research that shows petting a dog or cat can lower blood pressure.) As Goodavage observes elsewhere, "The irony is that soldier dogs make war a little more human."[58]

The psychological comfort that MWDs provide by their presence and associations with American familial life constitute one way that combat canines metaphorically "rescue" soldiers and Marines. A second, more literal way that MWDs "rescue" American troops is through their ability to detect explosives through their superior olfactory organs. The emergence and wide-spread use of improvised explosive devices by Iraq and Afghan insurgents, the leading cause of American combat fatalities, resulted in the expansion of the MWD program in 2004 and the creation of a Specialized Search Dog program.[59] SSDs are trained to search for explosives off leash, conferring the advantage of working at a distance from troops and providing a buffer zone around explosives. Should a SSD accidentally trigger an IED, the dog would take the hit rather than the soldiers and Marines on the mission, thus saving human lives. In Afghanistan, which is one of the countries most heavily seeded with landmines that were planted during the Soviet Occupation, SSDs are a particularly valuable presence in combat units. Their bomb-sniffing abilities render them, so to speak, as preventive-rescue agents of the armed forces. Indeed, Lucca saves the Special Forces soldiers on her patrol by inadvertently setting off the IED that injures her, but at a distance from the troops who are out of harm's way. Over the course of her military career, she had completed four hundred explosive-detection missions "with no injuries other than her own," and, thus, saved numerous soldiers and Marines (266).

In the fraught environment of the battlefield, the relationship that develops between MWDs and their handlers is extraordinarily close, as evidenced by the reactions of Lucca's second handler Marine Corporal Juan Rodriguez following her injury. Not only do he and the other Green Berets risk their lives protecting Lucca while they await evacuation, but he never leaves her side, even sleeping next to her in the hospital kennel, in the period leading up to her surgery and during her recovery. Rodriguez's insistence on remaining by Lucca's side makes perfect sense given that MWDs and their handlers are together 24/7 on combat tours, and handlers would be especially attuned to the necessity of offering the comfort of close proximity to their canine partners during the trauma of injury. As Goodavage observes, "Being together 24/7, where one life depends on the other, creates the kind of deep bonds that handlers say nothing can compare to in civilian life" (177–178). Handlers acknowledge at several places in *Top Dog* how their MWDs are "like a part" of them, they are "in synch," and "the best dogs and handlers became more like each other over time" (163–164). The process of training a dog for a "job," Donna Haraway notes, can be "subject-changing" for both canine and human; under life-and-death circumstances, the relationship between the two must become profound.[60]

For Lucca, that bond develops with two handlers: Marine Staff Sergeant Chris Willingham and Marine Corporal Juan Rodriguez. Her first handler, Willingham, serves several tours with Lucca before deciding to take a break from combat and focus on his family. To this end, he accepts a position as a detachment commander at the American embassy in Helsinki. Willingham chooses Rodriguez as his replacement handler, entrusting Lucca to the Marine Corporal on the basis of his confidence in Rodriguez's skills, but makes it clear that he expects to adopt Lucca on her retirement from active duty. After her injury, however, in acknowledgement of the bond between MWD and Marine that is forged through surviving such a traumatic experience together, Willingham offers Rodriguez the opportunity to adopt Lucca in his stead. Rodriguez, for his part, wants "to give Lucca the best home possible," which means life with a family rather than a single man (251). The decision is made to fly Lucca to Willingham in Finland via a transit stop in the United States.

In contrast to international rescue dogs for whom the "airplane is an instrument in a series of subject-transforming technologies," insofar as the "social contract" of their birth is replaced with the one of their "adopted" land, MWDs experience the airplane as the metaphoric bridge between military and civilian life.[61] Having already acquired symbolic American citizenship through her combat tour, Lucca's plane ride becomes an opportunity to reaffirm her US nationality by ritually marking her transition to retirement with ceremonies associated with the homecoming of soldiers and Marines. American Airlines arranges for a water cannon salute to welcome the plane on its arrival at O'Hare; over the intercom, a flight attendant explains that the salute is "in honor of a marine hero returning home" and describes Lucca's military service to the other passengers (256). On the ground, a five-person color guard and two women "holding large photos of Lucca in front of a marine flag" escort Lucca and Rodriguez, parade-style, to their departure gate (appropriately Gate K9), where speeches by airline officials and the singing of the national anthem conclude the homecoming ceremonies (256). The airplane journey, in effect, supersizes

Lucca's status as an American citizen. In the absence of a universal military draft, service in the all-volunteer armed forces signifies an uber form of patriotism, the willingness to die for one's country when the state does not require the obligation of such sacrifice from all its citizens. The honors accorded to her, typical of those used to celebrate returning military personnel, affirm a version of canine personhood and emphasize her enhanced patriotism.

In Helsinki, the Willinghams, along with "about fifteen Finnish television, newspaper, and web photographers and reporters," greet Lucca and Rodriguez (259). And so begins a second career as a minor celebrity and canine ambassador for MWDs, which has Lucca spreading cheer among injured veterans and terminally ill children, and being inducted into the Veterans of Foreign Wars. In the penultimate scene of the memoir, six-year-old Claire Willingham, with Lucca at her feet, draws a picture of the two of them. This tableau of domestic tranquility promises a happily-ever-after ending for its injured canine protagonist, Lucca, who has become "a live-in member of the Willingham family" (292). As in its civilian counterpart, the MWD variation of the canine-rescue narrative features a teleological plot that moves toward an affirmation of US citizenship and the integration of the canine protagonist into the nuclear family. The heteronormative nuclear family, consequently, gets constructed as the locus of sociality for the nation, the significance of which I treat in this chapter's conclusion.

Bringing the War Home: *Max* and the Critique of the War on Terror

Like *Saving Cinnamon* and *Top Dog*, the novel and film both titled *Max* proffer the family as the primary unit of society, but similarities between the larger ideological projects of these texts end here.[62] The novel and film represent the long-term physical and psychological impact of war on both nonhuman and human subjects. Perhaps more damning, however, the plot involves a Marine trafficking in illegal weapons, which he has procured in Afghanistan, that are destined for purchase by Mexican drug cartels. In its acknowledgement of an illegal economy centered on weapons trafficking and the drug trade, *Max* superimposes two realities of the contemporary Afghan and Pakistani economies onto the US—aspects that had their origins in the Cold War and American support for the Mujahideen, which now threaten the long-term stability of the region. In spite of the novel's and film's sentimental banality, they demonstrate the aftershocks of US intervention by showing how violence ripples out from the periphery to the core in the illicit transnational flow of drugs and guns.

Told from the third-person limited point of view of Justin, the younger brother of a Marine who has died in combat in Afghanistan, the novel draws on representational clichés of dysfunctional American families, such as the angry teenager, the emotionally repressed father, and the bewildered mother, who ineffectually attempts to mediate between the two. Resentful of his older brother Kyle, a MWD handler who died in combat in Afghanistan, Justin feels burdened by his parents' expectations to live up to the example set by Kyle, a high achiever in their small town of Lufkin, Texas. He is uninterested in his studies, disdainful of working at his father's storage business, and appears most animated when playing video games. Indeed, Justin seems headed down the path of criminality insofar as he sells pirated copies of video games to a local thug Emilio, the cousin of his best friend. We learn that the trade in video games constitutes the tip of the iceberg of Emilio's illegal activities, which are part of a transnational network of an illicit trade in drugs and small arms and light weapons [SALW], spanning Afghanistan, Mexico, and the US.

As in *Top Dog* and other military versions of the canine-rescue narrative, the novel and film construct the MWD and the human in a reciprocal relationship of rescue to one other. Suffering from canine PTSD, Max, Kyle's MWD, has been deemed too vicious for continued military service or adoption and is slated to be euthanized, much to the consternation of Justin's mother. Not himself comfortable around dogs, Justin has a calming effect on Max, who cautiously accepts a Kong and follows rudimentary commands from him. After hearing his mother's declaration that "[t]his family looks out for its own" in relation to Max, Justin determines to accept primary responsibility for the dog's care as a way of alleviating his mother's grief over his brother's death (51). Thus begins the building of trust between the boy and dog through the process of training, which has, to invoke Haraway, subject-altering effects: Max transforms from a snarling, ferocious beast to a protective pet and Justin changes from a petty criminal to an unofficial agent of the law, thwarting an illegal sale of SALW bound for a Mexican drug cartel.[63] Both boy and dog ultimately become socialized into the nuclear heteronormative family, the telos of the canine-rescue narrative.

More interesting than the theme of family cohesion and consolidation in this conventional narrative, however, are its critiques of US militarism and the Global War on Terror, which are represented as having physical and psychological effects of long duration. In addition to Max's canine PTSD, Justin's father, Mr. Wincott, a former Marine, has sustained a leg injury in Operation Desert Storm that leaves him with a permanent limp. The novel and the film initially characterize him as inordinately strict and unfeeling, implying that military discipline goes hand in hand with emotional frigidity. Lauded as a hero in their small town, the father becomes more sympathetic when he explains the ignominious nature of his injury to his son. While the film does not include this detail, the scene of the "combat injury" in the novel is "Al-Burqan" oil field in Kuwait, most likely a fictionalization of Burgan field, the largest sandstone oil field in the world and the second largest oil field overall.[64] The identification of an oil field as the location of Mr. Wincott's injury hints at the political economy of the Iraq War, which was ostensibly initiated by a dispute between Iraq and Kuwait over slant drilling. In the novel, the Marines stumble onto the oil field set ablaze by Iraqi soldiers. Although their mission is not explicitly explained, the fact that the scene situates American troops at an oil field suggests that the US government believes access to oil reserves is in the national interests and, consequently, recalls the Carter Doctrine that declared the right to use military force to maintain vital US strategic aims in the Persian Gulf.

A second critique of US militarism in relation to Mr. Wincott inheres in the acknowledgement of its inherent violence, a violence that can be directed toward its own soldiers and Marines during the proverbial fog of war. Mr. Wincott recollects his experiences on the very first day of his combat tour:

> . . . there was smoke everywhere. Our eyes were burning—you couldn't even see your hand in front of your face. Then shots went off. . . . So we returned fire. Only, it turns out, we were firing on nobody. Because the shots were coming from *behind* us. . . Friendly fire. . . The enemy was long gone, but no one could see a thing so our own guys were shooting at us. Accidentally. The guy next to me went down. Then I got hit. I took two bullets in my leg. One passed through the muscle, but the other. . . cracked right into my shinbone and shattered it like glass. (emphasis in the original 202–203)

A victim of so-called friendly fire, Mr. Wincott's limp from the injury becomes a permanent memento of wartime trauma, whose meaning is interpreted in Lufkin as a signifier of patriotic heroism rather than military bungling. Historically, fratricide most frequently results from situations where two or more units are supporting each other in combat. With the exception of the invasion of Panama, the Army estimates that US casualties from friendly fire have averaged between 10% and 14% for every conflict from World War II to Desert Storm. Friendly fire fatalities for Desert Storm weigh in at 12%, translating to a body count of 35 of the 298 US service members killed.[65] By attributing Mr. Wincott's injury to friendly fire, both the novel and the film restore to the cultural imaginary one aspect of "the repressed and buried reality" of the violence of Operation Desert Storm and the toll the national-security state extracts from its own citizens.[66] But there are limits to the narratives' critique of military violence, which cannot exceed its effects on US citizens to contemplate the devastating impact of Operation Desert Storm on Iraqis and the destabilization of the region inaugurated by that invasion.

A third critique of US militarism consists of *Max's* representation of the illicit transnational trade in SALW and drugs that the narrative connects to the Afghan war. The novel and film transpose the binary logic of hegemonic accounts of the Afghanistan intervention, which divides natives into "good" and "bad" ones, to the Marines themselves: the exemplary Marine, Kyle, plays saintly doppleganger to his childhood best friend, the immoral Marine, Tyler. Much of the plot centers on Tyler's attempts to sell military rifles and rocket launchers, which he has smuggled from Afghanistan, to a Mexican cartel. Both the book and movie impute Tyler's motives to greed; as Tyler tells Justin, a gun that could net him $600 in the United States sells for "just a shade over three thousand dollars" in Mexico (190). In describing a supply chain that identifies Mexico as the market for illegal gun sales from the US, *Max* accurately captures the historical reality that thousands of small arms seized annually by Mexican authorities can be traced to the US.[67] The Government Accounting Office calculates that over 73,000 guns confiscated in Mexico between 2009 and 2014 originated in the US, the majority of which came from Arizona, California, and Texas, the setting of *Max*. A little over half of these weapons could not be traced to their first retail sale.[68]

Globally, the illicit trade in SALW tends "to be concentrated in areas afflicted by armed conflict, violence, and organized crime," where the demand for weapons is high.[69] Civil wars and regional conflicts also contribute to the existing arsenals of weapons and their proliferation into new territories through the "'ant trade'—numerous shipments of small numbers of weapons that, over time, result in the accumulation of large numbers of illicit weapons by unauthorized end users."[70] The film version of *Max* opens in Afghanistan with best friends Kyle and Tyler walking point with Max. After successfully locating a weapons cache in a village, we see the troops individually questioned by their commanders, who have noticed a small discrepancy between the number of weapons tallied at the discovery location and those turned in after the mission. Such discrepancies are a recurring pattern with this unit, we learn. Shortly afterwards, Kyle confronts Tyler about siphoning off weapons. In the next scene, a visually chaotic spectacle of combat, Kyle gets shot, which kills him on the spot. Lurking in the periphery of the scene is Tyler, whose role in the ambush is ambiguous. Has he taken the opportunity to eliminate Kyle to avoid detection for smuggling arms? Has he conspired with insurgents to plan the ambush? Or is he also caught off guard by the attack, escaping injury only by chance? The opening sequence, thus, embeds Tyler in the transnational ant trade and establishes doubts about his character and the sincerity of his feelings for his childhood friend.

Both the novel and the film *Max* recognize the existence of complex commodity chains that underwrite the ant trade and weapons trafficking more generally. The putative villain Tyler explains to Justin, "'My business? I'm just a little fish in a big pond.' Tyler's tone had taken on a hint of disdain, like he was being forced to explain something obvious to a child. 'The big fish sell weapons all over the world and make a lot of money doing it. Then they send wide-eyed hicks like me and Kyle out there to get shot at with those very same weapons, so they can cry big crocodile tears, salute the flag, and sell some more.'" (192). While the antecedents of "fish" and "they" are vague, Tyler's references to saluting the flag and selling weapons allude to US corporations, who in actuality dominate the global arms trade. According to the Stockholm International Peace Research Initiative, US companies racked up arms sales of $209.7 billion in 2015.[71] Lockheed Martin, Boeing, Raytheon, Northrup Grumman, and General Dynamics topped the list.[72] Tyler's comment captures the structural irony of the military-industrial complex: US companies make enormous profits off the sale of weapons abroad, which are legal at the point of sale but then circulate in grey or black markets and often end up being used by insurgents against US troops, which then becomes a justification for the sale of more arms to the national-security state.[73] The sale of weapons abroad and the amassing of profits for US companies generate defense contracts and the additional sales of armaments to the US government in what becomes a giant feedback loop of dollars and death.

Tyler's explanation misses one critical dimension of how SALV enter the gray and black markets. As C.J. Chivers reveals, many such weapons have been distributed by the Pentagon to various security forces in Iraq and Afghanistan, who then sell them on the black market, sometimes utilizing the internet and Facebook accounts for such transactions. Although a conservative estimate for the number of arms dispersed in this fashion in Iraq and Afghanistan is 1.45 million, the Pentagon has inexplicably only recorded the serial numbers of 700,000 of these weapons, facilitating the illegal sales of the remaining undocumented arms.[74] Contra *Max*'s representation of US troops as arms traffickers, Iraqi and Afghan soldiers and members of their respective police forces are more likely to desert and sell their weapons than the Americans. Other weapons become available on the black market through their outright theft from Afghan, Iraqi, and US security forces.

The book and the movie are also not completely faithful representations of the illicit transnational trade in drugs, ignoring Afghanistan's dubious status at the time of this writing as the supplier of 90% of the world's supply of heroin. The narratives demarcate drugs and guns on the basis of geography, associating the drug trade with Mexican cartels and arms trafficking to rogue US Marines in Afghanistan. Since the 1980s and the resistance to the Soviet Occupation the two commodities had become deeply imbricated in Afghanistan. Ahmed Rashid describes the intertwining of the Mujahideen, Pakistani ISI agents, and the CIA in the production and circulation of opium and weapons.[75] "Donkey, camel and truck convoys carried weapons into Afghanistan" and raw opium out of the country to Pakistan, where it was refined into heroin and eventually bound for markets in Europe via Central Asia and the Gulf states.[76] Dubbed the "Golden Crescent," Pakistan, Afghanistan, and Iran had replaced the "Golden Triangle of Laos, Myanmar, and Thailand as the lead producer of opium" by the late 1980s.[77] With US efforts to crack down on the drug trade in Pakistan during the 1990s, the refinement of opium shifted to Afghanistan.[78]

Since the US invasion in 2001, the drug economy has become pervasive. Competing with the Mujahadeen warlords for drug profits, the Taliban initially embraced the cultivation of poppies. As Rashid notes in his magisterial study *Descent into Chaos*, the Taliban's policies toward opium production subsequently changed and the regime then discouraged poppy cultivation as a strategy to win international recognition.[79] For their part, after being demobilized and disarmed by the UN, following the fall of the Taliban, the Mujahideen warlords were given positions in the Interior Ministry during President Hamid Karzai's administration, in effect, "blurring [the] lines" between "powerful figures who trafficked in drugs and those who protected drug traffickers."[80] In the last few years, the Taliban has become a cartel in its own right, trafficking in heroin in order to finance its insurgency.[81] If anything, the Afghan government—from the local level to the national one—has emerged as a competitor with the Taliban for control over the illegal drug trade.[82] Competition between former warlords, government officials, and insurgents for market share now characterizes the illicit drug economy. Given the vast amounts of profit that can be made from opium, it is not surprising that cultivation in Afghanistan has significantly increased, as have the rates of addiction in the country and surrounding Central Asian states.[83]

The failure of the novel and film versions of *Max* to represent this aspect of the transnational drug trade in the face of their critique of the violence of US intervention in terms of its physical and psychological costs to soldiers and WMDs and their exposure of the political economy of the circulation of SALW is not startling. The narrative flags those unintended and negative consequences of US imperialism that can be resolved: physical injuries such as Mr. Wincott's can be treated, canine PTSD can be overcome, and rogue soldiers can be disciplined. But to acknowledge that the Afghan government has become a major player in the transnational trafficking of heroin would be to expose the utter sham of the US's democratizing project, one of the belated rationales for its intervention. The Afghan government's drug trafficking raises fundamental questions about the nature of the rule of law and its relation to democracy. In a context where government officials routinely engage in criminal activities, what does the rule of law even mean? And in the absence of the rule of law, how can those civil institutions that are the hallmark of democracy even exist, let alone, flourish? Ultimately, the active involvement of Afghan government officials in a rather robust drug trade reveals the complete failure of US intervention in the region.

Max's critique of the US intervention in Afghanistan, and to a lesser extent in Iraq, meets its historical limit in containing the Global War on Terror's harmful impact to its effects on military families. The violence of intervention reverberates from the periphery, rattling the metropole, but it can be calmed through the soothing ministrations of the patriarchal family. Like its nonfictional counterparts *Saving Cinnamon* and *Top Dog*, *Max* ends with a consolidation of that heteronormative formation: father and son have reconciled and taken cautious steps to forge a loving relationship, and Max's position in the family seems assured given that Mr. Wincott has gotten rid of his outdoor crate, allowing the former WMD to move into the home and complete his transition to family pet. In the final scene of both the novel and film, the Wincotts, including Max, are gathered in the kitchen. The presence of Carmen, Justin's girlfriend, in this scene, helping Mrs. Wincott in the kitchen, holds out the promise of the social reproduction of the family. Against the backdrop of rogue soldiers disciplined and a transnational drug deal disrupted, the family-ever-after ending of *Max* intimates that a happily-ever-after ending to the Afghan intervention is in the offing.

Conclusion

The canine-rescue narrative's stock ending of the incorporation of the stray dog or MWD into the structure of the nuclear family illustrates Lauren Berlant's contention that one consequence of Reaganite conservatism has been that "nostalgic images" of a normative "familial America. . . define the utopian context for citizen aspiration."[84] For Berlant, American citizenship has increasingly become "a condition of social membership produced by personal acts and values, especially acts originating in or directed toward the family sphere."[85] She astutely observes that "the American fetus" and "the American child," those subjects who themselves cannot enact the responsibilities of citizens, acquire a "supericonicity" and provide the grounds for politicized discourses of morality and for the formulation of reactionary legislative policies.[86] I follow Uddin in adding dogs to Berlant's categories of "infantile citizens."[87] But whereas Uddin explores what canines signify about "citizenship as a set of actions or inactions, as a definition of personhood, as a way of moving through and imagining the nation," my concern is to consider how stray dogs and MWDs displace Afghan civilians as affective objects of identification in need of rescue and healing by American soldiers and, hence, to investigate how they become alibis for humanitarian intervention.[88]

Such displacements have several major consequences. First, the canine-rescue narrative has a very limited engagement with the politics of US intervention in Afghanistan other than to consider its effects on military families. While a few uneasily acknowledge some of the contradictions of the US prosecution of war, for example, pointing out the irony of a military brass that objects to dogs scavenging the corpses who have been killed by US troops in the first place, thus offering a limited opening for a critique of military intervention, *Saving*

Cinnamon and *Top Dog* are blithely indifferent to the larger context of their production.[89] The US invasion and occupation of Afghanistan have created the conditions of possibility for the development of a strong attachment between a soldier and dog, but these memoirs never engage that context.

After appearing in 2007 under the title *44 Days Out of Kandahar*, the updated edition titled, *Saving Cinnamon,* was published by St. Martin's in 2009. By 2006, during the period when Sullivan would have been completing the memoir, news coverage of Afghanistan, both in the print media and on the three major television networks, had significantly waned. Although the Tyndall Report, which tallies the number of minutes devoted to coverage of particular stories on the nightly newscasts of ABC, CBS, and NBC, reported that coverage of the Iraq War was the top story in 2007 (1157 minutes), direct coverage of Afghanistan did not even make the list of top twenty stories.[90] Yet the Afghan war surfaced indirectly in broadcast coverage devoted to the political implosion of Pakistan (165 minutes), the increasing numbers of disabled American military personnel (160 minutes), and the problems faced by US military families (119 minutes).[91] By 2015, the publication year for both *Top Dog* and *Max*, network coverage of the Iraq and Afghan wars had become even more anemic: the Tyndall Report rated the Iraq civil war and fight against ISIS as the twentieth most covered story (113 minutes), while Afghanistan did not make the list at all. That year, the number one spot went to winter weather stories, which garnered 377 minutes of coverage by the networks.[92] Network television's coverage of Afghanistan evidences a kind of national narcissism whereby the conflict can be experienced only through its effects on US soldiers and their families. So perhaps it is not surprising that all three of the texts are equally myopic in their concern to delineate a byproduct of the war—canine rescue—in terms of its impact on a military family.

Saving Cinnamon, Top Dog, and *Max* are more varied in the extent to which they represent the horrors of military conflict, ranging from not at all to providing a somber backdrop for the plot. *Saving Cinnamon* fails utterly in this regard, never mentioning the traumatic injuries sustained or fatalities caused by ground-level explosives, drones, and aerial bombardment; the violent deaths that result from landmines; and the not infrequent incidents of suicide bombings and casualties caused by so-called "friendly fire." In contrast, *Top Dog* records the painful losses and injuries of WMDs, their handlers, and US troops, and also acknowledges the military's efforts to win hearts and minds through venturing into rural communities to train Afghan local police. Impending doom and the potential deaths of US security forces, human and canine alike, cast a pall over this memoir. Of the three texts, *Max* most directly grapples with the relationship between the battlefield and the homefront, showing how military violence has lasting consequences for wounded combatants and is implicated in transnational crime syndicates.

Notwithstanding these variations in their representations of the US intervention, none of these narratives explores the impact of the war on ordinary Afghan civilians, a second characteristic of the canine-rescue narrative. The human costs of this conflict remain hidden. In this respect, the canine-rescue narrative mirrors the military's unwillingness to disclose civilian casualty figures. Definitive civilian casualty figures for this war are impossible to determine as the US and NATO only track injuries and deaths among their own troops and not among Afghans.[93] ISAF began a tally of civilian casualties in 2008, but it did not consistently release this information to the public. While the United Nations Mission in Afghanistan [UNAMA] started to keep such records in 2007, it did not regularize its methodology for collecting this information till 2009.[94] Demographers have explained the difficulty of conducting both direct and indirect body counts in Iraq and Afghanistan; all the serious studies have limitations and most likely underestimate casualties. Analyzing data from UNAMA, the Mine Action Coordination Centre of Afghanistan, and the Afghan Ministry of Defense, Neta C. Crawford estimates, as of August 2016, that approximately 111,000 people (31,000 of whom are civilians) have been killed in this conflict, and the number of injured is over 116,000. Civilian casualties have increased since 2014, the majority of which resulted from insurgent violence.[95] These statistics do not account for the considerable loss of life that accrues from tangential aspects of conflict such as disruptions of agricultural production and the distribution of food, resulting in widespread malnutrition and starvation, and a healthcare system that has struggled to rebuild itself after decades of war and to cope with tuberculosis, malaria, and cholera, and chronic shortages of trained healthcare personnel, medicines, and vaccines. None of the conditions that make quotidian life precarious for most Afghans are represented in the canine-rescue narrative.

Responding to geopolitical violence following 9/11, Judith Butler has asked, "Who counts as human? Whose lives count as lives? And, finally, *What makes for a grievable life*?"[96] She worries that Afghans, Arabs, and Palestinians have been disarticulated from the category of the "human" "as "it has been naturalized in its 'Western' mold by the contemporary workings of humanism."[97] When the US government refuses to tally Afghan casualties, the answer to the question of whose lives do not count is explicit. When the dead cannot even be counted, what chance have they to be grieved outside the intimacy of their families and local communities? What does it say about the American public that we can marshall sympathy for Afghan strays and MWDs in the absence of our outrage for these uncounted dead?

The canine-rescue narrative appeals to an American public enamored by the articulation of dogs and family that has become normative in this society over the last few decades. Representations of stray dogs and MWDs, to invoke Goodavage, "make war a little more human" but in ways that enable the elision of certain groups of people, namely Afghans.[98] The effacement of Afghans and their replacement with dogs indicate that the only consequence of US militarism that Americans are culturally willing to assimilate is the mute and abject nonhuman, who has become the new avatar of the native, colonized subject. The canine-rescue narrative indexes the ways in which the categories that once girded American exceptionalism such as the family, democratic citizenship, and social mobility are now in crisis. When the iconic citizen and exemplary American dreamer is a dog, we have a requiem for the democratizing project that has lost its persuasive capability to interpellate ordinary people into civic life.

In the meantime, Afghan civilians are fleeing the violence and destitution in their country in record numbers and are being denied asylum in Europe and the US. The latent suspicion of refugees in the US has escalated with the 2016 election of a no-nothing, openly xenophobic and Islamophobic president who has mainstreamed racist attitudes toward immigrants, economic migrants, and refugees of color. The Trump administration has slashed the number of refugees allowed into the country under President Obama from 110,000 annually to 45,000, and it is threatening to reduce the number further to 25,000.[99] Over the course of the long Afghan War, stray dogs have been rescued and WMDs have been adopted into loving families. For Afghan civilians, however, no rescue has ever been proffered. Such are the achievements of US intervention: canine citizenship and failed states.

Chapter 4

The Retributive-Justice Narrative

• •

Osama bin Laden as Simulacra

Introduction

On Halloween evening in 2001, I opened my front door to more than one trick-or-treater dressed as a diminutive Osama bin Laden, a costume choice over which I puzzled. Did it correspond to the Celtic origins of the holiday, when the dead were believed to visit the living, potentially ruining crops and creating mischief and thus necessitating masks and disguises to frighten the spirits away? Had bin Laden come to represent the limits of evil in mass culture, transforming into *the* paradigmatic figure to scare ghosts and goblins? This meaning of the costume would be eerily prescient, given bin Laden's elusiveness and ability to evade detection for a decade by a state with unprecedented surveillance technology and lethal power. The referent for the costume choice that was to scare away spirits itself became a ghost, a common trope used by journalists to describe Osama bin Laden in the decade after the 9/11 attacks: bin Laden had disappeared, periodically emerging in grainy videos, a spectral presence who haunted the mediascape of the Global War on Terror. Alternatively, was the costume a form of comic, visual mimicry (small children dressed as a tall, austere jihadist) and a way to gain mastery over the fear that had swept the country? Or did the costume attest to bin Laden's transformation into a simulacrum, an image that floats free of any referential relation to the historical person? The children were not dressing up as an actual political actor, I concluded, but in the guise of a de-referentialized media icon, which could be mobilized for different purposes.

This Halloween costume, with its multiple valences, acts as an appropriate trope for the "meanings" associated with Osama bin Laden in the narratives I analyze in this chapter, which construct bin Laden as terrorist bogeyman who becomes a justification for the US war machine and as a comic signifier who becomes a vehicle to criticize the Global War on Terror. Mark Owen's SEAL Team Six memoir, *No Easy Day: The Firsthand Account of the Mission that Killed Osama Bin Laden*, and Abhishek Sharma's Indian independent film, *Tere bin Laden*, represent competing versions of bin Laden with very different ideological inflections.[1] Owen's text demonstrates both continuities and ruptures with the Cold War paradigms of masculinity that are the subject of chapter 1. While continuities inhere in *No Easy Day's* representation of American masculinity as overdetermined by technological prostheses, race, and gender, the current iteration of military manhood seems incapable of the empathy that characterized its Cold War counterpart. So too does the representation of the "native" differ from those earlier accounts; instead of the brave Afghan warriors of yore, we have the native rendered as terrorist in the terms delineated by Jasbir Puar as constituting one strand of "homonationalism."

Puar argues that the universal abjected status of women and queer subjects in Third World cultures has become an alibi for counter-terrorism and military interventions, even as constructions of (primarily) Muslim men as "terrorists" are queered. She explains that "terrorists are quarantined through equating them with the bodies and practices of failed heterosexuality, emasculation, and queered others."[2] *No Easy Day* genders and sexualizes Osama bin Laden in an idiom that denigrates his masculinity in contrast to the hegemonic masculinity it aligns with SEALs. Yet the representation of hegemonic masculinity undoes a clear distinction between the US's imperial adventures abroad and its brutal subjugation of internal populations at home. Thus, Owen's disdain for the rule of law unwittingly reveals the law as sham insofar as the memoir suggests that there are no constraints on the state's arbitrary use of force, which can be deployed against noncitizen terrorists and citizens alike.

The sexual pathologization of Muslim men as terrorists invokes the older use of the word "queer" as a slur against homosexuals; since the late 1980s, "queer" has been appropriated as an empowering self-description for a wide range of nonnormative sexual identities. Its verb form "to queer" means to playfully signify on dominant cultural and political codes, a form of narrative jouissance enacted by *Tere bin Laden*. If *No Easy Day* draws on highly sexist and homophobic language in its construction of Osama bin Laden, *Tere bin Laden* queers such representations by slyly insinuating that Bush and bin Laden are sweethearts, casting doubt on the veracity of official state representations of terrorism, and highlighting the invented nature of propaganda. The film's screenplay has the CIA and ISI collaborating to stage fake footage of Osama bin Laden with a look-alike, Noora, a chicken producer, in order to precipitate an end to the Global War on Terror. By using the vehicle of a poultry farmer to be bin Laden's look-alike, the film makes bin Laden both into a figure of ridicule and into a spokesperson of a broadly felt negative attitude toward US military power as being a cynical cover to monopolize natural resources, such as oil, and as being disproportionate in its realization. Stuart Hall advocates getting inside the image itself as a means of disrupting stereotypical representations of specific communities; new meanings can arise from the gap between the media image and our expectations of how a particular group should be represented, he explains.[3] In associating Osama bin Laden, the paradigmatic face of Islamic terror, with Noora, a simple and affable man, within the generic conventions of a Bollywood comedy, *Tere bin Laden* presents a counter-hegemonic analysis of the Global War on Terror that queers and unsettles rather than reinforces the dominant narrative of this military intervention.

I begin by examining President Bush's explanation for the Global War on Terror, which is informed by his religiosity and belief in retributive justice, a concept that underwrites Owen's desire to punish bin Laden as "payback" for 9/11. Analyzing hegemonic masculinity in *No Easy Day*, along with its pejorative construction of Osama bin Laden as queer, I then unpack how the status of the law reveals continuities between imperialism abroad and the treatment of people of color at home. To challenge Owen's insistence on positing terrorism as an exceptional form of violence, I turn next to bin Laden's speeches; the pronouncements of both bin Laden and Bush share a structure of feeling rooted in vengeful violence. Isomorphic parallels in the logic of violence in Bush's and bin Laden's pronouncements lend credence to *Tere bin Laden's* takedown of the Global War on Terror. Incorporating excerpts of bin Laden's speeches into the dialogue, Sharma, the film's director, simultaneously capitalizes on the figure of bin Laden and highlights the invented nature of state propaganda. If bin Laden exists as a simulacra, a fiction generated by opportunistic individuals and states, as the film proposes, *Tere bin Laden's* brilliance is to assert that new fictions can be written that bring the Global War on Terror to an end. The film enables a larger critique of the Afghan intervention as dependent on an account of the world that does not reference actual conditions but that facilitates the US consolidation of power and capital through the continuous play of memes and simulacra.

President George W. Bush and Retributive Justice

The September 11, 2001 attacks thrust bin Laden into prominence on the global stage in a way that the bombings he had masterminded earlier of the US embassies in Kenya and Tanzania in 1998 and the USS Cole in 2000 had not. On that day, nineteen militants, armed with low-tech box cutters, hijacked four airplanes and turned them into lethal weapons in a coordinated, devastating suicidal mission that killed nearly 3,000 people in New York City, the Pentagon, and a field in Pennsylvania. The global range of the attacks commanded attention: eighty countries were represented among the victims and many people around the world expressed sorrow for the tragedy, though others rejoiced in perceiving the attacks as punishment for the US's deadly actions abroad.[4] After reviewing the passenger manifests of the doomed aircrafts, the G.W. Bush administration determined that Al-Qaeda and Osama bin Laden had organized the attacks.[5] At the time, bin Laden had holed up under the protection of the Taliban in Afghanistan, where he had previously established training camps for the Mujahideen during the Soviet era, which were later used to instruct jihadists. In the weeks following the attacks, President Bush gave a series of speeches, issuing a warning to the Taliban to shut down the "terrorist training camps" and "hand over leaders of the Al-Qaeda network."[6]

In spite of their sometimes tense relationship with Osama bin Laden, the Taliban refused the president's demands for several reasons, including their gratitude for bin Laden's earlier assistance to the Mujahideen as well as *Pushuntunwali*, the ethical-cultural code governing hospitality that requires giving sanctuary to guests. However, Omar Mullah, the putative leader of the Taliban, did convene a large assembly of clerics in Kabul to deliberate on the question of bin Laden's complicity in the attacks; he addressed the gathering, noting that if the US had proof of bin Laden's guilt, it should provide evidence to the assembly, which would determine his fate. While the G.W. Bush administration did not comply, the clerics recommended that bin Laden be asked to voluntarily leave the country in order to avert war, a request he ignored.[7] The US then commenced its war on a nation-less concept, "terrorism," by bombing targets within a nation, Afghanistan. Within the first two months of the bombing campaign, a terrible reciprocity was established between the initial terrorist attacks and the violence of war: nearly 3,800 Afghans died as a result of the US bombing campaign, surpassing the 2,996 people who had been killed by the hijacked airplanes.[8] Bin Laden himself eluded capture or injury for the next decade until his assassination by SEAL Team Six in 2011.

On September 11, 2001, then President George W. Bush took to the airwaves to reassure a horrified nation that was reeling from shock. While he did not name any suspects for the attacks, his brief speech contained several themes that would become leitmotifs in the coming weeks and months such as the claim that terrorists hate "our way of life," the resolve to bring the perpetrators to "justice," and the declaration of a "war on terrorism." This first speech was overlaid with Christian resonances, including a quotation from Psalm 23 about "the valley of the shadow of death" and fearing "no evil" in the company of the Lord.[9] Several days later, Bush called the "war on terrorism" a "crusade," reverting to a medieval-era conflict as an explanatory model for this most modern of wars.[10] References to God also peppered a speech he delivered at the National

Cathedral during a National Day of Prayer and Remembrance Service on September 14, 2001. President Bush reminded the gathered assembly that God's intentions were sometimes opaque: "God's signs are not always the ones we look for. We learn in tragedy that his purposes are not always our own."[11] Although not discernible to people, "This world He created is of moral design."[12] Elsewhere in the same speech, Bush emphatically asserted that "Americans do not yet have the distance of history. But our responsibility to history is clear: to answer these attacks and rid the world of evil."[13] Together, these references to justice, divine inscrutability, and assurance of a morally ordered world implied that the United States had a Christian duty to pursue and punish the terrorists, paving the way for religious retribution.

Less than two weeks later, Bush addressed a joint session of the 107th Congress, on September 20, 2001, this time attributing guilt to Osama bin Laden and Al Qaeda. He also toned down the Christian rhetoric, even though subtle references to a gendered God persisted, and he made overtures to Muslims, assuring them that the war was not against them per se but in opposition to "terrorists" who "practice a fringe form of Islamic extremism that has been rejected by Muslim scholars and the vast majority of Muslim clerics—a fringe movement that perverts the peaceful teachings of Islam."[14] Describing Al Qaeda as "a collection of loosely connected terrorist organizations," Bush explained the organization's culpability for bombing the US embassies in Kenya and Tanzania and the USS Cole.[15] Their goals, according to the president, were to overthrow "existing governments" in Egypt, Jordan, and Saudi Arabia; "to drive Israel out of the Middle East"; and to expel Christians and Jews from large swaths of Africa and Asia. Drawing a lineage for Al Qaeda, he made it heir to fascism, Nazism, and totalitarianism.[16]

As for the United States, Bush opined, Al Qaeda's attacks had been motivated by antipathy to the American way of life: "They hate our freedoms—our freedom of religion, our freedom of speech, our freedom to vote and assemble to disagree with each other." The US was targeted "because we stand in their way," he said.[17] In his gloss on Al Qaeda and Osama bin Laden, Bush failed to mention that their origins extend back to the 1980s, when they were allies of the US in Afghanistan during its Cold War rivalry with the Soviet Union.[18] Blowback, in other words, was instrumental to Al Qaeda's emergence in the late nineties but absent in the president's exegesis.

Sternly admonishing the Taliban to hand over Osama bin Laden and other Al Qaeda leaders, Bush characterized the conflict as a war between "freedom" and "fear." And he threw down the gauntlet, putting the world on notice: "we will pursue nations that provide aid or safe haven to terrorists. Every nation, in every region, now has a decision to make. Either you are with us, or you are with terrorists. From this day forward, any nation that continues to harbor or support terrorism will be regarded by the United

States as a hostile regime."[19] The declaration that any country discovered giving sanctuary for terrorists would be a legitimate target for US military action would become one of several foreign policy principles lumped together as the Bush Doctrine.[20]

The combination of Christian piety, moral certitude, and rhetorical aggressiveness in Bush's speeches illustrates his friends' and journalists' assessment of the role faith played in his decisions. In a *Frontline* documentary, several individuals comment on his deep belief in Christianity, which was infused with a view of the world as based on stark distinctions between good and evil, on the one hand, and a genuine respect for religious pluralism, on the other (hence, the outreach to Muslims and the attempts to discourage Islamophobia among the public).[21] A member of the United Methodist Church, George W. Bush understood himself to be God's agent on earth. Wayne Slater, a reporter for the *Dallas Morning News*, reveals that privately "Bush had said. . . that he is a person chosen by God at this particular point and time to represent the interests, not only of a nation, but the guidance of God at a troubled time in the country."[22] For Bush, evil does not exist in the world, "as an abstract idea, a philosophy, but [is] something that's real and tangible."[23] A family friend describes the "tempering effect" of religion on Bush, who could be "brutal," "apologetic," and "self-righteous" without its moderation.[24] The editor of the progressive Christian journal *Sojourner*, Jim Wallis, sees in Bush a quasi "American Calvinist," spouting an "American civil religion" as opposed to an "evangelical biblical faith," with the result that "church and nation" become confused in his presidential actions.[25]

Bush's fundamentalist belief system and his decision to launch an aerial campaign and ground invasion against bin Laden and the Taliban as punishment for the September 11 attacks are partially consistent with the concept of retributive justice, often associated with the Biblical eye-for-an-eye law of retaliation. Such approaches to justice value punishment over deterrence or rehabilitation. According to Alec Walen, retributive justice rests on three principles: 1) perpetrators of certain acts, particularly "serious crimes, morally deserve to suffer a proportionate punishment"; 2) a moral good is accomplished when "some legitimate punisher gives them the punishment they deserve"; and 3) the intentional punishment of "the innocent" or the infliction of "disproportionately large punishments on wrongdoers" is "morally impermissible."[26] To its proponents, retributive justice differs from vengeance in being impersonal and giving its administrators no pleasure in punishment.[27] The Latin root of "retribution" is "re + tribio, which means 'I pay back,'" vocabulary that Owen employs in *No Easy Day* as well.[28] For George W. Bush, the 2001 invasion of Afghanistan constituted payback for bin Laden, Al Qaeda, and the regime that sheltered them, delivered through US security forces and its commander-in-chief, acting as God's agents on earth.

The concept of proportionality and the moral prohibition against intentionally punishing the innocent constitute two key aspects of retributive judgment. Evaluated on those criteria, Bush's invasion flunks the morality test for retributive justice. Since its introduction during World War I, aerial bombardment has dramatically increased the number of civilians killed during armed conflicts. The president must have been cognizant of this basic fact of modern warfare, and yet he made the moral and political calculation that apprehending Osama bin Laden and punishing Al Qaeda were worth the large loss of life that would result from a bombing campaign. Once the hostilities commenced, American bombs fell on the Kajakai Dam Power Station, the Kabul Telephone Exchange, and Al Jazeera television station—making communication and emergency relief difficult—and they also landed on trucks and buses filled with refugees. Anti-personnel cluster bombs exploded in urban areas. Responding to the death of ninety-three civilians in a farming village, who had been killed by US gunships, a Pentagon official shamelessly commented, "The people there are dead because we wanted them dead."[29] The official's comment gives credence to Achille Mbembe's contention "that the ultimate expression of sovereignty resides, to a large degree, in the power and the capacity to dictate who may live and who must die."[30] In the first two months of the US intervention, Afghan casualties numbered in the thousands, exceeding the total victims of 9/11, and that figure would rise to over 111,000, including 30,000 civilians, during the next sixteen years.[31] Judged from criteria of proportionality and harm done to the innocent, these figures expose the sham of claiming retributive justice.

The casualty figures also supply supporting evidence for Osama bin Laden's oft-repeated assertion that the US has been waging war on Muslims and has been callous to the loss of civilian lives around the world. While the term "terrorism" is generally restricted to acts committed by non-state actors, it is worth considering what happens to our understanding of conflict when the definitional focus shifts from the *agents* of violence to the *nature* of the violence itself. If we define terrorism as violence against civilians enacted in order to coerce particular political outcomes, as Eqbal Ahmad urges, it is impossible to avoid the conclusion that states are also capable of terrorism and that US military intervention in Afghanistan comprises one such instantiation.[32] The callousness and casualness with which American politicians and military officials over multiple successive administrations have continued to dispense armaments against people in foreign lands, raining death and destruction from the air on combatants and civilians alike, provides a clear answer to the question of why they hate us. Whether or not they hate our freedoms, they might justifiably hate how the US exercise of sovereignty "is to exercise control over mortality and to define life as the deployment and manifestation of power."[33] That form of sovereignty finds its expression in the summary execution of bin Laden without due process, a topic which I consider next.

Queering bin Laden: *No Easy Day* and Techno-Military Masculinity

Matt Bissonnette's account of the assassination of Osama bin Laden, *No Easy Day*, written under the pseudonym Mark Owen, with coauthor Kevin Maurer, subscribes to the themes of G.W. Bush's 9/11 speeches, particularly in the assumption that the Afghan intervention and execution of bin Laden constitute retributive justice. A bildungsroman about the making of an elite Navy SEAL, the autobiography opens with Owen's boyhood determination to become a SEAL after reading a Vietnam War memoir by a former SEAL. From the Soviet occupation of Afghanistan when US government officials invoked the Vietnam War as an aspirational goal for drawing the USSR into a similar military quagmire, as I described in chapter 1, to the ongoing power of stories of Vietnam-era SEAL heroism to inspire new generations of US Marines and soldiers, the Vietnam War continues to be the palimpsest underwriting the American cultural dominant of war. Indeed, the text's construction of hegemonic masculinity eerily echoes the Vietnam War representations analyzed by Susan Jeffords, who observes that "the production and technologization of the male body" becomes "an aesthetic of spectacle."[34]

Structured as a teleology that culminates in bin Laden's execution, Owen's narrative is centrally about the production of a techno-military masculinity that finds its legitimization and actualization in retributive justice. *No Easy Day* reveals how this particular gendered and racialized subjectivity is dependent on surveillance technology and sophisticated weapons that render Owen into a quasi cyborg. Read against the grain, the memoir discloses the fragile nature of life under the US rule of law, more often represented by Owen as burdensome bureaucracy, which can be jettisoned at will by agents of the state.

Techno-military masculinity has four characteristics: extreme physical fitness, dependency on technological prosthetics, Euro-American male superiority, and disdain for civilian authorities. *No Easy Day* describes the process by which candidates qualify for the United States Naval Special Warfare Development Group, requiring them to excel at a grueling physical and psychological selection and training regime. Candidates begin each day with timed swims, long runs, push-ups, pull-ups, and other sundry activities, including pushing cars and buses (13). This exhausting routine is a prelude to the real work of the day—learning the skills that these fighters will need in their capacity as the Navy's elite counter-terrorism unit, conducting hostage rescue missions, tracking war criminals, and eliminating Al Qaeda operatives in Afghanistan and Iraq (12). Training entails learning close-quarters combat, boarding ships under secrecy, parachuting onto land and water, wielding different weapons, devising contingency plans, generally all under extreme conditions of hot or cold temperatures. Only the most physically fit SEALs, who have two deployments under their belt, apply to be part of this unit, called the "Green Team" (19). In terms of their physical capacities, combat skills, and mental toughness, these men are the crème de la crème, the pinnacle of military masculinity.

Proficiency in the use of weapons and becoming comfortable with the technological equipment that enhances the SEALs' fighting capability are important aspects of training. Four-tube night vision goggles, thermal scopes, and customized weapons with "individual modifications on the trigger and grips" render the SEALs into quasi cyborg sailors with superhuman sensory powers to see people in the dark and to kill them (45). Constant audio contact between members of the SEAL teams during the raid on bin Laden's compound also features in their success. The advantages of being outfitted with these technological prosthetics, a crucial aspect of techno-military masculinity, are augmented by the use of surveillance drones and communication equipment. Not only did continuous surveillance footage from drones in the weeks leading up to the attack hint at bin Laden's presence, but the entire raid was live-streamed to Admiral McRaven, the head of Joint Special Operations Command, who was in Jalalabad, Afghanistan; CIA director Leon Panetta, in Langley, Virginia; and President Obama and members of his cabinet, in the White House Situation Room in Washington, DC.

If extreme fitness and technological prosthetics define the physical aspects of techno-military masculinity, raced and gendered elements inform its ideological unconscious, which emerges in descriptions of the unit's humor. Pranks are common in the squadron, consisting of surreptitiously draping a lace bra that has been filched during a raid on an Iraqi village on unsuspecting marines and planting a "giant twelve-inch black dildo" (discovered earlier in an abandoned Miami hotel) in quotidian situations during deployment tours. Owen encounters the dildo, nicknamed the "Staff of Power," strapped to his steering wheel, and cheerfully deposits it in turn in "a random helmet in one of the equipment bags" (81). Both items have symbolic import in the US. Although it was not a common occurrence, burning bras became associated with the women's lib movement of the 1960s.[35] And since slavery, black men have been overdetermined in mainstream American culture as embodying hypersexuality that was coded as a threat to white women. The dildo's moniker, "Staff of Power," also resonates with the phrase "Black Power," which became prominent during the Civil Rights Movement. Beyond the juvenile pleasure of encountering sexual objects in such a high-pressure environment, Owen never explains why such gendered and raced objects might elicit merriment. Presumably, the humor resides in the stark contrast between the masculinity and the unmarked whiteness of the SEALs and the femininity of lingerie and the blackness of the sex toy. By making these things into objects of ridicule, the SEALs symbolically contain the threat posed by women and African American men to this version of fraternity among warriors. Apropos of the performative logic here, it seems worth noting that the SEALs are a primarily white unit with African Americans only making up 2% of the force.[36]

Owen's uneasiness with women extends to his characterization of bin Laden as an effeminate man, or as "queer" in the word's pejorative sense. Busting into bin Laden's bathroom during the raid, he finds a box of Just For Men hair dye, which Owen speculates bin Laden "must have used on his beard" for how else to explain his youthful appearance. This detail also appears in Peter L. Bergen's *Man Hunt: The Ten-Year Search for Bin Laden from 9/11 to Abbottabad*. Bergen additionally broadcasts the salacious tidbit that "Avena syrup—a sort of natural Viagra made from wild oats" was discovered in bin Laden's residence and speculates that it is a "clue as to how the fifty-four-year-old bin Laden was able to give each wife 'what is enough for her.'"[37] Frequently surfacing in articles covering bin Laden's death, these two details code him both as feminine in the vanity associated with coloring his hair and as having unnatural masculine sexual appetites by virtue of his polygamy.[38] Significantly, these details construct him as inauthentic (a dyed beard) and inadequate (dependent on erectile aids)—as a phony, in other words.

To bin Laden's vanity and sexual dysfunction, Owen layers on the suggestion that he was a coward for failing to defend himself and his family during the raid on his home. Discovering an unloaded AK-47 and Makarov pistol on the shelf above the doorway where bin Laden was initially wounded, Owen moralizes in highly gendered language: Bin Laden "hadn't even prepared a defense. He had no intention of fighting. He asked his followers for decades to wear suicide vests or fly planes into buildings, but he didn't even pick up his weapon. In all my deployments, we routinely saw this phenomenon. The higher up the food chain the targeted individual was, the bigger a pussy he was. The leaders were less willing to fight. It is always the young and impressionable who strap on the explosives and blow themselves up" (249). The slang meanings of "pussy" include a timid man, as well as female genitalia. The term is not uncommon in the US military, where it is used to socialize recruits into a version of hegemonic masculinity and mark their difference from women, who are perceived as weaker and second-rate warriors.[39] These passages support Puar's assertion that "negative connotations of homosexuality were used to racialize and sexualize Osama bin Laden: feminized, stateless, dark, perverse, pedophilic, disowned by [natal] family (i.e., fag)." She notes that "the evilness of bin Laden is more fully and efficaciously rendered through associations with sexual excess, failed masculinity (i.e., femininity), and faggotry."[40]

Imperial sentiments also augment these gendered and racialized attitudes: the "pro words," single-word messages chosen to efficiently relay information among combatants on missions, are Native American-themed, and bin Laden is given the name "Geronimo" (168).[41] Referring to bin Laden as the great Apache warrior, the SEAL team unconsciously draws connections between

a prior Anglo settler colonialism in the continental US and the current iteration of US imperialism in Afghanistan. Eva Cherniavsky has pointed out how
"U.S. history is marked by a *convergence* of nationalism and colonialism" in
a dynamic whereby territory is assimilated and internalized into the borders
of the nation-state even as certain populations have their labor expropriated
under colonial rule and are simultaneously "forcibly externalized with respect
to what is constituted as the space of an 'American' national politics and culture."[42] Here we have the figurative expulsion of Geronimo from the symbolic
space of the nation and his projection onto bin Laden, an enemy of the state.
The linguistic conflation of bin Laden and Geronimo makes explicitly visible
an American project that collapses internal and external threats and enacts
violence both inside and outside its territorial borders.

State violence has a conflicted relationship to the rule of law, which does
not encompass many aspects of light-footprint warfare (the use of drones, for
example) or whose representatives feel no compulsion to answer to its authority, such as soldiers and police officers who kill with impunity. Disdain for
the rule of law and civilian authorities saturates *No Easy Day*, illustrating the
historical limits of bourgeois democracy as it travels abroad. That is to say, the
internal contradictions of a state that differentiates among those living inside
its borders, granting rights and privileges to some and denying those same rights
and privileges to others, will inhere in the mobile version of that state as it
exports lethal force outside its territorial boundaries.

The Rule of Law as the Sham of Law

Owen explains his motivation to join the SEALs in the idiom of retributive justice that featured prominently in President G.W. Bush's speeches following the
September 11 attacks. The religious inflections of retributive justice have the
peculiar effect of disarticulating punishment from the rule of law by positing
it as a divine mandate. The moral and theological rationale in effect substitutes
for the juridical one. Owen's disdain for the rule of law is also articulated in
his contempt for civilian authorities, particularly President Barack Obama and
Vice President Joe Biden, and his impatience with the paperwork associated
with combat procedures.

These attitudes surface in the extrajudicial killing of bin Laden. Owen
pays lip service to the rule of law when he relays the instructions given by a
"lawyer from either the Department of Defense or the White House"—it
is all the same to him—about the mission. In response to a question about
whether the raid on bin Laden's compound is a "kill mission," the lawyer
replies, "If he is naked with his hands up, you're not going to engage him. I
am not going to tell you how to do your job. What we're saying is if he does
not pose a threat, you will detain him" (177). Earlier in the text, Owen has

described his frustration that insurgents have become cognizant of the rules of engagement that forbid the outright shooting of unarmed men (142). Not infrequently, insurgents surrender to the special operations forces with their hands up and weapons in a different room to avoid being killed during raids. In spite of the lawyer's directive, in the very next chapter, Owen and his fellow SEALs "debate. . . where in the body you should attempt to shoot Bin Laden." The chest, they agree, represents a better target than his face insofar as "Everybody is going to want to see" the picture of bin Laden's corpse (192). From their conversation, it appears that bin Laden's assassination has been predetermined.

A casual and callous approach to killing, in general, permeates *No Easy Day*. For one, Owen never voices any qualms over the moral and ethical dimensions of combat. Describing the first time he kills someone during a mission in Iraq, he recalls, "I didn't have time to dwell on it nor did I have any feelings about it. This was the first person I'd ever shot and with all the time I'd spent thinking about how it would make me feel, it really didn't make me feel anything. I knew that these guys in the house had already tried to kill my friends on the first floor and they wouldn't hesitate to do the same to me" (62). Nor does he bother to explain the fate of women, children, and elderly and infirm men who are in the homes raided by the US Special Forces. It is as if his belief in retributive justice codes the killing of any insurgents as a moral good, freeing him from the inconvenience of an ethical reckoning for his actions, let alone a legal one. The casualness with which Owen recounts killing illustrates how "we" (his fellow citizens) require our soldiers and Marines to become psychopaths incapable of empathy with other humans. As I argued in chapter 3, canine compassion is our preferred emotional attachment and outlet for our armed forces.[43]

The account of bin Laden's death illustrates that the rules of engagement can be easily shunted aside without consequences. He is shot by an unidentified "point man" when he peers out of his bedroom doorway. As the point man muscles bin Laden's wives into a corner of the room, Owen and another SEAL make for bin Laden's inert body. He recounts, "We saw the man lying on the floor at the foot of his bed. He was wearing a white sleeveless T-shirt, loose tan pants, and a tan tunic. The point man's shots had entered the right side of his skull. Blood and brains spilled out of the side of his skull. In his death throes, he was still twitching and convulsing. Another assaulter and I trained our lasers on his chest and fired several rounds. The bullets tore into him, slamming his body into the floor until he was motionless" (236). The sartorial details in this passage seem to be a non sequitur if one does not recall the lawyer's instructions: a naked bin Laden with his hands up in the air was to be captured not killed. Neither of these conditions applied in a literal interpretation of legal counsel, and the commandos apparently felt carte blanche to shoot him point-blank in what appears to be an extrajudicial killing.

Owen attributes cowardice to bin Laden's failure to defend himself during the raid on his compound, which does not tally with the assessment offered by those who fought alongside bin Laden in the past. During the resistance to Soviet occupation, bin Laden impressed many of his Arab and Afghan Mujahideen cohort with his willingness to endure hardship and risk his personal safety in battle. Because bin Laden is dead and consigned to a watery grave, we cannot ascertain his reasons for not resisting in the SEAL Six attack. But it seems plausible that he knew the rules of engagement and assumed that he would be detained if he offered no resistance. He might have calculated that the publicity of his detention and the possibility of a civil trial, which was more likely under an Obama administration than the G.W. Bush one, would have provided a platform to disseminate his grievances with the US and his rationales for establishing a caliphate. In Owen's world view, this possible interpretation of bin Laden's actions does not arise.

Whether the SEALs were given explicit instructions by the Obama administration to kill bin Laden during the raid, Owen does not reveal. Even if no such directive was delivered, it could be that the SEAL team interpreted the lawyer's statement that he was "not going to tell [them] how to do [their] job" as a green light to eliminate bin Laden (177). It is certainly the case that President Obama escalated the number of targeted killings, primarily through drone attacks, ordering four times as many in his first two years in office as the previous administration.[44] While the number of civilians killed in such attacks declined as a result of policy changes designed to minimize such casualties over the course of his term, the legal framework for targeted killings remains sketchy and subject to debate. Initially, the Authorization for the Use of Military Force, passed by Congress several days after 9/11, gave then President Bush broad authority to pursue those responsible for the attacks. Later, Obama invoked Article 51 of the UN Charter and the right to self-defense as a justification for targeting Al Qaeda and Taliban operatives.[45] The Obama administration also claimed the right to target suspects in other countries without securing their permission in the event that those countries were unwilling or unable to neutralize the threat. Obama ordered the raid on the Abbottabad compound without notifying the Pakistani government out of a suspicion that elements of the security apparatuses were in cahoots with bin Laden; the failure to inform the Pakistani government violated its sovereignty.[46] As Philip Alston, the former Special Rapporteur of the United Nations Commission on Human Rights, observes regarding Extrajudicial, Summary, Or Arbitrary Executions, such self-delegated powers are too expansive and could "result" in "chaos" if other states likewise insisted on the right "to kill people anywhere, anytime."[47]

Such diplomatic and legal protocols most likely would not play well with Owen who expresses impatience with the procedural aspects of combat missions. From the PowerPoint slides required for the approval of missions to the paperwork that needs to be filled out afterwards, procedures intended to regulate the use of force are rendered as bureaucratic nuisances that impede counterinsurgency. He grouses, "It felt like we were fighting the war with one hand and filling out paperwork with the other. When we brought back detainees, there was an additional two or three hours of paperwork. The first question to the detainee at the base was always, 'Were you abused?' An affirmative answer meant an investigation and more paperwork" (141). Particularly galling to Owen is the likelihood that captured insurgents will be released after a few days because they had "worked their way through the system" through their knowledge of the rules of engagement (142). For him, the law is clearly a detriment to the administration of a moral right, which rests, in turn, on the predicates that all captives are insurgents and all insurgents have no rights.

Owen's irritation with the rule of law extends to civilian authorities, of whom he is quite dismissive. To receive approval for the mission, the SEALs perform the final dress rehearsal of the assault for an audience of unidentified civilian "VIPs." He gleefully recalls that as "the helicopter started its hover over our fast-rope location, the rotors kicked up a maelstrom of rocks and dust, blasting the VIPs and forcing them to run in the opposite direction. I chuckled as I watched a few of the women stagger away on their heels" (178). No sympathy here for an unofficial dress code that enjoins uncomfortable, impractical shoes for professional women. Owen's assessment of Vice President Joe Biden is also uncharitable. Biden tells "lame jokes," seems like a "nice guy," but reminds him "of someone's drunken uncle at Christmas dinner" (292).

Owen's greatest contempt, however, is directed at President Obama, whom he suspects of claiming all the glory for successful SEAL missions that occur during the president's tenure: the rescue of Captain Richard Phillips who had been captured by Somali pirates and the assassination of bin Laden. Before the Abbottabad mission, one SEAL member cynically observes that they will "'get Obama reelected for sure'" (193). "We had seen it before when he took credit for the Captain Phillips rescue," Owen writes. "Although we applauded the decision-making in this case, there was no doubt in anybody's mind that he would take all the political credit for this too" (193). When Obama makes his televised remarks following the mission, Owen reluctantly admits that he doesn't "think [the president's] speech was bad at all," robbing the Marines of the opportunity to talk "smack" about their commander-in-chief. Yet Owen churlishly refuses to sign his name to the flag that was carried on the mission, which would be given to the president. Along with a few of his teammates, he "scribbles a random name" on this gruesome memento (291). The fact that Owen agrees with Obama's decisions in the Phillips rescue and grudgingly approves of his speech indicates a visceral dislike of the president not anchored in an assessment of Obama's actual job performance.

Nowhere does Owen acknowledge the challenges of the decision-making process and the coordination among different branches of the government that the raid required. In authorizing the attack, Obama had to weigh conflicting advice from his cabinet members and various intelligence agencies, and he had to assess the risks posed by the mission not only to the SEAL teams, but also to civilians in the vicinity of the compound and to relations with the Pakistani government. For Owen, the mission's success resides in the physical prowess and bravery of the elite Marines who conducted it. While CIA analysts draw his praise, elected officials do not, suggesting a troubling aspect of the inability of techno-military masculinity to grasp the importance of having the armed forces subordinate to civilian authorities.

There is seeming deep irony in the juxtaposition of two conservative themes that circulate in the public sphere: Bush's charge that Al Qaeda and bin Laden "hate our way of life," and the desire to untether the military from civilian control and to loosen restraints on its use of force. In theory, "our way of life" and the individual liberties Americans enjoy depend on the rule of law embedded in a democratic system over which civilians exercise oversight. In practice, the "our" in the phrase "our way of life" has all too often been restricted to specific individuals based on their identities. To put it crassly: wealthy, white men have historically enjoyed these rights while minoritized subjects have not and, not infrequently, have been targets of state violence themselves. The emergence of Black Lives Matter in 2013 brought public attention to what African Americans have known for a long time: they are disproportionately maimed and killed by law enforcement within the territorial boundaries of the US. Given the extremely low rate of conviction for police officers charged with killing African Americans, it is difficult to avoid the conclusion that the rule of law serves and protects agents of state violence rather than victims of its brutality.[48] Owen's memoir reveals that the rule of law can be jettisoned when hunting foreign threats. In its disclosure of details such as the black dildo and the code name "Geronimo," *No Easy Day* unwittingly exposes the racialized nature of the rule of law that affords protections to Euro Americans, but not to African Americans, other people of color, and foreigners who can be summarily executed because they are perceived as threats by the state.

Payback or Payout?

No Easy Day contains familiar narrative conventions from the genre of life writing, such as an explanation for the imperative to tell and a gloss on the narrator's representative status in relation to their community. As with many other memoirs of individuals recounting important events, Owen explains his motivations for writing as a desire to contribute to the historical record, which has been distorted, in his opinion, by the media (xii). The imperative to tell is complicated in Owen's case by two factors: co-authorship with Kevin Maurer and the fact that he had signed a non-disclosure agreement that is standard for those in Special Operation Forces. It is difficult to generalize about the significance of co-authorship because the memoir offers no explanation of the collaboration. Indeed, the only acknowledgements of Maurer's textual presence are the phrase "with Kevin Maurer" in smaller type under Mark Owen's name on the book cover and a short biography on the inside of the book jacket, identifying him as "the author of four books, including several about special operations" and as having been embedded with various US armed forces in Afghanistan, East Africa, Haiti, and Iraq. We have no way of knowing what role Maurer took in the shaping, organization, and telling of Owen's story.

Notwithstanding the nondisclosure agreement, Owen also neglected to submit the manuscript for government review prior to publication, triggering an investigation by the Department of Justice. Both parties reached a settlement that has him paying the US government all proceeds from the sale of the book (a *New York Times* bestseller) and movie rights, totaling over $6.6 million.[49] *No Easy Day's* publication also revealed fault lines among the SEAL fraternity, initiating an argument between Owen and fellow SEAL Six team member Robert O'Neill over who fired the fatal shot.[50] Whereas Owen credits the anonymous point man, who led the charge into bin Laden's bedroom, with the killing and notes that he and an unidentified comrade then fired pointblank into the twitching body, O'Neill claims that his was the lethal shot, an assertion he later retracted.[51] The competing versions of bin Laden's death led the *Huffington Post's* Igor Bobic to quip, "At this point, who didn't shoot bin Laden?"[52]

At issue in the question of who fired the fatal shot are lucrative book deals and gigs to be had on the motivational-speaker circuit, on the one hand, and the code of ethics for the SEALS, on the other. According to the *New York Times*, several SEAL Six members blamed Owen for revealing tactical information in his book and in a *60 Minutes* interview that could endanger SEAL units. One retired SEAL operator commented, "It was ingrained in us to be 'silent professionals.' Guys getting out, and writing books, going on TV or doing other things this public flies against that core value."[53] Shortly after publishing a second book, again co-authored with Keven Maurer, *No Hero: The Evolution of a Navy SEAL*, which he did submit for government review, Owen was scheduled for another appearance on *60 Minutes*. Fox News had booked a competing interview around that time with "The Shooter," as O'Neill had dubbed himself. Both interviews were heavily promoted by the networks prior to airing. The advance publicity probably provoked Rear Admiral Brian Losey, then head of the Navy SEALS, and Force Master Chief Michael L. Magaraci to send the SEALs a letter, reminding them of the "SEAL Ethos" that discourages seeking "public notoriety and financial gain" for their service.[54]

Owen's violation of the "SEAL Ethos" resulted in his informal excommunication from the SEAL brotherhood: some of his comrades have cut him off and his former commander requested that his contact information be deleted from Owen's phone.[55] Owen's name has reputedly been added to a rock at Virginia Beach Seal Team Six base that designates which former members "are no longer welcome at the command, including former SEALS who have violated a series of unwritten codes of conduct among the unit."[56]

Throughout *No Easy Day*, Owen emphasizes the strong fraternity and camaraderie among his Special Forces cohort even as everyone else (civilian authorities, intelligence analysts, Iraqis, and Afghans) elicits his scorn and antipathy. Yet the post-publication history of *No Easy Day* belies his representation of the fraternity forged through techno-military masculinity. Instead, we have the spectacle of SEALs jostling for credit for their role in assassinating bin Laden.[57] Owen's stated desire of "serving up a little payback" to bin Laden more accurately resembles an anticipation of a payout from sales of his memoir and speaking fees (3). Rather than the conventional ending of the bildungsroman which has the return of a smarter, seasoned protagonist reintegrated into the community, we have Owen alienated from the SEAL brotherhood and no wealthier or wiser from his travails.

Osama bin Laden and Reactive Violence

If retributive violence animates Bush's oratory and Owen's memoir, bin Laden's vision was grounded in the notion of "reactive violence." Reactive violence resembles retributive justice in its reliance on a logic of reciprocal brutal punishment. Bin Laden abhorred the exercise of US sovereignty through its self-appointed right to kill people, particularly in the Muslim world, and this revulsion informed his conceptualization of "reactive violence." Expressed in the idiom of "jihad," his rhetoric additionally mirrored the religiosity of George W. Bush's pronouncements but from an Islamist perspective.[58] Indeed, when Bush likened the War on Terror to a "crusade," bin Laden accused the president of plagiarism. "So Bush has declared in his own words, 'crusade attack,'" bin Laden wryly noted. "The odd thing about this is that he has taken the words right out of our mouth."[59] Bin Laden and Bush had a simplistic understanding of the crusades as solely a religious conflict between Islam and Christianity, an idea debunked by historians, who have explored how migration, expansionism, and cultural clashes between nomadic and pastoral people also played a role in these wars. The invocation of this medieval reference by both men speaks to a shared sectarian view of the world and a parallel structure of binary thinking.

As Bruce Lawrence points out, bin Laden frequently justified the use of violence against Western civilians as a form of "reactive terror—a response to what he perceives as the much greater terror exercised by the West over an incomparably longer period of time."[60] Remarking on the lack of equivalence between the violence visited by the US on other territories—Iraq, Hiroshima and Nagasaki, and Palestine, among others—and that perpetrated by Muslims on the West, bin Laden repeatedly called for, in his words, a "recalculation" of the human tally of political violence and a "settling of accounts" with the US, insisting on a moral calculus that recognized non-Western casualties.[61] Attacks against the US, in his opinion, were self-defense: "This is a defensive *jihad* to protect our [e.g., Muslim] land and people," he emphasized.[62]

To the question posed to him by several journalists about the ethics of "killing innocent civilians" as part of his defensive jihad, bin Laden had three responses. The first justification inhered in his elaboration of reactive violence. In an October 20, 2001 interview with Tayser Alluni, then head of the Kabul bureau of *Al Jazeera*, bin Laden explained,

> It is very strange for Americans and other educated people to talk about the killing of innocent civilians. I mean, who said that our children and civilians are not innocents, and that the shedding of their blood is permissible? Whenever we kill their civilians, the whole world yells at us from east to west, and America starts putting pressure on its allies and puppets. Who said that our blood isn't blood and that their blood is blood? What about the people that have been killed in our lands for decades? More than 1,000,000 children died in Iraq, and they are still dying, so why do we not hear people that cry or protest, or anyone who reassures or anyone who sends condolences?[63]

Particularly repulsive to bin Laden had been the brutal effects of the US-led UN sanctions against Iraq, which magnified the human misery caused by the earlier deliberate destruction of its infrastructure—highways, power plants, sanitation and water treatment facilities—during the 1991 military campaign headed by the US. The loss of Iraq's infrastructure, combined with the UN sanctions, resulted in a large number of preventable deaths, especially of children, from malnutrition and water-borne illnesses. Although it did not get much coverage in the American press, the UN Food and Agricultural Organization released a study in 1995 estimating that 567,000 Iraqi children under the age of five had died as a result of the conditions created by sanctions. When Lesley Stahl asked then Secretary of State Madeleine Albright on *60 Minutes* whether the deaths of half a million children were "worth" the "price," Albright notoriously replied, "I think this is a very hard choice, but the price—we think the price is worth it." The Stahl-Albright exchange was widely reported in the Arabic-language media, contributing to resentment against the US in the region for its destabilization of Iraq and the profound suffering it had caused in the country.[64]

Bin Laden had a second response to questions about the ethics of killing civilians in relation to the 9/11 attacks, insisting that the targets were military and financial rather than civilian. He explained, "we didn't set out to kill children, but attacked the biggest center of military power in the world, the Pentagon, which contains more than 64,000 workers, a military base which has a big concentration of army and intelligence" officials.[65] His characterization of the Pentagon as a military target was accurate, but the claim that the World Trade Center [WTC] was not a civilian target was specious, resting on the fact that it was neither "a children's school" nor "a residence."[66] Its victims, according to bin Laden, "were part of a financial power," the very "men that backed the biggest financial force in the world, which spread mischief throughout the world."[67] This perception of the WTC conflated finance capitalism with the US state. Putting aside the issue of whether the state acts in concert with financial elites, a perusal of the WTC tenants reveals health care providers, union offices, television stations, real estate businesses, and law firms among others.[68] All of these enterprises were part of civil society and relied on a precarious low-wage workforce, living in one of the most expensive cities in the world, to furnish support services such as cleaning, cooking, serving food, and security, along with other forms of often invisible labor. The occupants of the buildings also consisted of people of various races, ethnicities, and gender identities. In addition, the WTC was not uniquely an *American* target, housing as it did offices for Chinese, German, Japanese, Korean, Swiss, and Thai businesses. More than a few tourists, domestic and foreign, were also in the Twin Towers during the attack. For all these reasons, bin Laden's contention that the WTC was populated by elite American men who were not properly civilians and thus deserved to die is absurd. And the implication that anyone deserved to die, regardless of economic status and background, is chillingly offensive.

The third justification for the killing of American civilians, in bin Laden's opinion, was the fact that the US is a representative democracy. American civilians had freely elected the politicians who had waged war on Muslims. He pointed out, "the American people are the ones who choose their government through their own will; a choice which stems from their agreement to its policies. . . . The American people have the ability and choice to refuse the policies of their government, and even to change it if they want."[69] This view of the representativeness of American democracy seems almost quaint in the present era when gerrymandered districts, voter ID laws, the Electoral College, and dark money in political campaigns have delivered the White House to the 2016 presidential candidate who lost the popular vote by a count of nearly three million. Even in the 2000 presidential election, the winner of the popular vote, Al Gore, conceded the presidency to George W. Bush, on the basis of the 5-4 Supreme Court decision, *Bush v. Gore*. As recent history evidences, the occupants of the White House and the halls of Congress do not always reflect the will of the majority of American voters.

Along with assuming the representative character of the American political system, bin Laden concluded that Americans support the policies of their government. Contra his sense of a unified polity, the US has been deeply divided and ideologically polarized for the last several decades. Those divisions were apparent in the widespread protests by Americans against both the invasions of Afghanistan in 2001 and Iraq in 2003. Before the hostilities had begun against both these countries, protests numbering into the thousands took place in big cities such as Chicago, New York, San Francisco, and Seattle, and also in small towns such as Bloomington, Indiana. Many Americans feel frustrated by their government. Their inability to mount successful opposition to its policies speaks more to the severe constraints of the current iteration of representative democracy than it does to their lack of empathy for others and commitment to human rights, although to be sure there is a significant contingent of Americans who support the war effort. In any event, Bin Laden's pious invocation of the responsibilities of citizenship was spurious given his contempt for democracy; in its place, he envisioned an Islamic theocracy and he advised Americans to convert and join the *ummah,* the worldwide community of Muslims.[70]

Expressing several other grievances in his call for jihad against the US, bin Laden framed his campaign as an imperative in the face of Muslim humiliation in places such as Bosnia, Chechnya, Kashmir, Lebanon, and Somalia. Along with the US invasion of Iraq, Israel's occupation of Palestine, now stretching into its fiftieth year and financed by the US, garnered the lengthiest reflections in his speeches and interviews, which made frequent references to the enemy "Jews," "Zionists," and "Crusaders." He had a few other quarrels with the US too, namely its support for authoritarian regimes in the Middle East and the desecration of Mecca and Medina through its civilian presence and establishment of military bases in Saudi Arabia. Another source of aggravation, in bin Laden's view, was the US's favorable relations with China, India, and Russia, all countries that had oppressed Muslims. He was also furious that the US and other Western countries profited from purchasing oil from Middle East countries at below-market rates.[71]

Together, these resentments, according to Michael Scheuer, shaped Al-Qaeda's three-point agenda to rid the Muslim world of the US, "destroy Israel and the oppressive Muslim tyrannies," and punish the "heretical Shia," an agenda that was to be enacted sequentially rather than simultaneously.[72] Scheuer remarks on the ironies of the consequences of the 9/11 attacks apropos of bin Laden and Al Qaeda's agenda. Where bin Laden had wanted to dislodge the US from the Middle East, Bush's 2003 invasion of Iraq entrenched US forces in the region. (The Iraq invasion was justified through a questionable interpretation of intelligence that claimed Saddam Hussein had weapons of mass destruction and the insinuation that there were links between his regime and the World Trade Center attacks.) Where the Taliban's Afghanistan had provided an inspiring example of a pure, Islamic society for bin Laden, the 2001 invasion ousted that regime from power. The fallouts from the September 11 attacks were the opposite of those bin Laden had originally envisioned.

A perusal of Bin Laden's speeches and interviews reveals a startling convergence between his rationales for the 9/11 attacks and Bush's explanation for the invasion of Afghanistan. Both justifications are rooted in a religious idiom and draw on tropes from the Crusades. Bin Laden's conceptualization of reactive violence is not dissimilar to Bush's rhetoric of retributive justice; each term assumes its dialectical opposite, which it aligns with extreme criminality, thus presenting itself as a righteous embodiment of divine justice. The reciprocal nature of the violence of terrorism and of war suggests a continuation of hostilities till either a horrific equilibrium is established or the complete annihilation of one side by the other is achieved. Bin Laden warned that "as they [the Americans] kill us, without a doubt we have to kill them, until we obtain a balance in terror."[73] Unfortunately, Bush, and Obama after him, took the bait, ramping up the aerial bombing of Afghanistan and escalating the use of drones. The mounting death toll of Afghans and devastation of the country through the US-NATO air campaign fuels more terrorism, which triggers more bombings from coalition forces in a cycle of perpetual war.

Osama bin Laden as a Vehicle of Critique

Quotations from bin Laden's speeches make cameo appearances in Abhishek Sharma's Indian independent comedy, *Tere Bin Laden*, and are central to how the film playfully queers the Global War on Terror by suggesting that its principal agents are acting out dramatic roles rather than engaging in terrorism or counterinsurgency.[74] Sharma draws on "real history"—bits of bin Laden's speeches and rumors about him that have swirled around the world—to illustrate how the Global War on Terror exists as a deliberate "fiction" created by self-serving government officials. As part of his research for the film, he watched both real and fake Osama bin Laden footage.[75] It has become a truism of feminist and queer studies to acknowledge the performativity of gender.[76] *Tere bin Laden* queers conventional and hegemonic depictions of Osama bin Laden by quite literally representing his identity as a performance by a naïve poultry farmer. In lieu of the "Osama bin Laden as evil incarnate" of Bush's and Owen's account, the film offers up the terrorist as campy performer complete with exaggerated acting and comic accoutrements. By the film's end, the range of identities unveiled as performances has expanded to include US cabinet officials and Pakistani celebrity journalists, suggesting that the War on Terror is less about counter-terrorism than it is an opportunity for the personal advancement of individual Americans and Pakistanis, who earn their positions by bamboozling the public through their simulacra of professional competence.

A madcap comedy about an ambitious Pakistani journalist, Ali Hassan, who stages a fake video of Osama bin Laden as his golden ticket to immigrate to the US, *Tere Bin Laden* explores the unholy trinity among governments (US and Pakistan), the transnational bourgeoisie, and global media, which conspire to produce different versions of Osama bin Laden for their own separate purposes. The astuteness of the film's analysis of the Global War on Terror and global media resides in its insertion of representatives from different segments of Pakistani civil society into a transnational economy of representation and images associated with bin Laden, in which these classes simultaneously critique US foreign policy and become complicit with it.

"Tere Bin Laden" literally means "Your bin Laden," but also yields the pun, "Without you, Laden," and the joke of the film centers on the absence of Osama bin Laden himself. The title's double meaning implies that, regardless of the actual bin Laden, he becomes the perfect empty signifier, whatever "you" (governments and their militaries, the transnational bourgeoisie, and the global media) make him. For the Pakistani intelligence services and US military, bin Laden represents an opportunity to create a media narrative in which they figure as statesmen determined to negotiate a settlement to the Global War on Terror, largely to save face and distract attention from the colossal failures of their efforts to date.

The film queers the Global War on Terror primarily by revealing the fictional dimensions of US policy and secondarily by sending up masculinity as an exaggerated gender performance. In addition, Sharma illustrates how the national security state is a racial formation, and he spoofs the US military campaign in Afghanistan by literally rendering it into a cartoon. *Tere Bin Laden's* critique, at the same time, is not limited to Americans alone, but also includes a satirical glimpse of how elite Pakistanis are taken in with an idealized version of the American dream that constitutes a desire for upward mobility. The film depicts the fragile state of Pakistani civil society as constituted by a range of classes and aspirations that can be persuaded to cooperate with one another only in limited ways and as existing in an uneasy equilibrium with the state.

Amreeeka: The National Security State and the American Dream

Mistaken for a terrorist on a flight to the US, Ali has been permanently denied a visa to emigrate to "Amreeka," his destination of choice. In order to acquire a forged passport, he must give a large advance to a shadowy organization, Lashkar-E-Amreeka (a parody of Lashkar-e-Taiba).[77] Unable to afford the advance, he hits on the idea of fooling Noora—a poultry farmer, simpleton, and Osama bin Laden look-alike—into appearing in footage of the Al-Qaeda leader, which he plans to sell for a lucrative amount. First aired on *Live India* and then *News America*, the fake footage acquires a life of its own, gaining global distribution and precipitating political alarm in the US and financial markets worldwide. In response, the US government initiates a massive bombing campaign of Afghanistan. Stricken by the unleashing of American power on Afghanistan as a consequence of his video, Ali convinces Noora to make a follow-up tape addressed to President Bush in which Osama bin Laden suggests a ceasefire between the two sides. Comedic plot twists conspire to make US and Pakistani intelligence officers and government officials complicit in the production of Ali's Osama video sequel.

Tere's Bin Laden's opening scene sequence establishes its twin concerns with the United States as a national security state and the superficiality of segments of the Pakistani bourgeoisie, emphasizing the role played by global media in promoting the government's security agenda and creating an idealized version of the US among elite Pakistanis' imaginations. The film opens several days after September 11, 2001, in the Karachi airport, where Ali, an intrepid reporter for a down-market local television channel, frantically waits to use the restroom in time to make his flight to New York. A fellow traveler, who is wrestling to undo the knot on his *kurta-pajama*, responds to Ali's urgings to hurry by remarking that Ali must be going to New York to become a taxi driver, thereby suggesting that the United States offers limited economic opportunities for South Asian immigrants.

Immediately following this scene, the camera presents a medium close-up shot of Ali on board the flight as he rehearses for an audition as a newscaster; he reads aloud sample headlines, practicing different inflections of an Americanized accent: "America Becomes Suspicious of Muslims," "Bush Ready to Bomb Osama," and "Al Qaeda Behind Plane Hijacking." Scared by his repetition of the words "bomb" and "hijack," the skittish flight attendant screams, prompting a burly male passenger to restrain Ali, who is turned over to US authorities. The film then breaks into a Bollywood song and dance sequence, "Ullu da Pattha," which intersperses shots of Ali being interrogated and tortured by US authorities, gyrating female immigration agents, a "Federal Bureau" panel reviewing his case for deportation, a Karachi bazaar, multiple visits to the American embassy to secure a visa from a dour official, and Ali's fantasy object: a skimpily clad blonde woman in front of a craftsman-style bungalow.

The song sequence explicitly constructs the United States as a national security state that differentially treats those within its borders based on their racial identities and geographical origins. In addition to the racial profiling of Ali as a "terrorist" on the Go America flight that opens the film, after Ali's arrest, a continuous series of stills flashes across the screen, featuring mug shots of prisoners of different ethnicities. In the first still, a brown man holds a sign reading "Mexican." He is followed by a mug shot of a black man holding an "African" sign. A white male with a sign lettered "Peter" is next, and Ali and his "South Asian" sign round out the mix. While the others are marked as foreign subjects

("Mexican," "African," and "South Asian"), the white male prisoner is the only one granted a unique identity through the use of his first name and the absence of any geographic identification labels. In not marking Peter's geographic origins, the scene implies that the US national security state collapses geographic and racial identity, naturalizing American citizenship as white.

The threat of violence against foreign/ethnic subjects is signified by a large blood splatter in the background of Ali's mug shot. This threat is reinforced by visual references to interrogation that pepper the sequence: the blue shirts initially slap Ali while questioning him, and he is later strapped into a chair with electrodes protruding from his head. These images evoke the US's controversial record of using torture in military facilities in Afghanistan and Iraq to interrogate those designated as terrorist suspects, as their inclusion in the song sequence underscores the idea that terrorist suspects are inevitably racialized subjects in the eyes of the US state. That the state is incapable of discerning the finer distinctions between different political categories that it defines as constituting threats to its national security becomes apparent in the Federal Bureau panelists' responses to Ali. One official deems him an Al Qaeda member, another designates him Taliban, and a third reverts to the more comic label "Ullu da Pattha," a Punjabi phrase that literally translates into "son of an owl" (the equivalent of "son of a jackass") and is an invective used to insult someone's intelligence or judgment.

But if the song sequence aims to queer and expose the US as a racialized national security state, it also mocks middle-class Pakistanis who buy wholesale into the discourse of the American dream. The Pakistani man who taunts Ali in the men's room with the prospect of becoming a cab driver in New York vocalizes a reality for many South Asian immigrants, particularly Pakistanis, who have found employment driving taxis in New York.[78] This scene helps deflate the inflated rhetoric of the American dream that Ali has swallowed. His image—in the song sequence when he appears before the Federal Bureau board—features a background collage juxtaposing the Statue of Liberty, an eagle, the US flag, and the words "American Dream." Later in the sequence, we see him in the midst of a domestic fantasy complete with bungalow and blonde babe—an object choice of desire overdetermined by the complex sexual dynamics of colonial history—handing him a glass of milk and a hamburger. The presence of a small, white boy in the frame constructs the American dream as inhering in the marriage between heteronormative reproduction and property ownership. The lyrics of the song emphasize his pursuit of this fiction insofar as the refrain includes the line, "He's running behind the American dream," which implies that he's chasing after a dream that he will be unable to catch.

That Ali's construction of Amreeka is simplistic and almost cartoonish is indicated in the flashbacks to his childhood, which represent him as obsessed with the United States from a young age. The Superman bedspread adorning the adult Ali's bed hints that his understanding of the US has not matured with age. Even more significantly, the title of the song "Ullu da Pattha" is clearly a signifier for Ali himself. His aspirations to attain the American dream, the song's title insinuates, are idiotic and foolish.

This opening song sequence also implicates the global media as being complicit in the promulgation of the Global War on Terror and with disseminating a hegemonic version of the American dream. In the first scene, Majeed, an executive and reporter for the Pakistani Danka television station, does a "news" spot on the first American flight to depart from Karachi to New York following September 11, apparently newsworthy for the presence of a single Pakistani passenger, Ali, on the flight. At one level, the scene starkly demonstrates the unequal power balance between the US and Pakistan insofar as the presence of a single Pakistani passenger on the plane would not merit media coverage in the US. Yet after his detention by US authorities on suspicion of terrorism, the US media picks up the story and runs with it. A reporter from News America interviews the flight attendant, who gleefully claims that Ali "had a look of vengeance in his eyes as if he wanted to kill me." Shortly afterward, an anchor for the same station solemnly announces that "reports are coming in of bin Laden trying to affect peace in America," implying that Ali is bin Laden's agent. The hyperbole of the news segments both demonstrates media exaggeration of content related to the Global War on Terror and the unapologetically fictional quality of US journalism in which all things related to terrorism lead back to Osama bin Laden, even in the absence of any causal connections. According to *Tere Bin Laden's* logic, the media—rather than functioning as the watchdog of democratic processes—instead acts like the fourth branch of government, promoting views in line with the executive and legislative branches, in effect operating along the lines of an Althusserian ideological state apparatus.[79]

Similar to its US counterpart, Pakistani media, as portrayed in the film and embodied in Danka TV, has a tendency to cover inane human-interest stories geared toward entertainment. The song sequence intersperses footage of Ali, at work as a Danka correspondent, interviewing a proprietor of an umbrella shop about the optimum way to open an umbrella and a farmer about his sense of fulfillment from growing white, tubular radishes. Later in the film, Ali's assignment to cover a cock-crowing competition introduces him to Noora, the naive Osama bin Laden look-alike, who will become the unwitting lead in Ali's fake footage.

Two consecutive frames reinforce the sense that the media has played a formative role in Ali's internalization of the American dream. In one, Ali is posed against a background of a wall covered with television screens, all featuring the image of the Statue of Liberty, with the soundtrack blaring, "He's running blind behind the American dream." The next frame substitutes different stills of Ali's detention and interrogation for the images of the Statue of Liberty on the television monitors. In combination with the other scenes featuring News America and Danka television, these frames point to the power of media and its capacity to shape individual subjectivity such as Ali's, as well as to exist in a closed loop with the state, beaming propaganda and justifications for the Global War on Terror on its airwaves, and inciting the state to enact more exaggerated forms of coercion against those deemed terrorist suspects.

The Critique of the War on Terror

Tere Bin Laden begins with a standard disclaimer: "The characters and incidents portrayed in the film herein are fictitious and any similarity/resemblance to the name, character, and history of any person, living or dead, is entirely coincidental and unintentional. The film is a satire on the difficult times we are living in." This disclaimer is clearly a joke given that the title of the film contains a reference to Osama bin Laden; yet he only appears in the film as his simulacra, his look-alike—the poultry farmer, Noora—whom the film crafts as a vehicle to represent the film's critique of the Global War on Terror. US foreign policy is queered in several ways: through comic references to George W. Bush, through Noora's speeches in the fake bin Laden videos, and through the cartoonish representation of US military action in Afghanistan. Ali and his cameraman Gul are dispatched to cover a rooster-crowing contest for Danka television, where with a great deal of fanfare, the announcer introduces one contestant, "And now straight from the land of Bushes: the mighty Dubya *Pardesi* [foreigner], last year's champion." An obese rooster struts across the stage only to issue a puny crow. The rooster's incongruous bodily bulk in conjunction with the feebleness of his voice suggests a parallel with his namesake: in the Global War on Terror, when push comes to shove, a puffed up and crowing president is unable to deliver on such basic goods as bin Laden's capture.

Apart from this comic reference to President G.W. Bush, the weightiest critique of US foreign policy in the film emerges from the speeches of Osama bin Laden in the fake videos staged by Ali and his gang, and in the cartoonish representation of cynical US intelligence officials, who deliberately mislead the public. Tricking Noora into believing that he is making a tape about poultry farming for Saudi television, Latif—an Arab colleague of Ali and Gul's—provides an Arabic script for him to memorize. Unbeknownst to Noora, the crew switches the background images of stacked egg cartons and the accoutrements of poultry farming for visuals of a cave, the setting for many of the actual Osama bin Laden's videotapes. Indeed, the text of Noora's speech echoes the theme of reactive violence that is a leitmotif in bin Laden's actual speeches and interviews. With his arm raised in a gesture characteristic of the real bin Laden, Noora declares, "America will have to pay heavily for its continued atrocities in Iraq, Afghanistan, and the rest of the Middle East. Its hands are red with the blood of innocent Muslim children. America cannot wash away this blood without bleeding itself in return. The sacrifice of our Iraqi brothers and sisters will not go in vain." As I explained earlier in this chapter, bin Laden frequently invoked the image of blood alongside references to violence perpetrated against Muslim children in his speeches. The themes of US violence against Arabs and Afghans, the deaths of Muslim children, and the threat of retaliatory violence against Americans articulated in Noora's first fake bin Laden tape all have their historical antecedents in Osama bin Laden's actual speeches and interviews.

If the first fake bin Laden tape highlights Muslim grievances against the US, the second one alludes to the political economy of its foreign policy, expressing a widely held view among South Asians and American progressives that US foreign policy is largely driven by the desire to exert control over gas and oil energy sources. Rehearsing the script for a second bin Laden tape proposing a ceasefire, Noora addresses the US president as "My beloved ["*habibi*"], George Bush." The use of the endearment "*habibi*" marks a change in tone and affect, signaling a shift from the gravity of reactive violence to the comedic references to fried snacks that will soon follow. Noora's address of Bush as "habibi" also cheekily insinuates that the two men are lovers, adding to the film's queer critique. He then asks Bush, "How long can you use me as an excuse to go oil hunting?" "Stop these atrocities," he orders. Together, the interrogative and imperative sentences assert that bin Laden largely functions as an alibi for the US to identify new territory and sources of oil to exploit. A third fake bin Laden tape elaborates on the theme of President Bush's desire for oil. Disguised as bin Laden, Noora chides the American leader, "You used to dream of having oil fountains in your backyard. . . . Your sly ways took you straight to oil wells and now you bathe in Iraqi petrol and Afghani [sic] diesel every day."

As Eqbal Ahmad, among others, has maintained, oil and gas production and distribution have been a consideration of US foreign policy going back to the early 70s, as one way for the US to gain leverage over its allies in Japan and Europe, which needed energy sources to fuel the industrialization of their economies.[80] While I argued in the introduction to this book that the hunger for oil and gas no longer drives US economic aims in Afghanistan, the perception that it is a prime motivator of American foreign policy still persists. Indeed, the jockeying over strategic partnerships with the Central Asian countries between the US, UK, and NATO countries, on the one hand, and Russia and the People's Republic of China, on the other hand, has popularized the term "the New Great Game" to capture the new politics of oil, resurrecting the nineteenth-century term used to describe the political rivalry between Britain and Russia in the region.[81]

The third fake Osama bin Laden tape in *Tere Bin Laden* has Noora offering a truce to President Bush and inviting him to share fried foods. References to fried foods bookend Noora's charges that Bush washes in Iraqi and Afghan fuel.

He initially remarks, "My beloved Bushie: you've liked your meat deep-fried and oily since you were little," and cautions, "But don't be too greedy or you might end up an oily McBush burger." "Take my advice, drop this war," Noora qua bin Laden advises. "Come to my cave. We'll gorge on fried food ["*pakoras*"] together." Although clearly ridiculous, the references to fried foods literalize President Bush's—and by extension, America's—insatiable appetite for oil and gas even as Noora's invitation to consume *pakoras,* a savory South Asian fried snack, together alludes to the legendary codes of hospitality in the region. The affectionate form of address and the invitation to the intimate space of the cave further plays with the characterization of Bush and bin Laden as lovers.

The War on Terror as Cartoonish

Tere Bin Laden spoofs the Global War on Terror by using animation stills to signify its cartoonish elements. After the first fake bin Laden tape surfaces, Washington sends Ted Wood, the head of US intelligence, to Pakistan to formulate an appropriate response. Briefing CIA and Pakistan's ISI officials, Wood announces plans to launch "Operation Kickass": a campaign to target Afghanistan hourly with cruise missiles and B52 bombers. As he speaks, Wood illustrates his military strategy with visuals that consist of cartoon images of menacing-looking armed Afghans posed against a mountain background. The scene literally renders the Global War on Terror as a cartoonish enterprise and simultaneously evokes Secretary of State Colin Powell's February 3, 2003 testimony to the UN in which he claimed Iraq possessed weapons of mass destruction. Toggling between actual photographs of Iraqi weapons that no longer existed and line drawings of such weapons and mobile biological weapons labs, Powell made a sober case in support of the Bush administration's plan to go to war with Iraq, a case that he acknowledged was "not solid" a little over a year later.[82]

"Operation Kickass," the name given to this venture, also recalls the absurdity of the designation given to the US military campaign in Afghanistan, "Operation Enduring Freedom," and its ambiguous meaning. Does freedom itself endure or is freedom that which must be endured?[83] Additionally, the name invokes the US military doctrine of shock and awe and the use of overwhelming force, formulated in 1996 by staff at the National Defense University.[84] In keeping with the farcical nature of the film, *Tere Bin Laden* restricts the lethal effects of Operation Kickass to the deaths of domesticated animals. *Live India's* coverage of the breaking news of the operation reveals "heavy bombing in Afghanistan has caused severe casualties to livestock. America says this onslaught will continue till Osama is captured." In actuality, however, Operation Enduring Freedom has resulted in the deaths of numerous Afghans, though exact figures are impossible to determine given that official tallies of

Afghan casualties were not kept until 2007. As I explained in the last chapter, the refusal to tally Afghan casualties is indicative that their lives do not count and, to invoke Judith Butler, are not grievable.

The United Nations estimates that the casualty figure for Afghan civilians from 2007 to 2011 is 11,864.[85] Afghan civilian casualties from the start of the war in 2001 to 2007 are probably much higher, given the use of aerial power to prosecute the war. A US military pilot remembers that in the initial phases of the war, military aircraft were instructed to return for landings with far fewer bombs than in their initial payload.[86] Lieutenant Commander Peter Morgan recounts, "When this [Operation Enduring Freedom] kicked off, they were launching aircraft with unrecoverable loads. Basically, you had to drop."[87] Military officials now claim that better coordination between ground forces and navy pilots via satellite technology has reduced the number of civilian casualties from aerial bombardment.[88] Under the Obama and Trump administrations, the US military has ramped up its drone program in Afghanistan both for the purposes of surveillance and for firing missiles and dropping bombs; the surveillance drones are targeted at identifying individuals planting roadside bombs, which are the largest cause of US military casualties.[89] As P.W. Singer, an analyst with the Brookings Institution, has observed, the increased use of drones has the potential to increase civilian casualties. "Not everyone digging by the side of the road is automatically an insurgent," he notes.[90] In sixteen years of war, civilian casualties are estimated to be about 31,000 in an overall count of 111,000 dead.[91]

Tere Bin Laden's displacement of the violent consequences of the US bombing campaign from Afghan civilians to livestock enables the film to maintain its comedic element and is consistent with its improbable plot, which also exposes US intelligence officials as being callous to the lethal effects of their campaigns. When ISI agent Usman realizes that the Osama tape features a map with Urdu lettering in the background, he concludes that bin Laden is in Pakistan rather than Afghanistan. In response to his question about why the US is conducting a bombing campaign of Afghanistan when they know bin Laden is in Pakistan, Wood says, "We have a budget of 100 billion dollars for hunting down Osama. I can't spend all of that on sipping coffee." The political economy of foreign intervention, Wood insinuates, becomes geared to its own reproduction regardless of whether or not its strategic objectives have been met.

From September 11, 2001, till January 1, 2014, Operation Enduring Freedom has cost $686 billion for Afghanistan alone.[92] As a number of analysts have commented, Al-Qaeda no longer has a substantial presence in Afghanistan, where instead the Taliban has reinvented itself as a form of Pushtun nationalism in opposition to the US occupation of the country.[93] Just as the ISI agent Usman recognizes that Osama bin Laden's absence from Afghanistan should logically exempt the country from being targeted by the US military, we might ask whether the dwindling numbers of Al Qaeda insurgents there necessitates an ongoing US military presence in that country.

Wood's collaboration with Ali to produce the final fake bin Laden tape amplifies the cynicism of Wood's position on Operation Kickass and the film's representation of the continued military campaign against Afghanistan when intelligence officials know of bin Laden's absence there. After discovering that the Osama bin Laden taken into custody by intelligence officials is Noora, a poultry farmer and not archenemy number one of the US, Wood screams at Ali, "What will I say to the world? . . . . That we bombed Afghanistan for nothing?" Partly as a face-saving measure for Wood, and partly out of a desire to end the Global War on Terror and its attendant terror unleashed on Afghans, Ali proposes the ISI, CIA, and his motley crew collaborate to make a final Osama bin Laden tape offering a ceasefire to President Bush, which Bush accepts.

That the CIA actively participates in the production of the final fake bin Laden tape in *Tere Bin Laden* will not seem wholly improbable from a plot perspective insofar as numerous actual internet sites, many created by Americans, purport to unmask the agency's role in making the video released by the Bush administration in October 2001 as proof of bin Laden's complicity in the 9/11 attacks. For instance, the website "The Real Proof the Government Released a Fake Video of Osama Bin Laden!" walks viewers through points in the tape that do not tally with known aspects of bin Laden's person and character: the Osama in the tape, the narrator claims, is heavier, has a shorter nose, is wearing a ring and wristwatch (ornamentation unlikely in serious believers), and is right-handed (he was left-handed). This analysis appears on other websites as well, including one featuring an interview with bin Laden's fourth son, Omar, who claims that the man in the tape is not his father.[94] Perhaps because of the popularity of such sites, the BBC even acknowledged, in December 2001, the widespread skepticism toward the authenticity of this tape, particularly in the Arab world.[95]

Five years later, the BBC went on to make a three-part documentary, *The Power of Nightmares*, that historicizes the dialectical relationship between the rise of American neo-conservatives and radical Islamists and charts how US foreign policy has shifted from evidence-based decision-making to speculative fantasy reliant on the creation of manufactured threats. The final segment, "The Shadows in the Cave" (a combined reference to Plato's parable of the cave in the *Republic*, the Archangel Gabriel's revelation to Muhammad in a mountain cave, and the cave setting for many of bin Laden's speeches), presents the view that in pursuing Al-Qaeda, Western powers are largely chasing a "phantom enemy," whose actual menace is an "illusion" that serves the interests of groups such as politicians in an "age of cynicism" after the end of history and, apparently, of ideology as well.[96] In other words, if Osama bin Laden did not exist, he would have to be invented as a dark fantasy to provide the conditions of possibility for Western heroics.[97] The invention of imagined threats, of course, also resonates with the actual fabrication of evidence by Bush administration officials to justify going to war with Iraq.[98]

"The South Asian Perspective" and Pakistani Civil Society

Ali Zafar—the Pakistani pop idol who plays Ali Hassan's character in the film—insists that *Tere Bin Laden* provides a much-needed Pakistani view of the Global War on Terror and that this element of the film attracted him to the script. Appearing in an interview on *Dawn*, he claims that the film does not have any content that is ideological or offensive.[99] The Indian writer and director of *Tere Bin Laden*, Abhishek Sharma, voices similar sentiments in an interview which aired on the segment "Is There Room for Humour in the War Against Terror?" on the Riz Khan's show, September 6, 2010, on *Al Jazeera*. The fictional character of Ali, according to Sharma, represents a generalized "South Asian perspective" on both the Global War on Terror and the American Dream. Given the historic rivalry between Pakistan and India since the partition of the subcontinent in 1947, the collaboration between an Indian director and Pakistani actor itself is remarkable.

Yet the claim that the film represents a generalized South Asian perspective on the Global War on Terror seems disingenuous, given the range of opinions on the US military campaign in India and Pakistan among diverse communities (religious, ethnic, and territorial, for example); these communities are positioned differently vis-à-vis their respective nation-states, and they have specific histories of suffering and entitlement that inform their views of US foreign policy. If anything, *Tere Bin Laden* demonstrates the complexities of civil society as an assemblage of voluntary associations that consist of, among others, faith-based groups; entrepreneurial units; and ethnic, cultural, and professional organizations that interact in complicated ways and exist in an uneasy equilibrium with one another and with the state.

Noora's identity as a village bumpkin and his appearance (wearing the traditional *kurta pajama* and *pagari*, and sporting a beard) mark him as a certain kind of Muslim: the manipulated, simple Forrest Gump-like character through whom we see the depravity of the world. His character presents a stark contrast to the constant scheming of Ali, whose clothing and lifestyle identify him as a global cosmopolitan. The film mocks both subject positions, given the opening song sequence, which spoofs Ali and his infatuation with the American Dream, and the ending credits in which Noora's hip haircut, shaving of beard, and donning of stylish jeans, along with his transformation from rural poultry farmer to urban beauty salon owner, signify a comic conversion to Western modernity.

Tere Bin Laden concludes with the success of the final fake bin Laden tape. The Global War on Terror has come to an end. Ted Wood has been promoted to Secretary of the Defense. The Pakistani characters have used the profit from the clandestine sale of their first fake bin Laden tape to realize their dreams for various forms of literal and social mobility. Ali becomes a journalist celebrity and goes to the US accompanied by Gul, his cameraman-sidekick; Zoya, the make-up artist who transformed Noora into bin Laden for the tapes, opens a beauty salon; Latif, who masqueraded as a Saudi television executive to fool Noora into making the tape, becomes the best-selling translator of the volume *Osama On Peace*; and Querishi, the leftist who did bin Laden's voice-overs in the fake tapes, founds the Communist Party of Pakistan. Across the ideological spectrum—from the lower-middle class to the professional managerial class to the leftist intellectual class—members of Pakistani civil society, as do US government officials, act to advance their self-interests even when those are based on complete falsehoods or require the hoodwinking of naïve rural subjects. The film represents Pakistanis as maximizing their own interests, whether focused on emigration (Ali and Gul), entrepreneurship (Zoya and Latif) or the amassing of local political power (Querishi); the individual characters, in effect, behave in the same self-serving manner as states.

The film portrays South Asian aspirations in the global arena alongside local power negotiations among representatives of different elements of Pakistani civil society, who sometimes undermine one another and at other times cooperate in limited ways. Mutual suspicion initially characterizes the interactions between media operators (Ali and Gul), aspiring businesswomen and established entrepreneurs (Zoya and Noor), emergent intellectuals (Latif), and those engaged in oppositional politics (Querishi). Once they become persuaded that their interests coincide, they become a collective that alternates between accommodation and antagonism toward the Pakistani and US governments. *Tere Bin Laden's* contribution to discourses about Osama bin Laden and the Global War on Terror is to insert the Pakistani lower-middle and middle classes, as representatives of civil society, into the nexus of global media by emphasizing their role in producing and disseminating footage pertinent to the Global War on Terror, and thus exerting geopolitical agency. Adding to the repertoire of popular culture representations of Osama bin Laden, the film contributes a critique of the Global War on Terror from South Asia, a part of the world often viewed as at risk for generating political violence and terrorism.

Conclusion

As if life were imitating art, bin Laden was discovered in Pakistan, the setting of *Tere bin Laden*, where he had been hiding for years before his assassination in Abbottabad, Pakistan on May 2, 2011. One-time ally of the US, Osama bin Laden encapsulates the contradictory figurations of the "native" that circulate in the Global War on Terror: both heroic Cold War foot soldier in the 1980s and despicable terrorist mastermind in the 1990s and 2000s. I have argued in this chapter that since 9/11, the meanings associated with bin Laden have also varied, allowing him to function as a vehicle for very different agendas. He has become, on the one hand, a justification for military intervention in Afghanistan and, on the other hand, the means to critique the Global War on Terror as an invented fiction of the US. A close reading of President G.W. Bush's speeches following 9/11 discloses how the rationale to pursue bin Laden was couched in the idiom of retributive justice, the righteousness of retaliating against terrorist attacks, which provides the palimpsest for Owen's account of the assassination of bin Laden in *No Easy Day*.

Narratives such as *No Easy Day* give ideological support for US imperialism through their mobilization of homophobic sentiments and construction of bin Laden as queer, along with their representation of techno-military masculinity. Part of the intended audience for the book is school-aged boys, a demographic Owen hopes to inspire to become warriors and with whom he has experience through his consulting work with corporations that produce war-themed video games. Marines and SEALs function as live action superheroes, battling evil for the safety and glory of their country.

But the appeal of these narratives also extends to adults. Structured as a teleology that culminates in bin Laden's death, the memoir provides assurances of an eventual victory in the Global War on Terror even as the actual war is at a stalemate. From the intelligence gathered through what is quaintly called the "enhanced interrogation techniques" of detainees to the descriptions of highly sophisticated weapons and surveillance equipment, *No Easy Day* and similar combat memoirs help legitimate the national-security state by showcasing the prowess of its agents and its successes in counter terrorism. The machismo of Owen's text—his passion for guns and admiration for the National Rifle Association—valorizes techno-military masculinity and validates a vulgar strand of imperial ideology wherein geopolitical dominance becomes its own self-justification. These types of narratives make us feel good about our armed forces and safer in the knowledge that the bad guys will get their just desserts.

Tere bin Laden queers and destabilizes dominant narratives of this kind that circulate in the US through its exaggerated acting and outlandish plot. The film represents bin Laden as the creation of global media and the fictions generated by the American government, which gain a momentum of their own, influencing the course of the US intervention in Afghanistan. Like the young trick-or-treaters who opened this chapter, bin Laden functions as a de-referentialized media icon in the film, which provocatively suggests that counterinsurgency efforts are a joke: what is at stake instead is the necessity of sustaining the phantasm of an amorphous civilizational threat that feeds the military-industrial complex. *Tere bin Laden* exposes how the considerable expenditure on the Global War on Terror necessitates additional investment to prevent the US from losing face.

Bin Laden's Islamist version of geopolitical payback demonstrates striking similarities to Bush's retributive justice in its reliance on a religious idiom and a parallel logic. The discursive similarities suggest continuity and synergy between acts of terrorism and of war, between punishing crimes committed by non-state actors and vengeance inflicted by states in retaliation. Structured by a shared logic of revenge, retributive justice and reactive violence lead to an endless cycle of conflict and to perpetual war. Despite having different names, the violence of terrorism and of war are remarkably similar. Tariq Ali warns that "[t]o fight tyranny and oppression by using tyrannical and oppressive means, to combat a single-minded and ruthless fanaticism by becoming equally fanatical and ruthless, will not further the cause of justice or bring about a meaningful democracy."[100] The Global War on Terror has made the US seemingly into that which it deplores, till we remember that the ruthless prosecution of the Afghan intervention is the most recent expression of the long and violent historical continuum of American imperialism, dating back to the territorial expansion of settlers across the continent.

Postscript

Three Presidents, One Policy

In 2018, the second year of the Trump presidency, a popular dissenting narrative had emerged, holding him responsible for replacing the liberal, internationalist world order associated with Obama with protectionist, xenophobic nationalism. Adherents of this view believe the change from the Obama to the Trump presidency has precipitated a qualitative shift in the content and tone of foreign policy: diplomacy steeped in knowledge has been supplanted with naked mercantilism and the urbanity of one administration superseded by the vulgarity of another. The professorial bent of a president who, we are told, agonized over the morality of his foreign policy decisions has been replaced by the capriciousness of a corporate executive who does not believe in the universality of human rights or civil liberties and, as a result, is eager to obliterate foreign nationals with drones or other high-tech weapons. Taking a longer view, I want to make the case instead that US-Afghan policy is not so much about any particular president, but the imperial prosecution of a persistent war with fairly stable objectives across administrations, including the prevention of terrorism and "nation-building." Wide fluctuations in the number of troops deployed in Afghanistan across and within administrations give the false impression that Afghan policy has dramatically changed from Bush to Obama to Trump. It has not.

Making this point, Heng's "Afghanistan Strategy" cartoon published in the *New York Times* on August 24, 2017, a day after President Trump's speech "Remarks on the Strategy in Afghanistan and South Asia," features a revolving door identified as "Afghanistan." One soldier is entering the contraption and another one leaving it; an "EXIT" arrow directs the smiling soldier whereas a

"RE-ENTRY" sign explains the alarmed expression on his compatriot's face. Notably absent in this graphic are dates and the names of specific administrations. The editorial cartoon succinctly critiques Afghan policy over successive administrations; both Presidents George W. Bush and Barack Obama, within their individual tenures, alternated troop deployments with the drawdown of forces.[1] Early in his first term, President Trump increased the number of US troops deployed to Afghanistan in spite of his vociferous criticism of the Afghan War during his campaign and earlier denunciations on social media. (In one of several tweets, he declared on March 12, 2012, "Afghanistan is a total disaster. We don't know what we are doing. They are, in addition to everything else, robbing us blind.")[2] Lest *Times* readers miss the cartoon's indictment of the continuity in policy across administrations, the copy below elaborates, "President Trump announced on Monday a strategy for the war in Afghanistan. He did not provide details about the number of troops that would be committed or how his approach would differ from the failed strategies of his predecessors."[3] Employing a visual shorthand whereby two single soldiers represent fluctuations in the number of boots on the ground, the cartoon renders troop counts into a metonym for Afghan policy. On the whole, it accurately represents an overall imperial policy that has remained stable for seventeen years.

FIG. 1 "Heng on Trump's Afghanistan Strategy," Heng, *International New York Times*, August 24, 2017

Shared objectives across three presidential administrations cohere around delivering payback to Osama bin Laden, destroying Islamist insurgencies as a preventive measure against terrorism, and nation-building. The Bush administration invaded Afghanistan as retributive justice for 9/11, seeking to punish Osama bin Laden and to decimate Al Qaeda. While bin Laden eluded US forces till after Bush's term ended, his administration succeeded in degrading Al Qaeda. Obama assumed the presidency with a promise to end the wars in Afghanistan and Iraq. He initially hoped to withdraw troops from Afghanistan by 2014, though, as I noted in the introduction, the troop drawdown included provisions to maintain a semi-permanent military presence there. Scaling back his goals, Obama concentrated on building the Afghan security forces and maintaining "a modest unilateral counterterrorism capability against transnational threats."[4] Osama bin Laden was assassinated on his watch as well. Notwithstanding Trump's protestations otherwise, his declared aims are remarkably similar to Obama's; he would like to achieve an honorable exit from Afghanistan and to create stability to prevent ISIS or Al Qaeda from filling a power vacuum in the context of a nuclearized subcontinent. Even as they sought negotiations with the Taliban, all three American presidents have shared the desire to defeat the Taliban.

Nonetheless, what Heng's cartoon perceives as more of the same policy, President Trump tried to pass off as a "new strategy" in his August 23, 2017, speech; he claimed that his "new strategy" "dramatically" differed from his predecessor in significant ways. He declared that he would base Afghan strategy on an assessment of "conditions on the ground" rather than the "arbitrary timetables" for withdrawal announced in advance by President Obama during his term. American policy would now integrate "all instruments of American power—diplomatic, economic, and military—toward a successful outcome." The US would pressure Pakistan to cease providing "safe havens for terrorist organizations, the Taliban, and other groups that pose a threat to the region and beyond." His administration would pivot toward India in order to develop a "strategic partnership," particularly in terms of providing Afghanistan with "economic assistance and development." Finally, he pledged to "lift restrictions and expand authorities in the field" that had "prevented the Secretary of Defense and his commanders. . . from fully and swiftly waging battle against the enemy."[5] With the exception of basing his decisions on conditions on the ground and abdicating his authority for setting troop levels to his generals, Trump's "new strategy" recycles elements of the policies of his presidential precursors.

Recall that George W. Bush reversed the foreign policy stances he had espoused during his presidential run in 2000 when the *New York Times* had dubbed him a "reluctant internationalist," who was suspicious of nation-building.[6] After 9/11, he ordered the invasion of Afghanistan to punish and rout Osama bin Laden and Al Qaeda for their role in the attacks. In October 2001, as I described in chapter 4, the Bush administration began bombing Afghanistan, killing more civilians in the first month than had perished in the September 11 attacks. On the ground in Afghanistan, CIA agents and a small contingent of US Army Special Forces commenced their hunt for bin Laden. By the following month, the US had deployed about 1,300 troops to the region, a number that would steadily increase with some fluctuations to about 25,000 by December 2007, the tail end of Bush's term.[7]

During the interim in 2003, President Bush made the disastrous decision to invade Iraq on the basis of cooked-up intelligence under the pretext of defanging Saddam Hussain of WMDs. While those weapons never materialized, the invasion of Iraq succeeded in replacing an authoritarian regime with a failed state and resulted in a humanitarian catastrophe. Hundreds of thousands of Iraqis have died from US military violence and the deliberate destruction of their infrastructure, sectarian conflict, or the indirect consequences of war, notably disease and starvation—all in a country that once had one of the best healthcare systems in the Middle East. According to talking heads and policy wonks, the Iraq war had the pernicious effect of diverting attention and resources away from the military effort in Afghanistan, a theme that candidate Barack Obama hammered on the presidential campaign trail in 2007. Comparative troop deployment figures substantiate this charge. In 2003, the average US monthly troop levels in Afghanistan were 10,400, but in Iraq they were 67,700. In 2007 when then President Bush, responding to a dismal security situation in Iraq, ordered a troop "surge" of 30,000 US soldiers there, average US monthly troop levels in Iraq soared to 148,300 while hovering at 23,700 in Afghanistan.[8] During President Obama's first term in office, he made good on a campaign promise to dedicate more troops to Afghanistan, which rose to a high of 100,000 by 2011, only to fall to 8,400 by the end of his second term in 2016.[9] That number would rise to 14,000 troops under President Trump by September 2018.[10] In December 2018, Trump abruptly announced that the US would withdraw about 7,000 troops in the coming months, an announcement that surprised Afghan officials who were not given advance notice of this decision.[11]

Apart from the anemic military campaign in Afghanistan under Bush, three other aspects of his war policy are worth mentioning in relation to Trump's claim to a new policy: development, relations with India, and his embrace of high-tech warfare and drones. Contra Trump's assertion that the novelty of his own strategy inheres in the integration of military, diplomatic, and economic efforts, Bush purported to combine all three almost from the beginning of the invasion in 2001. Whatever else one concludes about his commitments to multi-lateralism based, for example, on his withdrawal from the Kyoto Protocol, Bush did pursue military partnerships with other countries, enlisting NATO members to create and lead the International Security Assistance

Force comprised of troops from forty-two countries. (Arguably, one of the Bush Administration's "diplomatic achievements" was to persuade the UN Security Council to establish ISAF, the first NATO mission to deploy outside of Europe.) As early as his first State of the Union Address in 2002, the majority of which was given over to the War on Terror, Bush had also emphasized collaborations with historic adversaries, among them India. "In this moment of opportunity, a common danger is erasing old rivalries," he boasted, "America is working with Russia and China and India, in ways we have never before, to achieve peace and prosperity. In every region, free markets and free trade and free societies are proving their power to lift lives."[12] To be sure, the equation of free markets and political freedom constitutes a version of the capitalist-rescue narrative that is the subject of chapter 2, but it also attests to the imbrication of diplomatic, military, and economic efforts in G.W. Bush-era Afghan policy.

Several months later, President Bush's commitment to extending economic and development aid to Afghanistan was the focus of his remarks at the Virginia Military Institute to the George C. Marshall ROTC award recipients. Bush evoked "Marshall's vision" to rebuild Western Europe as a "beacon to light the path that we, too, must follow" in Afghanistan. The achievement of "true peace," he opined, depended on giving Afghans "the means to achieve their own aspirations," which would require the creation of governance, a national army, and "an education system for boys and girls which works." He affirmed the need for a "moral victory that resulted in better lives for individual human beings" as being companion to a "military victory" and in the tradition of the Marshall Plan. Pointing to the clearing of minefields, rebuilding of roads, and improving of health care, Bush saw reconstruction as a crucial part of the Afghan mission.[13] All of these projects required substantial economic investment and the involvement of NGOs, of course, along with private corporations. Indeed, Secretary of State Colin Powell waded into hot water for referring to NGOs as "force multipliers" and for encouraging the military to use development aid to solicit intelligence.[14] Intertwining development and security efforts, the US legitimized the criticism of insurgents who claimed that NGOs were largely a front for the American military, thus placing aid workers at risk of being attacked.[15]

Eerily anticipating Trump's claim to be pursuing a "new" course of action in Afghanistan, President Obama used a similar vocabulary of novelty to describe a policy that continued much of his predecessor's with the exception of his troop surge. In his "Remarks on a New Strategy for Afghanistan," Obama announced the need for "a smarter, stronger and comprehensive strategy" that would "integrate our civilian and military efforts."[16] The policy would be jointly directed by Ambassador Richard Holbrooke and General David Petraeus, who was then serving as Commander in Chief of Central Command, encapsulating in its leadership the partnership between civilian and military efforts. Petraeus had been a vocal advocate for "winning hearts and minds" as a crucial component of counterinsurgency [COIN] strategy in Iraq and Afghanistan, literally writing the book on it. In the *Field Manual 3-24: Counter Insurgency*, Petraeus, along with his co-author Lieutenant General James F. Amos, opines that "Soldiers and Marines are expected to be nation builders as well as warriors" and "must be prepared to help reestablish institutions and local security forces and assist in rebuilding infrastructure and basic services."[17] To the military's charge, Petraeus and Amos add the facilitation of "establishing local governance and the rule of law."[18] COIN seeks to alienate local villagers from insurgents by rendering them "irrelevant" by providing security, "basic economic needs," "essential services" (water, electricity, sanitation, and healthcare), and "sustainment of key social and cultural institutions." Such lofty goals require coordination and partnership among the US military and civilian agencies, Afghan government, "other nations' defense and nondefense agencies," international organizations, NGOs, and private contractors.[19]

In theory, COIN advocates hope that the provision of these services and aid will improve "the basic quality of life" and increase support for "host-nation partners" by demonstrating that the governments of US-occupied countries are able to care for their citizens.[20] In practice, those goals have not been met. Yet to suggest, as President Trump did, that the Afghan strategy of his predecessors narrowly focused on military tactics defies the historical record on COIN, which is not to endorse those cynical efforts or to claim their success. The balance sheet for reconstruction includes a now familiar litany of squandered resources: funds siphoned through the corruption pipelines; malfeasance by corporations such as Black Veatch, DynCorp, and the Louis Berger Group; schools built that are furnished with textbooks from the 1970s and 1980s; dining facilities that lack kitchens; roads that began to crumble on their completion because of substandard construction; and health care clinics with no provision for running water, to name just several of many examples of wasted dollars.[21]

As if this record of failure was not depressing enough, much of the reconstruction aid has been funneled to building up Afghan security forces, again with dismal results. While exact figures are difficult to ascertain, given the haphazard and irresponsible accounting practices of the DoD, Catherine Lutz and Sujaya Desai estimate the total amount of US aid allocated for "relief and reconstruction" through fiscal year 2015 to be a staggering $109.9 billion.[22] The State Department only administers approximately 30% of this aid, which is directed to governance (courts and prisons), development (infrastructure, basic education, and technical-vocational training), and "immediate humanitarian assistance" (healthcare).[23] The DoD administers the remaining 70% of these reconstruction funds, which are devoted to security, including support for the Afghan military and police forces and battling narcotics trafficking. Results have not been encouraging: chronic troop shortages, a literacy rate of about

14% for Afghan soldiers, and opium production on the rise.[24] Moreover, the security situation remains dire in much of the country as the Taliban increases its territorial control and rival Islamist forces have entered the fray. Given the abysmal failure of COIN and reconstruction more generally under the Bush and Obama administrations, the Trump administration's pursuit of more of the same policy seems ill advised.

Additional continuities among all three administrations inhere in the worrisome expansion of executive powers, particularly in terms of national security and the use of drones. Each president has laid the foundation for his successor to build up the lethal power of the imperial state with devastating and deadly consequences for Afghans. Bush enthusiastically embraced the proverbial "Revolution in Military Affairs" [RMA], long-distance warfare that relies on communications technology and highly sophisticated weapons including robots and unmanned aerial vehicles. The legitimation and enlargement of RMA under Bush enabled Obama to escalate the number of drone attacks tenfold.[25] Obama's innovation was to swap out the surveillance and intelligence gathering missions of first-generation drones for the lethal capabilities of second-generation drones; advertised as "hunt and kill" hardware, these drones are aptly named "predators" and "reapers." Like Bush, Obama kept the number of attacks, the resultant casualties, and policies governing drones shrouded in mystery for the majority of his term in office; in the waning months of his presidency, he belatedly issued an Executive Order to add transparency and safeguards for the use of drones.[26] What Majed Akhter and Ian Shaw call "the dronification of state violence," a "technopolitical transformation" of state violence "centered on the intensely bureaucratic and automated delivery of death," became normalized and routinized under the Obama administration.[27] Obama's Executive Order permits the use of drones in non-conflict situations and created the space for Trump to eliminate even more restrictions on the armed forces and CIA. Not only has Trump loosened regulations on the deployment of drones, but he has ramped up the frequency of their attacks over Obama's.

Another potential continuity between the Trump and Bush administrations, which President Obama was not able to effectively foreclose, coheres around the use of torture. Then President Bush authorized "Enhanced Interrogation Techniques" [EIT] for "High Value Detainees" at "black sites," secret CIA prisons in Poland, Lithuania, Romania, and Thailand, where prisoners were subjected to cruel and inhumane treatment such as water boarding, cramped confinement, stress positions, and sleep deprivation lasting up to eleven days, among other forms of torture. At Bush's request, the Senate passed a bill legalizing EIT and granting immunity to CIA agents and others involved in the CIA's interrogation program.[28] On assuming office in 2009, then President Obama issued an Executive Order barring government employees or their agents from employing interrogation methods that were not listed in the *US Army Field Manual*. Because EITs were not named in the Army Field Manual, they were banned for all practical purposes. Subsequently, Obama managed to pass legislation stipulating that interrogation techniques had to be drawn from the *Army Field Manual*. This qualification problematically leaves open the possibility that the manual itself could be revised in the future to include EITs. In fact, the Secretary of Defense, a presidential appointment, is required to complete a thorough review of the manual every three years. Nothing prevents him or her from adding waterboarding or any of the other aforementioned torture methods to the list at the urging of whoever occupies the White House.[29]

The current occupant of the White House, Donald J. Trump, expressed his enthusiasm for EITs, especially waterboarding, while he was on the campaign circuit ("I love it," he remarked at a campaign rally in Indiana).[30] As president, he picked Gina Haspel, who ran a black site CIA facility in Thailand in 2002, to head the CIA, in effect, appointing an administrator in the torture bureaucracy to oversee intelligence gathering.[31] In 2005, Haspel had drafted a cable to the Bangkok black site, on her CIA supervisor's instructions, ordering the destruction of 92 torture video tapes, which was potentially a criminal act.[32] That *this* nominee by *this* president won Senate confirmation shows just how normalized torture has become. What should have been a closed, shameful chapter of the national security state now risks having its sequel written, but most likely not read, given the secrecy veiling such morally repugnant activities of dubious intelligence value. The CIA agents who subjected Abu Zubaydah, the first prisoner in a black site to endure prolonged EIT, to these techniques, along with both the Select Senate Committee on Intelligence and former CIA Director Leon Panetta's secret review of the program, concluded that such techniques are brutal and do not yield credible intelligence—an insight that Elaine Scarry's *The Body in Pain* delivered as far back as 1985.[33] Given the president's endorsement of torture and his selection of Haspel as CIA Director, it is not unreasonable to worry that EIT might come back into vogue. Equally alarming is a recent *New York Times* investigation revealing that the CIA's trained and equipped Afghan strike forces have been abusing and killing civilians in the countryside. These atrocities against civilians alienate Afghans and aid Taliban recruitment efforts.[34]

Wide fluctuations in troop levels disguise both the accretion of executive powers across three presidents and continuities in their policies regarding counterinsurgency and reconstruction. As I described in the introduction to this book, reconstruction efforts are geared more toward demonstrating progress in the short term than the creation of a sustainable and enduring infrastructure. They are thus directed to an American public, who wants to believe that military intervention is a form of humanitarianism; aid becomes not so much the means to help Afghans as it is intended to make Americans feel that we are making a positive difference in Afghanistan. A crucial function of aid and reconstruction, in other words, is as a form of propaganda meant to market the war as providing opportunities for Afghans and enabling them to enter the twenty-first century. The selling of the war as benevolent humanitarianism occurs at a high cost to Afghans, who bear the brunt of its violent prosecution. In a remark on drones that can be generalized to the entire war, Cian Westmoreland, a former drone technician, observes, "'With drones, our citizens don't have to physically come into contact with the people we are killing anymore, just like we don't come in contact with the animals we eat in our food. It allows us to live in illusionary worlds where we are deprived of the exposure to our own personal violent consequences and have very little incentive to improve how we interact with the world."[35]

Westmoreland's reference to "illusionary worlds" seems particularly apt during the Trump administration, given the ease with which White House officials exaggerate claims and peddle misinformation. (One thinks here of White House Press Secretary Sarah Huckabee Sanders' false assertion that the media tipped off Osama bin Laden about the US government tracking him through his mobile phone.)[36] According to the *New York Times,* "American officials routinely issue inflated assessments of progress that contradict what is actually happening there."[37] While it may be tempting to view this pretend narrative of progress as a novel feature of the current administration, given its propensity for lying, as I have attempted to demonstrate throughout *Intervention Narratives,* the stated objectives of US Afghan policy, dating back to the 80s, do not correspond to real threats and conditions on the ground. Whether Cold War paranoia about the perceived danger of the USSR, the simplistic belief in capitalism as a form of gender empowerment, the virtue of canine rescue, or the naïve faith in assassination as retributive justice, the stories Americans tell of the US engagement with Afghanistan are untethered from the reality of civil war and foreign power intervention.

Among other misleading information, US government officials claim that the Taliban only controls or contests 44% of districts, whereas military analysts place that figure at 61%.[38] Since 2017, the Taliban has gained control of more territory than it had in the previous sixteen years of the conflict. Rather than the pretend narrative of the Afghan government and US vanquishing the Taliban, the evidence points to the opposite. For all practical purposes, the war has become a hybrid between a struggle for national liberation from the US occupation and a civil conflict among Afghans with competing visions for their country. Popular descriptors of the war in the US media include "perpetual war," "forever war," "permanent war," and "endless war," all of which allude to the fact the conflict is at a stalemate and cannot be "won" militarily. To this extent, reports that the US has been engaged in direct talks with the Taliban since July 2018 are welcome, as are the Taliban and Afghan government's periodic ceasefires over the past few months. Yet the Taliban's refusal to allow Afghan government officials at the negotiating table does not augur well for a lasting solution to the conflict. Indeed, given the fate of informal talks with the Taliban during President Bush's tenure and direct talks with them by the Obama administration, it seems prudent to temper optimism at the prospects of a negotiated settlement.

As this book goes to press at the end of December 2018, Trump's projected drawdown of American troops over the next few months would seem to signal an impending end to hostilities. The drawdown of forces, as I cautioned in the introduction, could lead to the continuation of war through a greater reliance on long-distance, technological warfare from the air. Since taking office in 2016, the Trump administration has intensified its aerial campaign even as troop levels have been at a relative historic low over the last two years. According to UNAMA, aerial bombardment in 2017 by both US and Afghan forces resulted in the highest number of civilian casualties (295 deaths and 336 injuries) from when such records were first systematically kept in 2009.[39] My point is that war is not simply about boots on the ground, but that it inheres in the existent infrastructure of violence and the economic interests at play. We need to be alert to how and in what forms the war might continue even under the banner of peace.

US policy toward Afghanistan as a rational geopolitical calculation and as an exercise in counterinsurgency has been a grotesque failure. This obvious assertion leads to the conclusion that US-Afghan policy across three administrations is an effort to buttress an ideologically bad faith political project. Imagined relations cannot conceal the depravity of the real conditions on the ground. Rather than a conventional political gambit, the war in Afghanistan represents a bid for the concentration of US power and consolidation of capital that depends on intervention narratives and their de-referentialized accounts of the world. The ideological struggle is not for control of the narrative that will reconcile us to the real conditions of life; instead, the challenge is to ensure that the real world disappears altogether in favor of the sentimentality and emotive power of intervention narratives. In a similar sense, the political goal is not to contain "terrorism" per se, but to consolidate global power through the creation of permanent military bases in Afghanistan and to maximize the profits of particular industries such as defense and those involved in reconstruction, through the proliferation of endless, hallucinatory threats.

Mary Kaldor's analysis of the Afghan War as a "mutual enterprise" oriented toward "war without end" seems apt. She explains that "if we understand the 'War on Terror' as a mutual enterprise, whatever the individual antagonists believe, in which the US administration shores up its image as the protector of the American people and the defender of democracy and those with a vested interest in a high military budget are rewarded, and in which extremist Islamists are able to substantiate the idea of a global jihad and to mobilize young Muslims behind the cause, then action and counterreaction merely contribute to 'long war,' which benefits both sides."[40] As I have described in these pages, much of the capital shoveled into reconstruction has been either dissipated because of corruption or used to finance the insurgency.[41] The American public subsidizes private profits for entities who benefit from destruction and death in a significant redistribution of wealth from taxpayers to corporations. A fixation on three very different presidential styles—Bush's blandness, Obama's urbanity, and Trump's vulgarity—obscures this version of accumulation by dispossession and other essential continuities across three administrations, continuities that draw their life blood from imperialism.

Acknowledgments

This book has been a long time in the making, and the intellectual debts I have incurred are substantial. I feel particularly fortunate to have spent my academic career at Indiana University, which has provided a humane and lively intellectual environment that has nurtured inter- and multi-disciplinary discussions across the university. I have benefited from friendships and opportunities to learn from my colleagues, especially in terms of appreciating how different disciplines shape the ways we understand the world. Conversations about culture and politics, feminism, and theory in campus offices and over meals with Keera Allendorf, Gardner Bovingdon, Sara L. Friedman, Vivian Halloran, Scott Herring, Nur Amali Ibrahim, Christoph Irmscher, Karma Lochrie, Yan Long, Enrico Lunghi, Scott O'Bryan, Phil Parnell, Ron Sela, Jessica Steinberg, William Scheuerman, and Shane Vogel have been energizing. Patrick Brantlinger, my first chairperson in the English Department, has been a supportive friend of many years and has been available for on-demand consultation in his capacity as a walking archive of scholarly knowledge of imperialism and cultural theory. Ellen Brantlinger, a "surrogate mother," who passed away in 2012, is sorely missed; her memory continues to be an inspiration both for her scholarship on the importance of social class and her advocacy for public education.

Indiana University also provided institutional assistance in the way of time and resources to devote to writing. A travel grant from the College of Arts & Humanities Institute enabled me to participate in the Tepoztlán Institute for Transnational History of the Americas workshop on "Capitalism from Below," and a fellowship from New Frontiers in the Arts & Humanities allowed me to expand the Tepoz paper on the capitalist-rescue narrative into chapter 2. I have been additionally fortunate to have deans who have made it possible for me to pursue my research agenda by granting administrative course releases for directing the Cultural Studies Program in the College of Arts & Sciences and for chairing the International Studies Department in the Hamilton Lugar School of Global and International Studies. Thanks to Nick Cullather, Lee Feinstein, Jean Robinson, and Larry Singell for this much appreciated support. My sincere gratitude to Barbara Breitung for her friendship and efficient handling of quotidian administrative matters, which enabled me to focus on finishing this book.

For their suggestions on early iterations of portions of this manuscript, I am grateful to Patrick Brantlinger, Claudia Breger, Lessie Jo Frazier, Sara L. Friedman, Vivian Halloran, Susan Jeffords, John Lucaites, Jeffrey T. Kenney, Radhika Parameswaran, Jon Simons, and Fahad Yahya Al-Sumait. In addition to their friendship, Mona Bhan, Nattie Golubov, Jeffrey L. Gould, Stephanie Li, Laura E. Lyons, Alyce Miller, and Robyn Wiegman generously gave me feedback on chapter drafts and often on short notice. My thanks in particular to Mona for her Mona-ness and for teaching me about Kashmir, to Jeff for his historical sensibilities and skepticism of grand pronouncements on neoliberalism and the state, to Laura for shared commitments and thirty-one years of friendship, and to Robyn for her careful reading of my work and infectious delight at analyzing our current times. At Rutgers University Press, recommendations by Daniel Leonard Bernardi and Nicole Solano, along with the anonymous press reviewers, proved extremely helpful.

Srimati Basu and Eva Cherniavsky went above and beyond the call of friendship with their encouragement and willingness to read the entire manuscript. Srimati's deft editing skills and ability to discern the larger stakes of an argument have been invaluable. Kudos to her too for pioneering the concept of the "writing boot camp." The intellectual comraderie from sharing writing, fine cuisine, and libations that emerged during a Lexington weekend years ago (not to mention gales of laughter and the coinage of idiomatic expressions) has been a model for subsequent gatherings in Bloomington, Kitsap Peninsula, Plainfield, and Seattle. Eva's fierce commitment to the unionization of academic labor and advocacy for Palestinian sovereignty continue to be inspiring. Her theoretical acuity and sharp political analyses helped hone the arguments in this project. Thanks as well to Eva and Robyn for encouraging me to get the hell out of Dodge during my sabbatical. Enjoyable afternoon boot camps with them facilitated the completion of this book and aided in the processing, through humor, of the tragic, but farcical, nature of contemporary political life.

My extended family (biological and forged) have provided much support over the years. Sudesh and Samir Bose, my parents, nurtured in their children a curiosity about the world, respect for science, and the importance of contributing to one's community. Amaar and Mushtaq Ahangar, and Mona Bhan; Srimati Basu and Tiku Ravat; Amit, Avinash, and Simrun Bose, and Satinder Jawanda; Bharati, Kamal, and Saugato Datta; Carey Hattic and Suzanne Henry; Manjulika and Rajinder Koshal; Benjamin, Bipasa, Chris, and Mira

Nadon; Kevin Newsom and Radhika Parameswaran; Shay Bose and Flynn W. Picardal have my affection and appreciation for providing intellectual stimulation and creating many happy memories.

Finally, I have dedicated this book to Barbara Harlow. Quintessentially private and anti-sentimental, she would have abhorred a lengthy tribute. Suffice it to say, her former students, colleagues, and friends mourn her passing and miss her irony, sharp intellect, and facility at formulating dialectical sentences.

Portions of the introduction, chapters 2, 3, and 4 appeared as "Geopolitical Fetishism & Afghanistan," *Against the Current* 159 (July/August 2012); "A Cosmetic Cover for Occupation: The Beauty Academy of Kabul," *Against the Current* 142 (September/October 2009); "From Humanitarian Intervention to the Beautifying Mission: Afghan Women and Beauty Without Borders," *Genders* 51 (Spring 2010); "Canine Rescue, Civilian Casualties, and the Long Gulf War," *In/Visible War: The Culture of War in Twenty-First-Century America*, ed. Jon Simons and John Lucaites (Rutgers University Press, 2017); and "Without Osama: Tere Bin Laden and the War on Terror," *Covering Bin Laden: Global Media and the World's Most Wanted Man*, ed. Susan Jeffords and Fahad Yahya Al-Sumait (University of Illinois Press, 2015). I thank the editors at *Against the Current*, *Genders*, Rutgers University Press, and the University of Illinois Press for permission to reprint this material. I am also grateful to Heng for permission to reprint his cartoon "Afghanistan Strategy" from the *International New York Times*.

Notes

Notes to Introduction

1 I am sensitive to the criticism of the use of "America" and "Americans" to signify the US and its citizens, respectively, given that the terms also include Central and Latin America. Using "North America" in its stead risks criticism as well insofar as the term includes Canada and Mexico. In many parts of South Asia, the US is referred to as "America"—or more accurately, "Amreeka"—and I have stuck with this usage in spite of its obvious limitations.

2 Afghan casualty figures are taken from Neta C. Crawford's "Costs of War: Update on the Human Costs of War for Afghanistan and Pakistan, 2001 to mid-2016," Watson Institute, August 2016, accessed January 2, 2017, http://watson.brown .edu/costsofwar/files/cow/imce/papers/2016/War%20in%20Afghanistan%20 and%20Pakistan%20UPDATE_FINAL_corrected%20date.pdf. For US armed forces fatalities, see the Pentagon, May 5, 2017, accessed May 6, 2017, https://www .defense.gov/casualty.pdf.

3 For a breakdown of corporate ownership of the media, see "Who Owns What," *Columbia Journalism Review,* accessed May 7, 2017, http://www.cjr.org/resources / and "Who Owns the Media?" *Freepress,* accessed May 7, 2017, http://www .freepress.net/ownership/chart.

4 Jean Baudrillard, *Simulacra and Simulation,* trans. Sheila Glaser (Ann Arbor: University of Michigan Press, 1994), 1.

5 Gillian Whitlock, *Soft Weapons: Autobiography in Transit* (Chicago: University of Chicago Press, 2006), 3.

6 Edward Said, *Orientalism* (New York: Vintage Books, 1978), 11.

7 My focus in this book is on overt war. Of course, a perusal of US covert operations across the duration of the twentieth century reveals that armed conflict abroad more generally has been a normative part of the American experience. For an overview, see William Blum, *The CIA: A Forgotten History* (London and New Jersey: Zed Books, 1986) and *Killing Hope: U.S. Military and C.I.A. Interventions since World War II* (Monroe, Maine: Common Courage Press, 2004).

8 The three to one ratio is from Lee Shane's *Military Times* article, which cites the Congressional Research Service as a source. Lee Shane III, "Report: Contractors

Outnumber US Troops in Afghanistan 3-1," *Military Times*, August 17, 2016, accessed May 2, 2017, http://www.militarytimes.com/articles/crs-report -afghanistan-contractors. Anne Hagedorn gives the ten to one ratio in *The Invisible Soldiers: How America Outsourced Our Security* (New York: Simon & Schuster, 2014), 10.

9 Douglas A. Wissing, *Hopeless but Optimistic: Journeying Through America's Endless War in Afghanistan* (Bloomington: Indiana University Press, 2016), 35.

10 Karl Marx, *Capital: A Critique of Political Economy*, Vol. 1, trans. Ben Fowkes (New York: Penguin, 1990), 163.

11 William Pietz, "The Problem of the Fetish, I," *RES: Anthropology and Aesthetics*, no. 9 (Spring 1985): 5–17.

12 I am drawing on Robert K. Schaeffer's brilliant analysis of conflict discourse and temporality. See *Warpaths: The Politics of Partition* (New York: Hill & Wang, 1991).

13 David Harvey, *The New Imperialism* (New York: Oxford University Press, 2003).

14 Harvey, *The New Imperialism*, 29.

15 Harvey, *The New Imperialism*, 26.

16 Harvey, *The New Imperialism*, 27.

17 Harvey, *The New Imperialism*, 26.

18 Harvey, *The New Imperialism*, 26–27.

19 Harvey, *The New Imperialism*, 132–133.

20 See Laura E. Lyons, "Dole, Hawai'i, and the Question of Land under Globalization," *Cultural Critique and the Global Corporation*, ed. Purnima Bose and Laura E. Lyons (Bloomington: Indiana University Press, 2010), 64–101.

21 Kenneth Partridge, "Preface," *US National Debate Topic 2010-2011: The American Military Presence Overseas* (New York and Dublin: H.W. Wilson Company, 2010), xii.

22 Michael T. Klare, "Imperial Reach," *Nation*, April 7, 2005, accessed May 12, 2017, https://www.thenation.com/article/imperial-reach/.

23 In addition to Michael T. Klare, see Alexander Cooley, "US Bases and Democratization in Central Asia," *Orbis* v. 52 (Winter 2008): 65–90; Michael Mechanic, "Mission Creep," *Mother Jones*, August 22, 2008, accessed May 12, 2017, http://www.motherjones.com/politics/2008/08/mission-creep; Nick Turse, "The 700 Military Bases of Afghanistan," CBSNews, February 10, 2011, accessed May 12, 2017, http://www.cbsnews.com/2100-215_162-6193925.html and his "450 Bases and It's Not Over Yet," *Huffington Post,* February 13, 2012, accessed May 12, 2017, http://www.huffingtonpost.com/nick-turse/450-bases-and-its-not-ove_b _1273018.html.

24 Michael T. Klare, "Imperial Reach" and Nick Turse, "Base Desires in Afghanistan" TomDispatch.com, October 21, 2010, accessed May 12, 2017, http://www .tomdispatch.com/post/175310/tomgram%3A_nick_turse,_base_desires_in _afghanistan.

25 Klare, "Imperial Reach."

26 Nick Turse, "How Many Afghan Bases are There?" *American Conservative*, September 4, 2012, accessed May 12, 2017, http://www.theamericanconservative .com/articles/how-many-afghan-bases-are-there/.

27 Nick Turse, "450 Bases."

28 Nick Turse, "The 700 Military Bases."

29 David Vine, *Base Nation: How U.S. Military Bases Abroad Harm America and the World* (New York: Metropolitan Books, 2015), 7. Given that the 2014 bilateral

Security and Defense Cooperation Agreement between the US and Afghanistan includes a list of areas for US military use, these bases are likely in Kabul, Bagram, Mazar-e-Sharif, Herat, Kandahar, Shorab (Helmand), Gardez, Jalalabad, and Shindad (30). United States, "Security and Defense Cooperation Agreement Between the Islamic Republic of Afghanistan and the United States of America," September 30, 2014, accessed May 13, 2017, http://staging.afghanembassy.us /contents/2016/04/documents/Bilateral-Security-Agreement.pdf.

30 Qtd. by Turse, "450 Bases and It's Not Over Yet."

31 Wissing, *Hopeless but Optimistic*, 17.

32 Michael Shaw, "Rotor Wash, In/Visibility of the Afghan War, and My Excellent Weekend at Indiana U," April 16, 2012, accessed May 12, 2017, http://www .readingthepictures.org/2012/04/rotor-wash-invisibility-of-the-afghan-war-and-my -excellent-weekend-at-indiana-u/.

33 "Treaties," unlike "agreements," require ratification by the Senate by a two-thirds majority.

34 United States, "Security and Defense Cooperation Agreement Between the Islamic Republic of Afghanistan and the United States of America," September 30, 2014, accessed May 12, 2017, http://staging.afghanembassy.us/contents/2016/04 /documents/Bilateral-Security-Agreement.pdf. The US disavowal to establish permanent military bases is on page 2 of this agreement, and the reference to the US's continued right to exclusive use of military facilities occurs on page 11.

35 "Security and Defense," 28. Either party can terminate the agreement with two years' written notice (29).

36 Turse, "450 Bases."

37 Larry P. Goodson and Thomas H. Johnson, "U.S. Policy and Strategy Toward Afghanistan After 2014" (Carlisle Barracks: United States War Army College Press, 2014), 10.

38 Goodson, "U.S. Policy," 22.

39 Harvey, *The New Imperialism*, 19.

40 President Carter, State of the Union Speech, January 23, 1980, accessed May 9, 2017, http://www.jimmycarterlibrary.gov/documents/speeches/su80jec.phtml.

41 Qtd. by Sitaram Yechury, "America, Oil, and Afghanistan," *The Hindu Online*, October 13, 2001, accessed May 9, 2017, http://www.hindu.com/2001/10/13 /stories/05132524.htm.

42 In fact, the Clinton administration had also pursued negotiations with UNOCAL over a pipeline, ostensibly to bring different Mujahideen factions and the Taliban together over "the prospect of shared pipeline profits." See *The 9/11 Commission Report* (New York and London: W. W. Norton, no copyright), 111.

43 During the Bush administration, cozy relationships between government officials and the oil industry most probably facilitated negotiations. Ties between administration officials and the oil industry include US National Security Advisor Condoleezza Rice's membership on the board of directors of Chevron from 1991 to 2000; she famously had an oil tanker named after her till it was renamed "Altair Voyager" to deflect charges of impropriety. Secretary of Commerce Donald Evans and Secretary of Energy Stanley Abraham both worked for Tom Brown, an oil and gas exploration company. Vice President Dick Cheney was the CEO of Halliburton, a company that provides services such as drilling wells, building wells, and a host of other activities involved in oil and gas production. President George Bush himself hails from a family that has been in the oil business since

1950. The first Secretary of State in the Trump Administration, Rex Tillerson, was a former Exxon executive. The existence of these ties is not proof of individual corruption per se, but it does indicate the extent to which US political culture has become intertwined with corporate capitalism such that overlapping personnel and advisors, along with the proverbial revolving door, are the norm. See Ahmed Rashid's *Taliban* for a detailed account of negotiations over the oil and gas pipelines (London: Pan Macmillan Ltd., 2001). For ties between Bush administration officials and the energy industry, consult articles by Katty Kay in the *Guardian* ("Analysis: Oil and the Bush Cabinet," January 29, 2001, http://news.bbc.co.uk/2 /hi/americas/1138009.stm) and Kevin Phillips in *The Los Angeles Times* ("Bush Family Values: War, Wealth, Oil," February 8, 2004, http://www.commondreams .org/views04/0208-05.htm).

44 SIGAR, "Afghanistan's Oil, Gas, and Mineral Industries: $488 Million in U.S. Efforts Show Limited Progress Overall, and Challenges Prevent Further Investment and Growth," SIGAR 16-11 Audit Report, January 2016, accessed May 16, 2017, https://www.sigar.mil/pdf/audits/SIGAR-16-11-AR.pdf.

45 "United States Crude Oil Consumption by Year," IndexMundi, 2017, accessed May 15, 2017, https://www.indexmundi.com/energy/?country=us&product =oil&graph=consumption. For information on petroleum imports into the US, see the U.S. Energy Information Administration, "Frequently Asked Questions," April 4, 2017, accessed May 15, 2017, https://www.eia.gov/tools/faqs/faq .php?id=32&t=6.

46 Associated Press, "US 'Likely' Has Taken Over as the World's Top Oil Producer," *New York Times*, September 12, 2018, accessed September 23, 2018, https://www .nytimes.com/aponline/2018/09/12/us/ap-us-oil-production-us.html.

47 Dimitri Dolaberidze, "Kabul Launches Survey Work in TAPI Gas Pipeline Project," *Georgia Today*, February 27, 2017, accessed May 15, 2017, http:// georgiatoday.ge/news/5952/Kabul-Launches-Survey-Work-on-TAPI-Gas-Pipeline -Project.

48 Qtd. by James Risen, "US Identifies Vast Mineral Resources in Afghanistan," *New York Times,* June 13, 2010, accessed May 9, 2017, http://www.nytimes .com/2010/06/14/world/asia/14minerals.html?pagewanted=all.

49 SIGAR, "Afghanistan's Oil," Preface, no page. See also Keith Johnson, "U.S. Squandered $488 Million on Afghan Mining Projects," *Foreign Policy*, January 14, 2016, accessed May 17, 2017, http://foreignpolicy.com/2016/01/14/u-s-squanders -488-million-on-afghan-mining-projects-sigar/ and Antony Lowenstein, "Natural Resources Were Supposed to Make Afghanistan Rich. Here's What's Happening to Them," *Nation*, December 14, 2015, accessed May 17, 2017, https://www .thenation.com/article/resources-were-supposed-to-make-afghanistan-rich/.

50 See SIGAR, "Corruption in Conflict: Lessons from the U.S. Experience in Afghanistan," September 2016, accessed May 17, 2017, https://www.sigar.mil/. US enlisted military personnel, officers, and contractors have also been convicted of various kinds of fraud. See Julia Harte, "The Fraud of War: U.S. Troops in Iraq and Afghanistan Have Stolen Tens of Millions Through Bribery, Theft, and Rigged Contracts," *Slate*, May 5, 2015, accessed May 17, 2017, http://www.slate.com /articles/news_and_politics/politics/2015/05/u_s_troops_have_stolen_tens_of _millions_in_iraq_and_afghanistan_center_for.html.

51 Mark Landler and James Risen, "Trump Finds Reason for the U.S. to Remain in Afghanistan: Minerals," *New York Times*, July 25, 2017, accessed August 15, 2017,

https://www.nytimes.com/2017/07/25/world/asia/afghanistan-trump-mineral
-deposits.html.

52 M. Nazif Shahrani, "Introduction: The Impact of Four Decades of War and Violence on Afghan Society and Political Culture," *Modern Afghanistan: The Impact of 40 Years of War*, ed. M. Nazif Shahrani (Bloomington: Indiana University Press, 2018), 6.

53 SIGAR, Homepage, accessed May 17, 2017, https://www.sigar.mil/.

54 For an excellent analysis of reconstruction, see Fariba Nawa, *Afghanistan, Inc.: A Corpwatch Investigative Report*, (May 2, 2006), 28. Also available at: http://www
.corpwatch.org/article.php?id=13518.

55 Nawa, *Afghanistan, Inc.*, 8.

56 Qtd. by Nawa, *Afghanistan, Inc.*, 6.

57 Regarding the symbolic nature of current reconstruction efforts, Nick Cullather reminds us that they have their precursor in US development schemes articulated with "modernization" during the Cold War, which were equally disastrous. See his analysis of the 1940s Helmand Valley dam scheme, "Damming Afghanistan: Modernization in a Buffer State," *The Journal of American History* 89, no. 2 (September 2002): 512-537.

58 *Charlie Wilson's War*, directed by Mike Nichols, performed by Tom Hanks, Julia Roberts, and Philip Seymour Hoffman, (Universal Studios, 2007), film; Mohammad Yousaf and Mark Adkin, *Afghanistan—The Bear Trap: The Defeat of a Superpower* (Havertown, PA: Casemate, 1992, 2001); and Milton Bearden, *The Black Tulip: A Novel of War in Afghanistan* (New York: Random House Trade Paperbacks, 1998).

59 Gayle Tzemach Lemmon, *The Dressmaker of Khair Khana: Five Sisters, One Remarkable Family and the Woman Who Risked Everything to Keep Them Safe* (New York: HarperCollins, 2011) and Deborah Rodriguez and Kristin Ohlson, *Kabul Beauty School: And American Woman Goes Behind the Veil* (New York: Random House, 2007).

60 For a critique of the Feminist Majority Foundation's position on the intervention, see Ann Russo's "The Feminist Majority Foundation's Campaign to Stop Gender Apartheid: The Intersections of Feminism and Imperialism in the United States," *International Feminist Journal of Politics* 8, no. 4 (December 2006): 557–580.

61 Christine Sullivan, *Saving Cinnamon: The Amazing True Story of a Missing Military Puppy and the Desperate Mission to Bring Her Home* (New York: St. Martin's Griffin, 2009); Maria Goodavage, *Top Dog: The Story of the Marine Hero Lucca* (New York: New American Library, 2015); Jennifer Li Shotz, *Max: Best Friend, Hero, Marine* (New York: HarperCollins, 2015).

62 Lauren Berlant, *The Queen of America Goes to Washington City* (Durham, NC: Duke University Press, 1997), 21.

63 Mark Owen and Kevin Maurer, *No Easy Day: The Autobiography of a Navy Seal* (New York: Dutton, Penguin Group, 2012).

64 *Tere Bin Laden,* directed by Abhishek Sharma and produced by Pooja Shetty Deora and Aarti Shetty, (India: Walkwater Media, 2010), DVD.

65 Tom Engelhardt, *The End of Victory Culture: Cold War America and the Disillusioning of a Generation* (Amherst: University of Massachusetts Press, 2007), 5. "Although a racially grounded tale," Engelhardt writes, this plot "deflected attention from the racial horror story most central to the country's development— that of the African-American—and onto more satisfying borderlands of the imagination" (5).

66 Engelhardt, *The End of Victory Culture*, 313. Ashley Dawson and Malini Johar Schueller also remark on Bush's use of cowboy rhetoric in relation to the invasion of Afghanistan; see their "Introduction: Rethinking Imperialism Today," in their edited volume, *Exceptional State: Contemporary U.S. Culture and the New Imperialism* (Durham and London: Duke University Press, 2007), 14.

67 Dawson and Schueller, *Exceptional State*, 15.

68 Dawson and Schueller, *Exceptional State*, 15. For more on how American exceptionalism continues to haunt imperial mass culture, see the essays in Scott Laderman and Tim Gruenwald's edited volume, *Imperial Benevolence: U.S. Foreign Policy and American Popular Culture since 9/11* (Oakland: University of California Press, 2018).

69 Melani McAlister, *Epic Encounters: Culture, Media, and U.S. Interests in the Middle East, 1945-2000* (Berkeley and Los Angeles: University of California Press, 2001), 42.

70 Jill Dsis, "'Lost' Dog Brings Trump, Clinton Supporters Together in New Ad," CNN Media, November 7, 2016, accessed May 7, 2017, http://money.cnn .com/2016/11/07/media/pedigree-dog-election-ad/. It is not clear whether the spot, "A Vote for Good," is scripted or "documentary footage" of an actual experiment. The ad can be viewed on the CNN site. My gratitude to Megan Eaton Robb for bringing this spot to my attention.

Notes to Chapter 1

1 Chalmers Johnson, *Nemesis: The Last Days of the American Republic* (New York: Holt Paperbacks, 2006), 278.

2 Johnson, *Nemesis*, 278.

3 Susan Jeffords, *The Remasculinization of America: Gender and the Vietnam War* (Bloomington and Indiana: Indiana University Press, 1989), xi.

4 *Charlie Wilson's War*, directed by Mike Nichols (Universal Studios, 2007); Mohammad Yousaf and Mark Adkin, *Afghanistan—The Bear Trap: The Defeat of a Superpower,* (Havertown, PA: Casemate, 1992, 2001); and Milt Bearden, *The Black Tulip: A Novel of War in Afghanistan* (New York: Random House Trade Paperbacks, 1998). Please note that all references to Yousaf's and Bearden's texts will be cited parenthetically in the body of this chapter.

5 R.W. Connell and James W. Messerschmidt, "Hegemonic Masculinity: Rethinking the Concept," *Gender and Society* 19, no. 6 (December 2005): 832.

6 Bob Woodward, "U.S. Covert Aid to Afghans on the Rise," *Washington Post*, January 13, 1985, accessed November 20, 2017, https://www.washingtonpost .com/archive/politics/1985/01/13/us-covert-aid-to-afghans-on-the-rise/cf0e7891 -d900-4421-b72f-7760af19256d/?utm_term=.0c8c8750f282.

7 Rodric Braithwaite argues that the impact of the Stinger missiles on the battlefield was minimal in terms of changing the political calculus in Moscow, noting that Gorbachev had decided to withdraw a full year before their introduction. See his *Afgantsy: The Russians in Afghanistan 1979-89* (Oxford: Oxford University Press, 2011), 205. Jonathan Steele also shares this assessment. See his "10 Myths About Afghanistan," *Guardian* (US edition), September 27, 2011, accessed April 2, 2017, https://www.theguardian.com/world/2011/sep/27/10-myths-about-afghanistan.

8 Qtd. by William Schneider, "The Vietnam Syndrome Mutates. *The Atlantic*, April 2006, accessed November 20, 2017, https://www.theatlantic.com/magazine /archive/2006/04/the-vietnam-syndrome-mutates/304891/.

9 The key text here is Judith Butler, *Gender Trouble: Feminism and the Subversion of Identity* (New York: Routledge, 2006).

10 Douglas Schrock and Michael Schwalbe, "Men, Masculinity, and Manhood Acts," *The Annual review of Sociology* 35 (2009): 279. See also Demetrakis Z. Demetriou, "Connell's Concept of Hegemonic Masculinity: A Critique," *Theory and Society* 30, no. 3 (June 2001): 337-361.

11 Schrock and Schwalbe, "Men," 280.

12 See also Coll, *Ghost Wars*, 91. Evidently, Herring knew about and did not mind Charlie's traveling companions, noting "If a man wants to be with you, it doesn't matter what else he's doing" as she reveals in the documentary, *The True Story of Charlie Wilson,* produced by Aaron Bowden (2007, History Channel/Wild Eye Productions, 2007), DVD. In Bowden's documentary, more than one Pakistani intelligence agent expresses bafflement by Wilson's companions; Colonel Sultan Amir Imam admits: "I asked the CIA people, I said 'Who are these women?' They said this woman is a girlfriend. It was very strange. . . such an old man having such a young girlfriend, but probably only possible in the United States."

13 Rodric Braithwaite disputes the commonplace idea that the Soviets deliberately disguised landmines as toys, in part based on the assessment of the Mine Action Coordination Centre of Afghanistan. He speculates that the story arose as a combination of "western propaganda" and based on the fact that "butterfly mines" are made of "brightly coloured plastic," which "were directly copies from the American Dragontooth BLU-43/B and BLU-44/B mines, used in very large numbers in Indo-China." See Rodric Braithwaite, *Afgantsy: The Russians in Afghanistan 1979-89*, (Oxford: Oxford University Press, 2011), 235. In the final analysis, the Russians' intentions do not matter. The end result remained: Afghan children maimed and killed from lethal objects they had mistaken for toys.

14 Loch K. Johnson, "Covert Action and Accountability: Decision-Making for America's Secret Foreign Policy," *International Studies Quarterly*, Vol. 33, No. 1 (Mar., 1989): 87.

15 Qtd. by Gregory F. Treverton, "Covert Action and Open Society," *Foreign Affairs* 65, no. 5 (Summer, 1987): 996.

16 Johnson, "Covert Action," 88.

17 In the interviews featured on the DVD of the Hollywood blockbuster, Tom Hanks and the screenwriter Aaron Sorkin, whose credits include *A Few Good Men* and the *West Wing*, recount being riveted by George Crile's 2003 *Charlie Wilson's War* and feeling a compulsion to make a film based on the book. Hanks purchased the film rights to the text, and Sorkin approached Hanks about writing the screenplay. Mike Nichols (whose directing credits number *The Graduate, Who's Afraid of Virginia Wolfe,* and *Catch-22)* joined them, and Julia Roberts and Philip Seymour Hoffman signed on to play Joanne Herring and Gust Avrakotos respectively. In the bonus scenes, these talented individuals recount their amazement that neither had they heard of Charlie Wilson before reading Crile's book, nor had they known of US covert operations in Afghanistan during the eighties. Sorkin explains, "Charlie is a wonderful, brilliant flawed hero who put together this war that no one had heard about, the biggest covert war in US history."

18 Treverton, "Covert Action," 98.

19 Treverton, "Covert Action," 98.

20 For an analysis of the complexity of repression and Cold War geopolitics in El Salvador during the 80s, see Jeffrey L. Gould's *Solidarity Under Siege: The*

Salvadoran Labor Movement, 1970-1990 (Cambridge, UK: Cambridge University Press, 2019).

21 Treverton, "Covert Action," 116.

22 How Israel has acquired a large cache of Soviet weapons, the film does not reveal, though Crile explains that the Israelis had seized the arms from the Palestinian Liberation Organization when they invaded Lebanon in 1982 (131).

23 Qtd. by Michael V. Seitzinger, "Conducting Foreign Relations without Authority: The Logan Act," *Congressional Research Service*, March 11, 2015, accessed May 21, 2017, https://fas.org/sgp/crs/misc/RL33265.pdf.

24 For the history of the Logan Act and references to it in judicial decisions and by the State Department, see Seitzinger's "Conducting." Critics have accused private citizens such as Jane Fonda, Reverend Jesse Jackson, and Ross Perot of violating the Logan Act for their trips to Vietnam, Syria, and Southeast Asia respectively, but none of these individuals was officially sanctioned for their activities. The crucial distinctions between them and Wilson, however, are twofold: first, his status as an elected official could contribute to the perception that he was acting as an agent for the state even though he did not have the authority to negotiate weapons agreements; and, two, whereas the other private citizens conducted their business publically and could, thus, be challenged and held accountable for their actions, Wilson did not divulge the real purpose of his trips, placing him outside the purvey of any official or public scrutiny and all but eliminating the potential that he could be held responsible for his unauthorized negotiations. Unauthorized private citizens who initiate and conduct negotiations with foreign governments and agents represent only their individual convictions and not those of the larger social collective. As Loch K. Johnson points out in his history and analysis of the decision-making process for covert operations, a system of checks and balances between the executive and legislative branches vets those covert actions deemed "important" (95-96). Since the passage of the Hughes-Ryan Act in 1974—requiring a timely presidential finding for covert operations conducted by the CIA—and the Intelligence Oversight Act in 1980—which expanded the requirement for a presidential finding to *all* important covert operations and encouraged prior notification to Congress—the legislative branch has recognized the desirability of subjecting covert operations to congressional oversight and enabling its members to register their displeasure at particular operations and to curb them as deemed necessary (Johnson 97-98). Of course, even with such safeguards in place, as the Iran-Contra affair demonstrated, overzealous and lawless government officials, CIA agents, and private citizens have felt empowered to bypass such decision-making processes. The actual Wilson, in the DVD's bonus scenes, even admits to being a "rogue Congressman" who worked with a "rogue CIA agent" to aid the Mujahideen.

25 Coll, *Ghost Wars*, 101.

26 Coll, *Ghost Wars*, 131.

27 Eva Cherniavsky, *Neocitizenship: Political Culture After Democracy* (New York: New York University Press, 2017), 149. (original emphasis)

28 Chasing the Frog, "Charlie Wilson's War," No date, accessed April 2, 2017, http://www.chasingthefrog.com/reelfaces/charliewilsonswar.php.

29 Coll, *Ghost Wars*, 93.

30 Coll, *Ghost Wars*, 93.

31 For details of attacks inside the Soviet Central Republics, see Coll's chapter "Don't Make it Our War" in *Ghost Wars* and Brigadier Mohammad Yousaf's very precise

recollections in his chapter "Bear Baiting" in *Afghanistan—The Bear Trap*. If these cross-border incursions and sabotage missions had been discovered at that time, they could have ignited a full-scale war between the two superpowers.

32 Norman A. Graebner, Richard Dean Burns, and Joseph M. Siracusa describe how Reagan's virulent anti-communism and single-minded insistence on reading insurgency movements in Central America and Africa as puppeteered by the Soviet Union rather than motivated by local disparities in wealth and access to power resulted in disapproving editorials in *Der Spiegel, Frankfurter Allgemeine Zeitung, Il Messaggero, De Telegraaf, Le Monde*, and *The Sunday Time*s. Moreover, Europeans largely opposed Reagan's sanctions against the USSR in retaliation for General Wojciech Jaruzelski's crackdown against the Solidarity movement in Poland. President Reagan's inflated rhetoric of the military threat posed by the Soviets, the three authors note, also helped energize the anti-nuclear movement across Europe and the United States. See their chapter "Ronald Reagan and the Second Cold War," *Reagan, Bush, Gorbachev: Revisiting the End of the Cold War* (Westport: Praeger Security International, 2008).

    Responding to Reagan's characterization of the Soviet Union as an "evil empire," the Russian Orthodox Patriarch issued the important reminder that the Russia had borne great sacrifices during World War II and "had never waged war against the United States and does not intend to lift up a sword against it in the future" (qtd. in Graebner et al 52). By 1984, Reagan had softened his rhetoric against the Soviet Union in response to pressure from public opinion polls and editorials in the print media, and the advice of his Secretary of State, George Schultz.

33 Ronald Reagan, "Address before a Joint Session of the Congress on the State of the Union," February 6, 1985, accessed May 21, 2017, http://www.presidency.ucsb .edu/ws/?pid=38069.

34 Coll, *Ghost Wars*, 126-127.

35 Tomdispatch, "Chalmers Johnson, An Imperialist Comedy," *TomDispatch*, A Project of The Nation Institute, January 6, 2008, accessed April 3, 2017, http:// www.tomdispatch.com/post/174877/chalmers_johnson_an_imperialist_comedy.

36 Chalmers Johnson, "Imperialist Propaganda: Second Thoughts on Charlie Wilson's War," TomDispatch.com, January 6, 2008, accessed May 21, 2017, http:// www.tomdispatch.com/post/174877/%20chalmers_johnson_an_imperialist _comedy.

37 DeGuerin's legal team also managed to exonerate Robert Durst, the real estate heir who, as Herring explains, "killed his neighbor and cut him into pieces." Joanne King Herring and Nancy Dorman-Hickson, *Diplomacy and Diamonds: My Wars from the Ballroom to the Battlefield* (New York: Center Street, 2012), 7.

38 No author, "Socialite Joanne Herring Wins 'War,'" *New York Daily News*, December 22, 2007, accessed April 2, 2017, http://www.nydailynews.com /entertainment/gossip/socialite-joanne-herring-wins-war-article-1.276411. The shelf life of stinger missiles is a subject of debate. While some analysts believe the missiles are operational for ten to twelve years, others note that stingers reacquired through buy-back programs by the US in Afghanistan consistently work. See Scott Schuger's "Missing Missile Mystery: O Stinger, Where is Thy Death?" *Slate*, December 5, 2001, accessed December 29, 2018, https://slate.com/news-and -politics/2001/12/what-happened-to-afghanistan-s-missiles.html. (See Coll for an account of the US government's attempts to buy back stinger missiles.) A market for stingers, along with other "man-portable air defense systems," exists. From 1973

to 2014, David Wood writes, at "least thirty civilian aircraft have been downed by shoulder-fired missiles." See his "For Civilian Airliners, Shoulder-Fired Missiles still a Global Threat," *HuffPost*, July 23, 2014, accessed December 29, 2018, https://www.huffingtonpost.com/2014/07/23/civilian-airplanes-missiles_n_5614040.html.

39 For an appraisal of the end of the Cold War, see Norman A. Graebner, Richard Dean Burns, and Joseph M. Siracusa's *Reagan, Bush, Gorbachev: Revisiting the End of the Cold War*. The authors credit Gorbachev with the vision and personal courage to break through "the Cold War's ideological straitjacket that had paralyzed Moscow and Washington's ability to resolve their differences" (146). Their account suffers, however, from a tendency identified by Joe Slovo in his nuanced discussion paper on the collapse of the Soviet bloc, "Has Socialism Failed?" which is to posit socialism itself as being responsible for the "distortions" suffered under these regimes (Joe Slovo, "Has Socialism Failed?" Marxists Internet Archive, 1989, accessed May 21, 2017, https://www.marxists.org/subject/africa/slovo/1989/socialism-failed.htm). Graebner, Burns, and Siracusa opine: "Marx was not responsible for all the human error committed in his name, but his writings justified a system that disregarded human worth and destroyed the normal incentives for personal achievement" (48). It is difficult to reconcile this claim with the humanism that emanates from Marx's eloquent explanation of such concepts as commodity fetishism and alienation in *Capital* and the *Economic and Philosophic Manuscripts of 1844*.

40 Gillian Whitlock, *Soft Weapons: Autobiography in Transit* (Chicago: University of Chicago Press, 2006), 21.

41 What to call the 1857 rebellion is still a matter of debate, as historians deliberate over whether it constituted localized revolts or the precursor of the national liberation struggle. By positing the events as "a struggle between a metropolitan power and native insurgency," Gavin Rand observes, they miss "the complexity of the imperial military apparatus" which governed primarily by force through an army that relied on native soldiers. See his article, "'Martial Races' and 'Imperial Subjects': Violence and Governance in Colonial India, 1857-1914," *European Review of History* 13, no. 1 (Mar 2006): 1-20.

42 Sir George MacMunn, *The Martial Races of India* (London: Sampson Low, Marston & Co. Ltd., 1933), 2.

43 Kaushik Roy, "Race and Recruitment in the Indian Army: 1880-1918," *Modern Asian Studies* 47, no. 4 (2013): 1312-1313.

44 Roy, "Race," 1312. Roy notes that the discourse of martial races was not stable and riven with contradictions, "partly because its chief advocates were military officers and not trained anthropologists" and that it changed according to prevailing political circumstances. Although Kashmiris inhabited a mountainous region, he notes that they were not included in the martial races. Their exclusion from this category, Mona Bhan has suggested, probably arises from a close identification of Kashmir, at that time, with Brahmanism and the construction of high-caste Hindus as effeminate (personal conversation).

45 For the classic analysis of gender in colonial India, see Mrinalini Sinha's *Colonial Masculinity: The 'Manly Englishman' and the 'Effeminate Bengali' in the Late Nineteenth Century* (Manchester: Manchester U Press, 1995). See also Heather Streets' *Martial Races: The Military, Race and Masculinity in British Imperial Culture, 1857-1914* (Manchester: Manchester University Press, 2010).

46 Stephen Philip Cohen, *The Idea of Pakistan* (Washington DC: The Brookings Institution Press, 2004), 101.

47 After joining the Baghdad Pact in 1955, the Pakistanis would turn to the Americans to provide paradigms for training soldiers and restructuring the armed forces. See Cohen's chapter "The Army's Pakistan" in *The Idea of Pakistan*.

48 Cohen, *The Idea*, 98. He contends that these percentages have remained fairly stable over time.

49 Cohen, *The Idea*, 103-104. See also footnote 11 of chapter 3 on page 341.

50 Yousaf, *Bear Trap*, "Publisher's Note," no page.

51 Yousaf's memoir contains no citations.

52 Michael Cherniavsky, "Corporal Hitler, General Winter and the Russian Peasant," *The Yale Review* LI, no. 4 (Summer 1962): 548.

53 Cherniavsky, "Corporal Hitler," 549.

54 Cherniavsky, "Corporal Hitler," 548-549.

55 See the chapter "Organization, Armament, and Training of the Limited Contingent of Soviet Forces and Government of Afghanistan Armed Forces," in The Russian General Staff, *The Soviet-Afghan War: How a Superpower Fought and Lost*, trans. and ed. Lester W. Grau and Michael A. Gress (Lawrence, Kansas: University of Kansas Press, 2002). While the general perception remains that the Mujahideen defeated the Soviet Army, as Rodric Braithwaite points out, the 40th Army "won all its major battles and never lost a post to the enemy: a record which consoled its commanders." See his *Afgantsy*, 145.

56 Braithwaite, *Afgantsy*, 174.

57 See Braithwaite's chapter "Soldiering" in *Afgantsy*, for a description of bullying, *dedovshchina*.

58 Braithwaite, *Afgantsy*, 190-191. Braithwaite reports that most soldiers quit their habits after demobilization. These conditions are corroborated in Svetlana Alexievich's poignant and wrenching *Zinky Boys: Soviet Voices from the Afghanistan War*, an oral history of Soviet conscripts, their surviving family members, and civilian and medical personnel that also details the psychological toll of the conflict on these participants. Svetlana Alexievich, *Zinky Boys: Soviet Voices from the Afghanistan War*, trans. Julia and Robin Whitby (New York and London: W.W. Norton & Company, Inc., 1992).

59 Of course, the Soviet Union was racially and ethnically diverse. Many of the Soviet troops initially posted to Afghanistan were selected on the basis of their Central Asian backgrounds under the assumption that Afghans would be more sympathetic to a culturally similar occupying force. Later Soviet soldiers were primarily drawn from the non-Islamic republics of the USSR (Russia, Belorussia, Moldavia, Ukraine, Georgia, Armenia and the Baltic States) because they were perceived as being more reliable (Alexievich, *Zinky Boys*, xvi).

60 The Russian General Staff, *Soviet-Afghan War*, 23.

61 Troop estimates are based on the Braithwaite and the Russian General Staff. Yousaf puts the figure at 85,000 (*Bear Trap*, 44). See Braithwaite for more on the social class background of Soviet conscripts. Braithwaite notes that Soviet soldiers had a better rapport with Afghan peasants than the NATO soldiers currently deployed in Afghanistan because of their shared experiences of rural poverty (*Afgantsy*, 181).

62 The Russian General Staff, *Soviet-Afghan War*, xix.

63 Yousaf, *Bear Trap*, 103. See chapter 6, "The Pipeline," for a description of the distribution of aid. In 1987, the percentage allocation of weapons and ammunition

to the Seven Parties was: Hekmatyar 18-20%; Rabbani 18-19%; Sayaf 17-18%; Khalis 13-15%; Nabi 13-15%, Gailani 10-11%, and Mujaddadi 3-5% (105). Ahmad Shah Masoud, who, in Braithwaite's estimation was the only Mujahideen commander interested in institution building, received very little aid (*Afgantsy*, 185).

64 Coll, *Ghost Wars*, 101.

65 Yousaf, *Bear Trap*, 85. According to Yousaf, when he "queried how and why the Indians sold weapons that they knew would be used against their friends the Soviets, the CIA officer replied 'The Indians are mean bastards, not trustworthy at all. For money they would even sell their mothers.'" (85).

66 Coll, *Ghost Wars*, 48.

67 Qtd. in Coll, *Ghost Wars*, 158.

68 Coll, *Ghost Wars*, 160.

69 Coll, *Ghost Wars*, 159.

70 Yet the comparison is not without its ambiguity: great warrior the original Alexander might have been, but his venture on the subcontinent ultimately ended poorly given his death on his return journey.

71 Tim Weiner, "Two Senior C.I.A. Officials Lose Jobs in Spy Case Fallout," *New York Times*, October 13, 1994, accessed March 30, 2017, http://www.nytimes .com/1994/10/13/us/two-senior-cia-officials-lose-jobs-in-spy-case-fallout.html.

72 Weiner, "Two Senior," *New York Times*. For details on the Snitch Fax, see Tim Weiner, "C.I.A. Officer's Suit Tells Tale of Betrayal and Disgrace," *New York Times*, September 1, 1996, accessed March 30, 2017, http://www.nytimes .com/1996/09/01/us/cia-officer-s-suit-tells-tale-of-betrayal-and-disgrace.html and Mark Riebling, *Wedge: From Pearl Harbor to 9/11: How the Secret War Between the FBI and CIA has endangered National Security* (New York: Simon and Schuster, 2010), 446.

73 See Tim Weiner's interview, "Why I Spied; Aldrich Ames," *New York Times*, July 31, 1994, accessed March 31, 2017, http://www.nytimes.com/1994/07/31 /magazine/why-i-spied-aldrich-ames.html?pagewanted=all.

74 See Amir Wasim, "Ojhri Camp Tragedy Lives on: Cause Remains Undisclosed," *Dawn,* April 10, 2007, accessed April 1, 2017, https://www.dawn.com/news /241557; Amir Wasim, "20 Years On, Ojhri Camp Truth Remains Locked Up," *Dawn*, April 11, 2008, accessed April 1, 2017, https://www.dawn.com/news /297623; and Shaikh Aziz, "The Ojhri Camp Disaster—Who's to Blame?" *Dawn*, February 7, 2017, accessed April 1, 2017, https://www.dawn.com /news/1237794.

75 Interview: Milt Bearden, "Hunting Bin Laden," *Frontline*, first broadcast in April 1999; updated and broadcast on September 13, 2001, accessed April 2, 2017, http://www.pbs.org/wgbh/pages/frontline/shows/binladen/interviews/bearden .html.

76 Jonathan Steele, *Ghosts of Afghanistan: The Haunted Battleground* (Berkeley: Counterpoint, 2011), 136.

77 Qtd. in Steele, *Ghosts of Afghanistan*, 131.

78 Jonathan Steele, *Ghosts of Afghanistan*, 136.

79 George W. Bush, "Address to the United Nations General Assembly," *Selected Speeches of President George W. Bush, 2001-2008*, November 10, 2001, (pages 86-87), accessed June 11, 2017, https://georgewbush-whitehouse.archives.gov/infocus /bushrecord/documents/Selected_Speeches_George_W_Bush.pdf.

80 Stephen M. Grenier, "Framing the War in Afghanistan." *Coalition Challenges in Afghanistan: The Politics of Alliance*, eds. Stephen M. Grenier and Gale A. Mattox (Stanford University Press, 2015), 1. [online edition]

81 Abdulkader Sinno, "Partisan Intervention and the Transformation of Afghanistan's Civil War," *American Historical Review* (December 2015): 1812.

82 Sinno, "Partisan," 1816.

83 Sinno, "Partisan," 1816-1817.

Notes to Chapter 2

1 Opportunities to present portions of this chapter at the 2014 Tepoztlán Institute for the Transnational History of the Americas, Ohio State University, and the University of Kentucky were helpful in conceptualizing this chapter. In particular, Franci Chassen-Lopez, Rachel O'Toole, Paul Bonín-Rodríguez, and Adam Warren provided constructive feedback. In addition, I am grateful to Nur Amali Ibrahim for reading suggestions on the relationship between capitalism and Islam.

2 Gayle Tzemach Lemmon, The Dressmaker of Khair Khana: Five Sisters, One Remarkable Family and the Woman Who Risked Everything to Keep Them Safe (New York: HarperCollins, 2011) and Deborah Rodriguez and Kristin Ohlson, *Kabul Beauty School: An American Woman Goes Behind the Veil* (New York: Random House, 2007). Please note that all citations to these two texts will be noted parenthetically in the body of this chapter. Other Western women have also written books on Afghan women in recent years. Examples include Saira Shah's The Storyteller's Daughter (New York: Random House, 2003) and Åsne Seierstad's The Bookseller of Kabul (New York: Back Bay Books, 2002).

3 Gayatri Chakravorty Spivak, "Can the Subaltern Speak?" in *Marxism and the Interpretation of Culture*, ed. Cary Nelson and Lawrence Grossberg (Urbana and Chicago: University of Illinois Press, 1988), 297. Anila Daulatzai cautions against the limitations of analyzing current realities in Afghanistan solely through the category of "gender," which tends to obscure the historical and political genealogies of suffering, themselves long products of military interventions and the policies of international aid agencies. See her "The Discursive Occupation of Afghanistan," *British Journal of Middle Eastern Studies* 35, no. 3 (December 2008): 419–435. For a gloss on critical concepts in post-colonial feminism and their bearing on the US intervention in Afghanistan, see Kevin J. Ayotte and Mary E. Husain's "Securing Afghan Women: Neocolonialism, Epistemic Violence, and the Rhetoric of the Veil," *NWSA Journal* 17, no. 3 (Fall 2005): 112–133. For a cogent analysis of media coverage of the US intervention in relation to "saving" Afghan women, see Carol A. Stabile and Deepa Kumar's "Unveiling Imperialism: Media, Gender and the War on Afghanistan," *Media, Culture & Society* 27, no. 5 (2005): 765–782.

4 Anne McClintock, *Imperial Leather: Race, Gender and Sexuality in the Colonial Contest* (New York and London: Routledge Inc., 1995), 41.

5 I am paraphrasing Ananya Roy's gloss on the iconicity of the Third World woman, who becomes a signifier for global poverty and the site for investing both empathy and capital. See her *Poverty Capitalism: Microfinance and the Making of Development* (New York and London: Routledge, 2010), 33.

6 Lila Abu-Lughod, "Do Muslim Women Really Need Saving? Anthropological Reflections on Cultural Relativism and Its Others," *American Anthropologist* 104, no. 3 (September 2002): 783–790 and Miriam Cooke, "Saving Brown Women,"

Signs: Journal of Women in Culture and Society 28, no. 1 (Autumn 2002): 468–470. Jasbir Puar extends the analysis of women's rescue, demonstrating how imperial discourses assimilate queer desire in complicated ways both constructing queer subjects as objects of humanitarian intervention and pathologizing Muslim men as terrorists on the basis of projections of queer identity. See her *Terrorist Assemblages: Homonationalism in Queer Times* (Durham and London: Duke University Press, 2007). I take up her analysis in chapter 4 on constructions of Osama bin Laden.

7 Spivak, "Can the Subaltern Speak?," 297.

8 Cooke, "Saving Brown Women," 469.

9 Katherine Mayo, *Mother India* (New York: Harcourt, 1927), 22. For an excellent analysis of the controversy surrounding the publication of this book, see Mrinalini Sinha's *Specters of Mother India: The Global Restructuring of an Empire* (Durham and London: Duke University Press, 2006).

10 Purnima Bose, *Organizing Empire: Individualism, Collective Agency & India* (Durham and London: Duke University Press, 2003), 112.

11 David Harvey, *The New Imperialism* (Oxford: Oxford University Press, 2003), 144.

12 Harvey, *New Imperialism*, 19.

13 This latter distinction perhaps accounts for the heavy toll that modern warfare takes on civilians. Eighty percent of the casualties of modern warfare, according to Amnesty International, are civilian, a fact obscured by the use of terms such as "smart bombs" and "surgical strikes," which imply the precise elimination of military targets with minimum "collateral damage." Amnesty International, *It's About Time! Human Rights Are Women's Rights* (New York: Amnesty International Publications, 1995), 29.

14 Statista, "Percentage Distribution of Population in the United States in 2015 and 2060, by Race and Hispanic Origin," 2018, accessed September 28, 2018, https://www.statista.com/statistics/270272/percentage-of-us-population-by-ethnicities/.

15 Statista, "Distribution of Active-Duty Enlisted Women and Men in the U.S. Military in 2016, by Race and Ethnicity," 2018, accessed September 28, 2018, https://www.statista.com/statistics/214869/share-of-active-duty-enlisted-women-and-men-in-the-us-military/.

16 Laura Wides, "Fewer Foreign Nationals Enlisting in US Military Services," *Boston Globe*, April 17, 2005, accessed July 25, 2016, http://www.freerepublic.com/focus/f-news/1385607/posts.

17 The figure of women's military participation, 20%, has remained stable over the last decade. "Women in the United States Military," accessed July 25, 2016, http://usmilitary.about.com/od/womeninthemilitary/.

18 Elaheh Rostami-Povey, *Afghan Women: Identity & Invasion* (London and New York: Zed Books, 2007), 4.

19 CIA World Factbook, "South Asia: Afghanistan," last updated July 10, 2019, accessed July 22, 2019, https://www.cia.gov/library/publications/the-world-factbook/geos/af.html.

20 Rostami-Povey, *Afghan Women*, 23.

21 Rob Schultheis, "Afghanistan's Forgotten Women," *Genders* 28 (1998), accessed July 25, 2016, https://www.atria.nl/ezines/IAV_606661/IAV_606661_2010_51/g27_afw.html.

22 Thomson Reuters Foundation, "The World's Most Dangerous Countries for Women 2018," accessed September 27, 2018, http://poll2018.trust.org/.

23 Institute for Women's Policy Research, "Pay Equity & Discrimination," accessed September 28, 2018, https://iwpr.org/issue/employment-education-economic -change/pay-equity-discrimination/.

24 Gayle Tzemach Lemmon, "Entrepreneurship," accessed June 5, 2014, http://www .gaylelemmon.com/entrepreneurship/.

25 Ericka Beckman, *Capital Fictions: The Literature of Latin America's Export Age* (Minneapolis and London: University of Minnesota Press, 2013), viii.

26 Beckman, *Capital Fictions*, xi.

27 Robert Reich convincingly argues against the conflation of capitalism and democracy. See his "How Capitalism is Killing Democracy," *Foreign Policy*, October 12, 2007, accessed July 25, 2016, https://foreignpolicy.com/2009/10/12 /how-capitalism-is-killing-democracy/.

28 For more on corporate personhood, see Purnima Bose and Laura E. Lyons, "Introduction: Life Writing and Corporate Personhood," *Biography* 37, no. 1 (Winter 2014): i–xvii.

29 Beckman, *Capital Fictions*, xi.

30 See Srimati Basu's "V is for Veil; V is for Ventriloquism: Global Feminisms in *The Vagina Monologues*" for an excellent analysis of *The Vagina Monologues'* appropriation of Afghan women's experiences [*Frontiers: A Journal of Women's Studies* 31, no. 1 (2010): 31–62].

31 See Andrew Hartman, "'The Red Template': US Policy in Soviet-Occupied Afghanistan," *Third World Quarterly* 23, no. 3 (June, 2002): 467–489.

32 Jimmy Carter, "State of the Union Address 1980," Jimmy Carter Library, last modified March 30, 2016; accessed July 31, 2016, http://www.jimmycarterlibrary .gov/documents/speeches/su80jec.phtml.

33 Namely, Kazakhstan, Kyrgyzstan, Tajikistan, Turkmenistan, and Uzbekistan.

34 Whether the Soviets' intervention in Afghanistan initially qualified as an "invasion" is subject to debate insofar as President Noor Mohammed Taraki requested, in March 1979, the presence of Soviet ground troops to aid the Afghan army in its counterinsurgency efforts against the Mujahideen. Taraki was eventually overthrown and killed by his own Deputy Prime Minister Hafizullah Amin. Yet Amin also expressed his appreciation for Soviet assistance, noting, "The Soviets supply my country with economic and military aid, but at the same time they respect our independence and our sovereignty. They do not interfere in our domestic affairs" (qtd. in William Blum, *Killing Hope: U.S. Military and C.I.A. Interventions Since World War II* [Monroe: Common Courage Press, 2004, 342]). In spite of these sentiments, the Soviet military force stormed the presidential palace and Amin was shot dead and replaced with Babrak Karmal, the former vice president and deputy prime minister in the 1978 revolutionary government. Even the *Washington Post* admitted, "There was no [State Department] charge that the Soviets have invaded Afghanistan, since the troops apparently were invited" (qtd. in Blum, 342).

35 For casualty figures, see Noor Ahmad Khalidi's "Afghanistan: Demographic Consequences of War, 1978-1987," (*Central Asian Survey* 10, no. 3 [1991]: 101–126) and for the migration rate, see Aideen Aisha Rahimi's "The Afghan Exodus: Oral Histories of Afghan Refugees During the 1980s Soviet Occupation of Afghanistan" (master's thesis, California State University, Sacramento, 2009: 3). Rahimi's thesis is available at http://scholarworks.calstate.edu/bitstream /handle/10211.9/255/Aisha%20Thesis%20part%202%5B1%5D.pdf?sequence=1. Accessed July 31, 2016.

Rodric Braithwaite reveals the strange historical irony about the Mi-24 attack helicopters, which the US now outsources, along with pilots, from the Russian company Vertical-T to supply American Special Forces (*Afgantsy* 198).

36 Rüdiger Schöch, "Afghan refugees in Pakistan during the 1980s: Cold War politics and registration practice," UNHCR, Research Paper #157 (June 2008): 1.

37 See the head of the Afghan Bureau of the Inter-Services Intelligence from 1983–1987, Brigadier Mohammad Yousaf's account of covert operations in his memoir, written with Mark Adkin, *Afghanistan—The Bear Trap: The Defeat of a Superpower* (Havertown, PA: Casemate, 1992, 2001).

38 George Criles's *Charlie Wilson's War* (New York: Grove Press, 2003) and the film of the same name (Universal Studios 2007) credit Representative Charlie Wilson with increasing the appropriations for covert operations, making no mention of William Casey's pivotal role. Other sources such as Steve Coll's *Ghost Wars: The Secret History of the CIA, Afghanistan, and Bin Laden* (New York: Penguin, 2004) assign a minimal role to Wilson and a major one to Casey.

39 Since the 1980s, the Deobandi movement has become influential in Afghanistan, partly as a result of the establishment of madrasas in Pakistan, where many of the Taliban were initially educated. This tradition originated as an anti-colonial movement in north India, but developed into a revivalist strand of Sunni Islam that emphasized literal and puritanical interpretations of the religion.

40 Eqbal Ahmad, *Confronting Empire: Interviews with David Barsamian* (Cambridge: South End Press, 2000), 44. See also Ahmed Rashid's *Taliban: The Story of the Afghan Warlords* (London: Pan MacMillan, 2001) and Coll's *Ghost Wars*.

41 See Rashid's *Taliban* and his masterful *Descent into Chaos: The United States and the Failure of Nation Building in Pakistan, Afghanistan, and Central Asia* (New York: Viking, 2008).

42 Rashid, *Taliban*, 217–218.

43 Rashid, *Taliban*, 218.

44 Purnima Bose and Laura E. Lyons, eds., "Introduction: Toward a Critical Corporate Studies," *Cultural Critique and the Global Corporation* (Bloomington: Indiana University Press, 2010), iv.

45 Michael Denning, "Wageless Life," *New Left Review* 66 (Nov/Dec 2010): 80.

46 Denning, "Wageless Life," 80.

47 Mahmood Mamdani, *Good Muslim, Bad Muslim: America, the Cold War, and the Roots of Terror* (New York: Doubleday, 2004).

48 As a side note, it is worth mentioning that the shopkeepers who are Kamila's customers decide to source their ready-made items from her rather than their regular Pakistani suppliers. They, thus, opt for an import-substitution model of development, which seems like a better route given the dynamics between peripheral, semi-peripheral, and core economies described, albeit with different nuances, by both Andre Gunder Frank ("The Development of Underdevelopment," *Monthly Review* 18, no. 4 (September 1966): 17–31) and Immanuel Wallerstein ("The Rise and Future Demise of the World Capitalist System: Concepts for Comparative Analysis," *Comparative Studies in Society and History* 16, no. 4 [September 1974]: 387–415).

49 Amira Mittermaier summarizes the literature on the relationship between Islam and capitalism in her "Trading with God: Islam, Calculation, Excess," *A Companion to the Anthropology of Religion*, first edition, ed. Janice Boddy and Michael Lambek (West Sussex: John Wiley and Sons, Inc., 2013): 274–275.

50 Mittermaier, 276. As her bibliography attests, Mittermaier is explicitly drawing on M. M. Bakhtin's notion of "heteroglossia," which he delineates in *The Dialogic Imagination* (Austin: University of Texas Press, 1981).

51 Laura Bush, "Radio Address by Mrs. Bush," *The American Presidency Project*, November 17, 2001, accessed July 31, 2016, http://www.presidency.ucsb.edu/ws/?pid=24992.

52 Bush, "Radio Address."

53 Bush, "Radio Address."

54 Ellen McLarney, "The Burqa in Vogue: Fashioning Afghanistan," *Journal of Middle East Women's Studies* 5, no. 1 (Winter 2009): 2–3.

55 McLarney, "Burqa," 3.

56 Kathy Peiss, "Educating the Eye of the Beholder—American Cosmetics Abroad," *Daedalus* 131, no. 4 (Fall 2002): 101.

57 Peiss, "Educating," 101.

58 McLarney, "Burqa," 3.

59 McLarney, "Burqa," 3.

60 Saira Shah, *Beneath the Veil*, videorecording, Hardcash Productions; Channel Four Television Corp., produced and directed by Cassian Harrison (New York: Multivision Media Monitoring, 2001). CNN, Transcript. *Beneath the Veil: The Taliban's Harsh Rule of Afghanistan*, aired August 26, 2001, accessed July 31, 2016, http://transcripts.cnn.com/TRANSCRIPTS/0108/26/cp.00.html.

61 Perhaps unavoidably, this footage also has an alienating effect on viewers. Shahira Fahmy writes of the ways in which media images of completely covered Afghan women militate against the establishment of an affective relationship between the viewer and the photographic subjects in the absence of visible facial expressions. See her article, "Picturing Afghan Women: A Content Analysis of AP Wire Photographs during the Taliban Regime and after the Fall of the Taliban Regime," *Gazette (Leiden, Netherlands)* 66, no. 2 (April 2004): 107. The RAWA footage, which is incorporated in Shah's film, unintentionally creates a social distance between the viewer and Afghan women by positioning them as completely shrouded, faceless victims of Taliban brutality.

62 Shah, *Beneath the Veil*, CNN Transcript.

63 Elaheh Rostami-Povey, "Women in Afghanistan: Passive Victims of the Borga or Active Social Participants?" *Development in Practice* 13, nos. 2 & 3 (May 2003): 269.

64 Elaheh Rostami-Povery, "Afghanistan," *Encyclopedia of Women & Islamic Cultures: Family, Law, and Politics*, ed. Suad Joseph and Afsaneh Najmabadi (Leiden and Boston: Brill Academic Publishers, 2005), 40.

65 Shah, *Beneath the Veil*, CNN Transcript.

66 Paula Black, *The Beauty Industry: Gender, Culture Pleasure* (London and New York: Routledge, 2004), 2.

67 Cynthia Enloe, *The Curious Feminist: Searching for Women in the New Age of Empire,* (Berkeley: University of California Press, 2004), 296.

68 Enloe, *Curious*, 294.

69 David M. Halbfinger, "After the Veil, a Makeover Rush," *New York Times*, September 1, 2002, accessed July 18, 2016, http://www.nytimes.com/2002/09/01/style/after-the-veil-a-makeover-rush.html.

70 Qtd. By Halbfinger, "After the Veil."

71 Beauty Without Borders, "Program Mission," 2003, accessed June 19, 2009, no longer available, http://www.heavenspa. com/clientmanager/Live/Sites/index.asp?CID=194.

72 Halbfinger, "After the Veil."
73 See her homepage, Kristin Ohlson, accessed September 28, 2018, http://www
.kristinohlson.com/about.
74 For reviews of Mermin's documentary, see Judith Stiles, "Beauty without Borders,"
The Villager, April 5–11, 2006, accessed August 2, 2016, http://www.thevillager
.com/villager153/beautywithout.html and Julia Stuart, "Beauty and the Burqa,"
The Independent, August 31, 2004, accessed August 2, 2016, http://www
.independent.co.uk/news/world/asia/beauty-and-the-burqa-542676.html.
75 Liz Mermin, *The Beauty Academy of Kabul,* [videorecording], Magic Lantern
Media; produced in association with BBC and Discovery Communications, Inc.;
produced in association with Wellspring Media, director and editor, Liz Mermin;
producers, Nigel Noble and Liz Mermin (2004, New York: New Video, 2006).
76 Mermin, *Beauty Academy.*
77 Mermin, *Beauty Academy.*
78 Mermin, *Beauty Academy.*
79 Mermin, *Beauty Academy.*
80 Mermin, *Beauty Academy.*
81 Debbie recounts the details of her courtship, along with her humanitarian zeal
for the beautifying mission, in her memoir, as well as in an interview with Michel
Martin, "A Beauty School in Kabul," *National Public Radio,* aired May 3, 2007,
accessed August 2, 2016, http://www.npr.org/templates/story/story.php?story
Id=9973298.
82 Sune Engel Rasmussen, "Vice-President Leaves Afghanistan amid Torture and
Rape Claims," *Guardian,* May 19, 2017, accessed September 28, 2018, https://
www.theguardian.com/world/2017/may/19/vice-president-leaves-afghanistan
-amid-torture-and-claims.
83 ISAF was disbanded in 2014 and replaced with the Resolute Support Mission. Both
security forces are under NATO command.
84 Lara Olson and Andrea Charron, "The Afghanistan Challenge: Hard Realities and
Strategic Choices," *The Afghanistan Challenge: Hard Realities and Strategic Choices,*
ed. Hans-Georg Ehrhart and Charles C. Pentland (Montreal and Kingston:
McGill-Queen's University Press, 2009), 84.
85 Jessica Mosby, "The Beauty Academy of Kabul," *The Women's International
Perspective,* January 5, 2008, accessed July 31, 2016, http://thewip.net/2008/01/05
/the-beauty-academy-of-kabul/.
86 Abby Ellin, "Shades of Truth: An Account of a Kabul School Is Challenged," *New
York Times,* April 29, 2007, accessed July 31, 2016, http://www.nytimes.com/2007
/04/29/fashion/29kabul.html.
87 Soraya Sarhaddi Nelson, "Subjects of 'Kabul Beauty School' Face New Risks," *All
Things Considered,* National Public Radio, aired June 1, 2007.
88 Nelson, "Subjects."
89 These activities are chronicled in a second memoir, *Margarita Wednesdays: Making
a New Life by the Mexican Sea,* as revealed in Jasmine Elist, "Q & A Deborah
Rodriquez: 'Kabul Beauty School' Author Turns to Mazatlan," *Los Angeles Times,*
June 17, 2014, accessed July 31, 2016, http://www.latimes.com/books/jacketcopy/
la-et-jc-deborah-rodriguez-kabul-beauty-school-author-margarita-wednesdays-
20140613-story.html.
90 Farai Chideya's interview with Liz Mermin, "Setting Up a Salon in the Land of
Burkas," Host Ed Gordon. *News and Notes.* National Public Radio, aired 8 May

2006, accessed August 2, 2016, http://www.npr.org/templates/story/story
.php?storyId=5390087.

91 Qtd. in Chideya, "Setting."

92 Kaweyan Business Development Services Training Topics, accessed July 31, 2016,
http://www.kaweyanbds.com/bds-trainings/kaweyan-bds.

93 Kaweyan International Labor Organization, accessed July 31, 2016, http://www
.kaweyanbds.com/bds-trainings/international-labor-organizationilo.

94 Casey Sutton, "Empowering Women through Business with Kaweyan Cabs,"
Thunderbird School of Global Management, Arizona State University, accessed
July 31, 2016, http://t4g.thunderbird.edu/blog/project-artemis-success-story
-kamila-sidiqi.

95 "Kamila Sidiqi: An Advocate for Afghan Women," accessed July 31, 2016, https://
vimeo.com/89015573.

96 Gayle Tzemach Lemmon, "How One Woman Rose from Dressmaker to Policy
Insider," *PBS Newshour*, aired March 26, 2015, accessed July 25, 2016, http://www
.pbs.org/newshour/bb/one-afghan-woman-rose-dressmaker-policy-insider/.

97 Human Rights Watch, "Country Summary: Afghanistan," January 2015, accessed
August 1, 2016, https://www.hrw.org/sites/default/files/related_material
/afghanistan_7.pdf.

98 Jonathan D. Ostry, Prakash Loungani, and Davide Furceri, "Neoliberalism Oversold?"
International Monetary Fund, *Finance & Development* 53, no. 2 (June 2016), accessed
July 26, 2016, http://www.imf.org/external/pubs/ft/fandd/2016/06/ostry.htm. See
also Branko Milanovic, *Global Inequality: A New Approach for the Age of Globalization*
(Cambridge, MA: Harvard University Press, 2016) for an account of how inequality
has *increased* within countries and *decreased* among countries.

99 United Nations, "Human Development Reports: Afghanistan," *The World's Most
Dangerous Countries for Women 2018*, accessed September 28, 2018, http://hdr
.undp.org/sites/all/themes/hdr_theme/country-notes/AFG.pdf.

100 Thomson Reuters Foundation, "Afghanistan," accessed September 28, 2018,
http://poll2018.trust.org/country/?id=afghanistan.

101 Roy, *Poverty*, 29.

Notes to Chapter 3

1 I benefited from opportunities to present portions of this chapter at the Annual
Conference on South Asia in Madison, the "Race, Place & Capital" Symposium
at Indiana University, and the conference in honor of Barbara Harlow at the
University of Texas. Dawlat Yassin generously shared her knowledge of Hadiths
pertaining to dogs with me, and I am grateful. A special thanks to Saleem, Sona, and
Tommy Bose, and Toby Steinberg for inspiration.

2 Rai Sahib Srendranath Bose was actually my great grandfather's younger brother,
but I have called him my great grandfather to acknowledge the fluidity of Bengali
kinship and the dynamics of extended families, in which relationships between
children and their uncles and aunts are often as close as those with their parents,
and great-uncles and great-aunts are effectively grandparents.

3 See Lieutenant Colonel Jay Kopelman and Melinda Roth's *From Baghdad, With
Love* (Guilford: The Lyons Press, 2006), Lieutenant Colonel Jay Kopelman's
From Baghdad to America (New York: Skyhorse Publishing, 2008), Terri Crisp
and Cynthia Hurn's *No Buddy Left Behind* (Guilford: The Lyons Press, 2012),

Mike Dowling's *Sergeant Rex: The Unbreakable Bond Between a Marine and His Military Working Dog* (New York: Atria Books, 2011), and Carey Neesley and Michael Levin's *Welcome Home Mama & Boris* (White Plains: The Reader's Digest Association, Inc., 2013). A slightly different version of Christine Sullivan's *Saving Cinnamon: The Amazing True Story of a Missing Military Puppy and the Desperate Mission to Bring Her Home* (New York: St. Martin's Griffin, 2009) was originally self-published as *44 Days Out of Kandahar* (New Hope for Animals, LLC, 2007).

4 Gillian Whitlock, *Soft Weapons: Autobiography in Transit* (Chicago, University of Chicago Press, 2007), 3.

5 Donna Haraway, *The Companion Species Manifesto: Dogs, People, and Significant Otherness* (Chicago: Prickly Paradigm Press, 2003), 5. Lisa Uddin, "Canine Citizenship and the Intimate Public Sphere," *Invisible Culture: An Electronic Journal for Visual Culture* 6 (2003), accessed September 5, 2013, http://www.rochester.edu/in_visibleculture/Issue_6/uddin/uddin.html.

6 My focus is in the development of middle-class, Anglo-American cultural attitudes towards dogs. I recognize that different cultural values attach to canines in ethnic and regional subcultures, where canines might be signifiers of masculinity as evident from the proclivity for pit bulls and dogfights in certain urban and rural cultures.

7 Katherine C. Grier, *Pets in America: A History* (Chapel Hill: U of North Carolina Press, 2006), 13.

8 Grier, *Pets*, 13.

9 Grier, *Pets*, 14.

10 Grier, *Pets*, 14. For an excellent analysis of commodification and alienation involved in the present-day production of meat, see Bob Torres's "Chained Commodities," *Making a Killing: The Political Economy of Animal Rights* (Edinburgh: AK, 2008). Carol Adams's *The Sexual Politics of Meat: A Feminist-Vegetarian Critical Theory* also unpacks this first contradiction within the context of providing a cultural history of representations of vegetarianism in the West (New York: Continuum, 2000).

11 Marshall Sahlins, *Culture and Practical Reason* (Chicago: U of Chicago P, 1976), 170–171. With thanks to Hayden Kantor for bringing Sahlins's book to my attention.

12 Grier, *Pets,* 15.

13 Grier, *Pets,* 275.

14 Grier, *Pets,* 275.

15 Grier, *Pets*, 281.

16 Grier, *Pets*, 282.

17 Grier, *Pets*, 286–288.

18 The Harris Poll, "More Than Ever Pets are Members of the Family," July 16, 2015, accessed December 30, 2016, http://www.theharrispoll.com/health-and-life/Pets-are-Members-of-the-Family.html.

19 Heidi Nast, "Loving. . . . Whatever: Alienation, Neoliberalism and Pet-Love in the Twenty-First Century," *ACME: An International E-Journal for Critical Geographies* 5, no. 2 (2006): 302. My gratitude to Majed Akhter for suggesting Nast's work to me.

20 Heidi Nast, "Loving. . . .," 307.

21 Insurance Information Institute, "Pet Statistics: Pet Ownership in the United States," accessed September 23, 2018, http://www.iii.org/fact-statistic/pet-statistics.

22 See the American Pet Products Association fact sheet, "Pet Industry Market Size & Ownership Statistics," accessed September 23, 2018, http://www.american petproducts.org/press_industrytrends.asp.

23 American Pet Products Association, "Pet Industry Spending Makes History: Surpasses $60 Billion," March 18, 2016, accessed January 3, 2017, http://media .americanpetproducts.org/press.php?include=146062.

24 Max Bearak and Lazaro Gamio, "The U.S. Foreign Aid Budget, Visualized," *Washington Post*, October 18, 2016, accessed September 23, 2018, https://www .washingtonpost.com/graphics/world/which-countries-get-the-most-foreign-aid/. Figures for the amounts that were granted to individual countries are available at http://beta.foreignassistance.gov/explore, but this website is not very user-friendly for searching and aggregating data. I am grateful to Keera Allendorf for her assistance navigating this site.

25 Fetch! Pet Care Inc. "Pet Industry Fact Sheet," accessed July 6, 2013, http://www .fetchpetcare.com/pet_industry_fact_sheet/.

26 James Vlahos, "Pill-Popping Pets." *New York Times Magazine*, July 13, 2008, 41.

27 Vlahos, "Pill-Popping," 41.

28 Theresa Fisher, "Dogs Get Anxiety, Too," *The Atlantic*, May 2, 2014, accessed December 30, 2016, http://www.theatlantic.com/health/archive/2014/05/dogs -who-take-prozac/360146/. While this number seems like an extraordinary jump in the sale of pharmaceuticals, Fisher does not specify whether it is restricted to behavior-modification drugs or represents the total sales of all pet pharmaceuticals.

29 Vlahos, "Pill-Popping," 63.

30 Neil Genzlinger, "Furry Best Friends Taking Over the Small Screen," *New York Times*, August 12, 2013, C3.

31 Vlahos, "Pill-Popping," 40.

32 Grier, *Pets*, 319.

33 C.B. Macpherson, *The Political Theory of Possessive Individualism: Hobbes to Locke* (Oxford: OUP, 1962). Macpherson has compellingly elaborated the theory of "possessive individualism" as a crucial component of the development of capitalism: societies are conceived of as exchanges between "free equal individuals related to each other as proprietors of their own capacities and of what they have acquired by their exercise" (3). For Macpherson, ownership comprises a significant component of individual human subjectivity in the nexus of market relationships that make up societies. Individuals not only "own" skills that can be exchanged on the market, but they also acquire and "own" possessions on the basis of those skills and market transactions. Pet individualism, in contrast, disarticulates animal subjectivity from ownership insofar as household animals are neither able to trade "their own capacities" nor are they able to accumulate possessions on the basis of these capacities.

34 When Leona Helmsley died in 2007, she created a $12 million trust for her Maltese, "Trouble." Associated Press, "Helmsley's Dog Gets $12 Million in Will." *Washington Post*, August 29, 2007, accessed July 17, 2013, http://www.washington post.com/wp-dyn/content/article/2007/08/29/AR2007082900491.html.

35 Oxford Centre for Animal Ethics, "Animal Language Sends Wrong Message." News Release, April 26, 2011, accessed July 11, 2013, http://www. oxfordanimalethics.com/2011/04/news-release-animal -language-sends-wrong-message/.

36 See the American Veterinary Medical Association's "Ownership versus Guardianship," June 2005, accessed July 11, 2013, https://www.avma.org /Advocacy/StateAndLocal/Pages/ownership-vs-guardianship.aspx.

37 See the AVMA's "Ownership versus Guardianship" for a lengthy list and explanation of the potential legal ramifications of changing the vocabulary of

ownership to guardianship. It is worth noting that existing state and municipal law permits the seizure of dogs under three categories: "the impoundment of loose or unlicensed dogs; the seizure of dangerous dogs; and the seizure of dogs that either appear rabid or as part of a rabies quarantine effort." For more information about these statutes, see Rebecca F. Wisch's "An Examination of State Dog Impound Laws," 2003, accessed July 11, 2013, http://www.animallaw.info/articles /ddusdogimpound.htm.

38 The Center for Media and Democracy's PR Watch, "How PR Sold the War in the Persian Gulf," (excerpted from John Stauber and Sheldon Rampton's *Toxic Sludge is Good for You*), accessed December 30, 2016, http://www.prwatch.org/books /tsigfy10.html#84.

39 John R. MacArthur, *Second Front: Censorship and Propaganda in the Gulf War* (New York: Hill & Wang, 1992), 54.

40 Heidi Nast, "Critical Pet Studies," *Antipode* 38, no. 5 (November 2006): 897.

41 Sullivan, *Saving Cinnamon*, 119. Please note that all citations to this text will be noted parenthetically in the body of this chapter.

42 Nast, "Loving. . . . Whatever," 302.

43 Maria Goodavage, *Top Dog: The Story of the Marine Hero Lucca* (New York: New American Library, 2015), 301–302. Please note that all citations to this text will be noted parenthetically in the body of this chapter.

44 In addition to Goodavage's *Top Dog*, see her *Soldier Dogs: The Untold Story of America's Canine Heroes* (New York: Penguin Group, 2012), Nigel Allsopp's *Cry Havoc: The History of War Dogs* (Sydney: New Holland Publishers, 2012), and Michael G. Lemish's *War Dogs: A History of Loyalty and Heroism* (Dulles: Brassy's, 1996).

45 Qtd. by Goodavage, *Soldier Dogs*, 9–10.

46 Allsopp, *Cry Havoc*, 80. Goodavage, in *Soldier Dogs*, puts the number of MWDs at 3,800 (18).

47 Allsopp, *Cry Havoc*, 77–80.

48 Allsopp, *Cry Havoc*, 47.

49 Goodavage, *Soldier Dogs*, 258.

50 Goodavage, *Soldier Dogs*, 267.

51 According to Goodavage, about five percent of MWDs return from deployment with Canine PTSD (*Soldier Dogs*, 231). See Nancy Schiesari's documentary *Canine Soldiers: The Militarization of Love* for more on PTSD and the training of MWDs (2016; Austin; Mo-Ti Productions).

52 Qtd. by Goodavage, *Soldier Dogs*, 25.

53 Linda Crippen, "Military Working Dogs: Guardians of the Night," US Army website, May 23, 2011, accessed September 24, 2016, https://www.army.mil /article/56965/Military_Working_Dogs__Guardians_of_the_Night.

54 Goodavage, *Soldier Dogs*, 274–275.

55 At 1,300 square miles, Yuma Proving Ground is one of the largest military installations in the West and also the facility where the army tests weapons systems.

56 Goodavage, *Soldier Dogs*, 48.

57 See, for example, Goodavage's *Soldier Dogs*, 45.

58 Goodavage, *Soldier Dogs*, 13.

59 US Army, "Public Intelligence: US Army Commander's Guide to Military Working Dogs (MWDs)," December 5, 2011, accessed January 2, 2017, https:// publicintelligence.net/ufouo-u-s-army-commanders-guide-to-military-working -dogs-mwds/.

60 Donna J. Haraway, *When Species Meet* (Minneapolis: U. of Minnesota Press, 2008), 57. For a moving account of the subject-changing nature of the handler-WMD relationship, see Michael Paterniti's "The Dogs of War," *National Geographic* (June 2014): 27-53. Paterniti describes the relationship between Marine Corporal Jose Armenta and his WMD, Zenit, before and after the IED incident that results in the amputation of both of Armenta's legs. Thanks to John Lucaites and Radhika Parameswaran for directing me to this article.

61 Haraway, *The Companion Species*, 93.

62 *Max*, directed by Boaz Yakin, 2015, WarnerBrothers, DVD. Jennifer Li Shotz wrote a novel based on Boaz Yakin and Sheldon Lettich's screenplay, *Max: Best Friend, Hero, Marine* (New York: HarperCollins, 2015). Please note that all citations to this text will be noted parenthetically in the body of this chapter.

63 Haraway, *When Species Meet*, 57.

64 "Burgan," PetroWiki, accessed December 7, 2016, http://petrowiki.org/Burgan.

65 Friendly fire casualties for the Panama Invasion are estimated at 6% and the averages do not include statistics from the Korean War. The army claims that friendly fire fatalities are significantly down in the current iteration of the Iraq War and in Afghanistan, but the numbers they cite are so low as to be viewed with suspicion by scholars. See Mark Benjamin, "Is the Army Lying about Friendly Fire Deaths?" January 15, 2009, accessed December 7, 2016, http://www.salon.com/2009/01/15/friendly_fire_6/.

66 Fredric Jameson, *The Political Unconscious: Narrative as a Socially Symbolic Act* (Ithaca and New York: Cornell University Press, 1981), 20.

67 "Small Arms Survey: Illicit Trafficking," accessed December 9, 2016, http://www.smallarmssurvey.org/weapons-and-markets/transfers/illicit-trafficking.html.

68 Bill Chapell, "In Mexico, Tens of Thousands of Illegal Guns Come from the US," National Public Radio, aired January 12, 2016, accessed December 9, 2016, http://www.npr.org/sections/thetwo-way/2016/01/12/462781469/in-mexico-tens-of-thousands-of-illegal-guns-come-from-the-u-s.

69 "Small Arms Survey: Illicit Trafficking."

70 "Small Arms Survey: Illicit Trafficking."

71 Stockholm International Peace Research Initiative, "Global Arms Industry: USA Remains Dominant Despite Decline," December 5, 2016, accessed December 9, 2016, https://www.sipri.org/media/press-release/2016/global-arms-industry-usa-remains-dominant.

72 Statista, "U.S. Companies Dominate The Global Arms Trade," December 7, 2016, accessed December 9, 2016, https://www.sipri.org/media/press-release/2016/global-arms-industry-usa-remains-dominant.

73 Grey markets involve the sale and distribution of goods through unofficial or unauthorized channels. For the distinction between "gray" and "black" markets, see Economy Watch, "Black Market, Black Economy, Gray Market, Gray Market [sic]," November 23, 2010, accessed December 10, 2016, http://www.economywatch.com/market/market-types/black-market.html.

74 C.J. Chivers, "How Many Guns did the US Lose Track of in Iraq and Afghanistan? Hundreds of Thousands," *New York Times Magazine*, August 24, 2016, accessed December 16, 2016, http://www.nytimes.com/2016/08/23/magazine/how-many-guns-did-the-us-lose-track-of-in-iraq-and-afghanistan-hundreds-of-thousands.html?_r=0.

75 Ahmed Rashid, *Taliban: The Story of the Afghan Warlords* (London: Pan Macmillan Ltd, 2001), 119.

76 Rashid, *Taliban*, 121.

77 Ahmed Rashid, *Descent Into Chaos* (New York: Viking Penguin, 2008), 319.

78 Rashid, *Descent*, 319.

79 Rashid, *Descent*, 319–320.

80 Rashid, *Descent*, 327–328.

81 Azam Ahmed, "Penetrating Every Stage of Afghan Opium Chain, Taliban Become A Cartel," *New York Times*, February 16, 2016, accessed December 14, 2016, http://www.nytimes.com/2016/02/17/world/asia/afghanistan-opium-taliban-drug-cartel.html.

82 Azam Ahmed, "Tasked With Combating Opium, Afghan Officials Profit From It," *New York Times*, February 15, 2016, accessed December 14, 2016, http://www.nytimes.com/2016/02/16/world/asia/afghanistan-opium-heroin-taliban-helmand.html?action=click&contentCollection=Asia%20Pacific&module=RelatedCoverage&region=Marginalia&pgtype=article. See also Emma Graham-Harrison, "Drug Trade Could Splinter Afghanistan into Fragmented Criminal State—UN," *Guardian* (US Edition), January 6, 2014, accessed December 14, 2016, https://www.theguardian.com/world/2014/jan/05/drug-trade-afghanistan-fragmented-criminal-state.

83 Ahmed, "Tasked With Combating Opium." Typically, farmers can earn nearly three times as much from an opium crop than they can from other crops. For more on rising addiction rates in Afghanistan and in the five central Asian republics, along with rapid increases in HIV/AIDS infection, see the chapter "Drugs and Thugs" in Rashid's *Descent Into Chaos*. Mathilde Simon's "The Drug Trade in Afghanistan: Understanding Motives behind Farmers' Decision to Cultivate Opium Poppies" also describes growing rates of drug addiction (*Foreign Policy Journal*, November 27, 2015): 1–13.

84 Lauren Berlant, *The Queen of America Goes to Washington City* (Durham, NC: Duke University Press, 1997), 3.

85 Berlant, *The Queen*, 5.

86 Berlant, *The Queen*, 6.

87 Berlant, *The Queen*, 21.

88 Uddin, "Canine Citizenship."

89 See Jay Kopelman's *From Baghdad, With Love* and Mike Dowling's *Sergeant Rex*. For a reading of Kopelman's text, see my "The Canine Rescue Narrative, Civilian Casualties, and the Long Gulf War," *In/Visible War: The Culture of War in Twenty-First-Century America,* ed. Jon Simons and John Lucaites (New Brunswick: Rutgers University Press, 2017), 188–207.

90 Andrew Tyndall, "Tyndall Report: 2007 Year in Review," accessed January 2, 2017, http://tyndallreport.com/yearinreview2007/.

91 Tyndall, "Tyndall Report: 2007."

92 Andrew Tyndall, "Tyndall Report: 2015 Year in Review," accessed December 28, 2016, http://tyndallreport.com/yearinreview2015/.

93 US casualties dating back to World War I are available on the Defense Casualty Analysis Website, accessed October 15, 2016, https://www.dmdc.osd.mil/dcas/pages/main.xhtml.

94 UNAMA, "Reports on the Protection of Civilians," accessed October 15, 2016, https://unama.unmissions.org/protection-of-civilians-reports. Reports dating back to 2007 are available on this site.

95 Nonetheless, the percentage of civilian casualties at the hands of pro-government forces has also increased since 2014. See Neta C. Crawford's "Costs of War: Update on the Human Costs of War for Afghanistan and Pakistan, 2001 to mid-2016," Watson Institute, August 2016, accessed January 2, 2017, http://watson.brown.edu /costsofwar/files/cow/imce/papers/2016/War%20in%20Afghanistan%20and%20 Pakistan%20UPDATE_FINAL_corrected%20date.pdf.

96 Judith Butler, *Precarious Life: The Powers of Mourning and Violence* (London and New York: Verso, 2004), 20.

97 Butler, *Precarious Life*, 32.

98 Goodavage, *Soldier Dogs*, 13.

99 Julie Hirschfield Davis, "White House Weighs Another Reduction in Refugees Admitted to US," *New York Times*, August 1, 2018, accessed September 24, 2018, https://www.nytimes.com/2018/08/01/us/politics/trump-refugees-reduction .html. For a detailed account of the bureaucratic impediments to acquiring refugee status under the Trump administration, see Sarah Aziza, "Donald Trump Isn't Just Slashing the Refugee Quota, He's Dismantling the Entire Resettlement System," *The Intercept*, August 15, 2018, accessed September 24, 2018, https://theintercept .com/2018/08/15/donald-trump-refugee-resettlement-quota/.

Notes to Chapter 4

1 Mark Owen and Kevin Maurer, *No Easy Day: The Autobiography of a Navy Seal* (New York: Dutton, Penguin Group, 2012). Please note: references to *No Easy Day* will be given parenthetically in the body of the text. *Tere Bin Laden,* directed by Abhishek Sharma and produced by Pooja Shetty Deora and Aarti Shetty, (2010, India: Walkwater Media), DVD.

2 Jasbir Puar, *Terrorist Assemblages: Homonationalism in Queer Times* (Durham: Duke University Press, 2007/2017), 47.

3 Sut Jhally (Producer and Director), (1997) *Stuart Hall: Representation and the Media*, US: Media Education Foundation.

4 Tariq Ali, *The Clash of Fundamentalisms: Crusades, Jihads, and Modernity* (London: Verso, 2002), 3. Ali cites examples of rejoicing at the 9/11 attacks in the non-Muslim world, reporting of incidents in Argentina, Brazil, China, Greece, and Nicaragua. He attributes these responses to resentment against US imperialism combined with anger at the deepening economic inequities produced by the global expansion of capitalism into a single market.

5 Peter Bergen, *Man Hunt: The Ten-Year Hunt for Bin Laden from 9/11 to Abbottabad* (New York: Crown Publishers, 2012), 25.

6 George W. Bush, "Address to the Nation on Operations in Afghanistan," *Selected Speeches of President George W. Bush, 2001-2008*, October 7, 2001, (page 75), accessed June 12, 2017, https://georgewbush-whitehouse.archives.gov/infocus /bushrecord/documents/Selected_Speeches_George_W_Bush.pdf.

7 Bergen, *Man Hunt*, 29. In 1998, Mullah Omar also promised Prince Turki bin Faisal that he would expel Osama bin Laden from Afghanistan, a promise that he did not ultimately honor. See "Responses to Al Qaeda's Initial Assaults," *The Final Report of the National Commission on Terrorist Attacks upon the United States*, Official Government Edition, (page 115), August 21, 2004, accessed June 19, 2017, http://govinfo.library.unt.edu/911/report/911Report_Ch4.pdf. In a December 1998 interview with *Al Jazeera*, the interviewer questions bin Laden about rumors

of tensions between the Taliban and him, which bin Laden denies. See "A Muslim Bomb," *Messages to the World: The Statements of Osama bin Laden*, ed. Bruce Lawrence, trans. James Howarth (London and New York: Verso, 2005), 83–85.

8 Seumas Milne, "The Innocent Dead in a Coward's War," *Guardian*, December 19, 2001, accessed June 22, 2017, https://www.theguardian.com/world/2001/dec/20/afghanistan.comment. Milne gives the exact number of dead as 3,767 with the important qualification that these are direct casualties of the invasion and do not include people who died later as a result of injuries sustained in the US campaign.

9 Qtd. in George W. Bush, "Address to the Nation on the September 11 Attacks," *Selected Speeches of President George W. Bush, 2001-2008*, September 11, 2001, (page 58), accessed June 15, 2017, https://georgewbush-whitehouse.archives.gov/infocus/bushrecord/documents/Selected_Speeches_George_W_Bush.pdf.

10 George W. Bush, "Remarks by the President upon Arrival," September 16, 2001, accessed June 21, 2017, https://georgewbush-whitehouse.archives.gov/news/releases/2001/09/20010916-2.html.

11 George W. Bush, "National Day of Prayer and Remembrance Service," *Selected Speeches of President George W. Bush, 2001-2008*, September 14, 2001, (page 60), accessed June 15, 2017, https://georgewbush-whitehouse.archives.gov/infocus/bushrecord/documents/Selected_Speeches_George_W_Bush.pdf.

12 Bush, "National Day of Prayer," 60.

13 Bush, "National Day of Prayer," 59.

14 George W. Bush, "Address to the Joint Session of the 107th Congress," *Selected Speeches of President George W. Bush, 2001-2008*, September 20, 2001, (pages 66–67), accessed June 15, 2017, https://georgewbush-whitehouse.archives.gov/infocus/bushrecord/documents/Selected_Speeches_George_W_Bush.pdf.

15 Bush, "Address to 107th Congress," 66.

16 Bush, "Address to 107th Congress," 68–69.

17 Bush, "Address to 107th Congress," 68.

18 Bin Laden assisted the Mujahideen in the 1980s by first providing aid to Pakistani NGOs delivering healthcare to insurgents, distributing funds to the fighters, and then constructing roads in Afghanistan to facilitate the distribution of weapons to the resistance. As his involvement with the Mujahideen deepened, bin Laden used heavy equipment from his family's construction business to create trenches, tunnels, and caves in the country. Tora Bora, the training camp he established for Arab fighters, along with the network of caves he dug in the mountains, proved a boon to him when he later dodged US attempts to capture him after the 9/11 attacks. During the resistance to Soviet occupation, bin Laden impressed many of his Afghan and Arab cohorts with his generosity, humility, and simplicity of lifestyle. See Michael Scheur, *Osama bin Laden* (Oxford and New York: Oxford University Press, 2011). Scheuer headed the CIA intelligence unit charged with finding bin Laden from 1996 to 1999 and presents a thoughtful analysis of bin Laden, his motivations, and overall strategies.

19 Bush, "Address to 107th Congress," 69.

20 Charles Krauthammer was the first to use the term "Bush Doctrine" in a June 4, 2001, *Weekly Standard* article, in which he referred to the Bush administration's unilateral withdrawal from the ABM Treaty and rejection of the Kyoto Protocol as heralding a significant foreign policy shift. In addition to naming "unilateralism," the Bush Doctrine acquired several other meanings which Krauthammer subsequently delineated in a 2008 *Washington Post* article: the US's right to attack

countries harboring terrorists; the right to engage in pre-emptive war; and the right to spread democracy around the world, even if it is at the end of a barrel of a gun. See his "Charlie Gibson's Gaffe," *Washington Post*, September 13, 2008, accessed June 12, 2017, http://www.washingtonpost.com/wp-dyn/content /article/2008/09/12/AR2008091202457.html.

21 "The Jesus Factor: The Spirituality of George W. Bush," *Frontline*, April 29, 2004, accessed June 16, 2017, http://www.pbs.org/wgbh/pages/frontline/shows/jesus /president/spirituality.html.

22 *Frontline*, "The Jesus Factor."

23 *Frontline*, "The Jesus Factor."

24 *Frontline*, "The Jesus Factor."

25 *Frontline*, "The Jesus Factor."

26 Alec Walen, "Retributive Justice," *The Stanford Encyclopedia of Philosophy*, ed. Edward N. Zalta, (Winter 2016 Edition), June 18, 2014, accessed May 31, 2017, https://plato.stanford.edu/archives/win2016/entries/justice-retributive/.

27 Walen, "Retributive Justice."

28 Walen, "Retributive Justice."

29 Milne, "The Innocent Dead." Milne quotes the Pentagon official in his article, which also includes the information about the bombing targets.

30 Achille Mbembe, "Necropolitics," Trans. Libby Meintjes, *Public Culture* 15, No. 1 (Winter 2003): 11.

31 Neta C. Crawford, "Costs of War: Update on the Human Costs of War for Afghanistan and Pakistan, 2001 to mid-2016," Watson Institute, August 2016, accessed June 17, 2017, http://watson.brown.edu/costsofwar/files/cow/imce /papers/2016/War%20in%20Afghanistan%20and%20Pakistan%20UPDATE _FINAL_corrected%20date.pdf.

32 Eqbal Ahmad, *Confronting Empire: Interviews with David Barsamian* (Cambridge, MA: South End Press, 2000), 95.

33 Mbembe, "Necropolitics," 12.

34 Susan Jeffords, *The Remasculinization of America: Gender and the Vietnam War* (Bloomington and Indianapolis: Indiana University Press, 1989), 1.

35 For a historical account of the association between bra-burning and feminism, see Susan Faludi, "The 'Trends' of Antifeminism: The Media and the Backlash," *Backlash: The Undeclared War Against American Women* (New York: Doubleday, 1991).

36 Tom Vanden Brook, "Pentagon's Elite Forces Lack Diversity," *USA Today*, August 6, 2015, accessed September 25, 2018, https://www.usatoday.com/story/news /nation/2015/08/05/diversity-seals-green-berets/31122851/. The SEALs performance of white masculinity starkly contrasts with what Melani McAlister calls "military multiculturalism" during the Gulf War, which constructed the US armed forces as a "diverse microcosm of U.S. society" to distinguish it from the earlier British imperial formation that rested on the ideological justification of the white man's burden. Military multiculturalism, she argues, was a logical result of increased immigration and growing sensitivity to race, following the struggles of the Civil Rights era. See her *Epic Encounters: Culture, Media, and U.S. Interests in the Middle East, 1945-2000* (Berkeley and Los Angeles: University of California Press, 2001), 42.

37 Bergen, *Man Hunt*, 15.

38 At the time of his death, bin Laden was married to three women (Khairiah Saber, Siham Sabar, and Amal Ahmed al-Sadah), separated from his first wife (Najwa Ghanhem), and divorced from a second one (Khadijah Sharif).

39 See Frank J. Barrett, "The Organizational Construction of Hegemonic Masculinity: The Case of the US Navy," *Gender, Work and Organization* 3, no. 3 (July 1996): 129–142.

40 Puar, *Terrorist Assemblages*, 46.

41 One is reminded here of Leslie Marmon Silko's powerful novel *Almanac of the Dead*, which suggests that the hundreds of photographs circulated of Geronimo bear little resemblance to the actual historical person or possibly persons who were Geronimo; the photographs are simulacra, in effect (New York: Simon & Schuster, 1991).

42 Eva Cherniavsky, "Subaltern Studies in a U.S. Frame," *boundary 2*, vol. 23, no. 2 (Summer 1996): 86–87.

43 The ease Owen expresses with killing starkly contrasts with soldiers of an earlier era. Carolyn Nordstrom has dismantled the myth that soldiers are innately aggressive, citing studies that demonstrate the reluctance of combatants through WWII to fire their weapons. She attributes the willingness of US soldiers to kill in more recent conflicts to the deliberate training regimes embarked on by the US armed forces after WWII, designed to overcome the aversion to killing. See her "Deadly Myths of Aggression," *Aggressive Behavior* 24, no. 2 (1998): 147–159.

44 Jonathan Masters, "Targeted Killings," *Council on Foreign Relations*, May 23, 2013, accessed July 30, 2017, https://www.cfr.org/backgrounder/targeted-killings.

45 Masters, "Targeted Killings."

46 For a description of debates about the most effective manner of targeting bin Laden and considerations about violating Pakistan's sovereignty, see Peter L. Bergen, "Courses of Action" and "The Decision," *Manhunt: The Ten-Year Search for Bin Laden From 9/11 to Abbottabad* (New York: Crown Publishers, 2012).

47 Qtd. in Masters, "Targeted Killings." For a succinct summary of the legal and moral issues raised by targeted killings, see Human Rights Watch, "Letter to Obama on Targeted Killings and Drones," December 7, 2010, accessed July 31, 2017, https://www.hrw.org/news/2010/12/07/letter-obama-targeted-killings-and-drones. Steve Coll also offers a thoughtful analysis of the use of drones and targeted killings in Pakistan. See his article, "The Unblinking Stare: The Drone War in Pakistan," *New Yorker*, November 24, 2014, accessed July 30, 2017. http://www.newyorker.com/magazine/2014/11/24/unblinking-stare.

48 Jasmine C. Lee and Haeyoun Park, "In 15 High-Profile Cases Involving Deaths of Blacks, One Officer Faces Prison Time," *New York Times*, December 7, 2018, accessed July 3, 2018, https://www.nytimes.com/interactive/2017/05/17/us/black-deaths-police.html.

49 Lolita C. Baldor, "Matt Bissonnette Settles 'No Easy Day' Case for $6.6M," *Christian Science Monitor*, August 20, 2016, accessed July 17, 2017, https://www.csmonitor.com/USA/Justice/2016/0820/Matt-Bissonnette-settles-No-Easy-Day-case-for-6.6M.

50 Matthew Cole and Anna R. Schecter, "Who Shot Bin Laden? A Tale of Two SEALs," *NBC News*, November 6, 2014, accessed August 8, 2017, http://www.nbcnews.com/news/investigations/who-shot-bin-laden-tale-two-seals-n241241.

51 Joby Warrick, "Ex-SEAL Robert O'Neill Reveals Himself as Shooter Who Killed Osama bin Laden," *Washington Post*, November 6, 2014, accessed July 22, 2017, https://www.washingtonpost.com/world/national-security/ex-seal-robert-oneill-reveals-himself-as-shooter-who-killed-osama-bin-laden/2014/11/06/2bf46f3e-65dc-11e4-836c-83bc4f26eb67_story.html?tid=a_inl&utm_term=.7d12f0fa4ac8.

52   Qtd. in Peter Grier, "Who Shot Osama bin Laden? Does it Matter?" *Christian Science Monitor*, November 7, 2014, accessed July 21, 2017, https://www.csmonitor.com/USA/Politics/Decoder/2014/1107/Who-shot-Osama-bin-Laden-Does-it-matter-video.

53   Qtd. in Christopher Drew and Nicholas Kulish, "Former Navy SEAL Team Member Investigated for Bin Laden Disclosures," *New York Times*, October 30, 2014, accessed July 21, 2017, https://www.nytimes.com/2014/10/31/us/former-navy-seal-matt-bissonnette-investigated-for-bin-laden-book.html?_r=1.

54   Kimberly Dozier, "'They Don't Call It SEAL Team 6-Year-Old for Nothing': Commandos Clash Over Tell All Book," *The Daily Beast*, November 2, 2014, accessed July 22, 2017, http://www.thedailybeast.com/they-dont-call-it-seal-team-6-year-old-for-nothing-commandos-clash-over-tell-all-book.

55   Matthew Cole and Anna R. Schecter, "Who Shot Bin Laden?"

56   Moreover, when he was still an active member of the SEALs, Owen had also profited from serving as a consultant for the video game "Medal of Honor: Warfighter" and had convinced six other teammates to join him, a judgment lapse that resulted in the Navy sending "letters of reprimand" to all seven men, thus compromising their future careers. See Matthew Cole, "Navy SEAL Turns Over Picture of bin Laden's Body, Faces Investigation of Business Ties," *The Intercept*, January 19, 2016, accessed July 22, 2017, https://theintercept.com/2016/01/19/navy-seal-turns-over-picture-of-bin-ladens-body-faces-investigation-of-business-ties/.

57   Owen's rejoinder to criticisms of his memoir is to point out that senior military officials have profited from publishing accounts of their work. "It's hard for me to take when I've been reading books my whole life about former special operations warriors, Army, Navy, Air Force, Marines," he observes, "There's how many former generals, how many former CIA directors, how many former secretaries of defense? How many of them all get out and write books?" He is especially incensed by the double standard he perceives in former CIA Director Leon Panetta granting access to information to *Zero Dark Thirty* director Kathryn Bigelow and her screenwriter Mark Boal; Panetta unwittingly disclosed details of the raid to Boal during a speech to the CIA, which Boal inexplicably attended unbeknownst to Panetta. Since then, the CIA has revised its procedures for interactions with the entertainment industry. See Cole and Schecter, "Who Shot Bin Laden?"

58   For an excellent genealogy of the term "jihad," including its modern meanings, see Asma Afsaruddin's *Striving in the Path of God: Jihad and Martyrdom in Islamic Thought* (New York: Oxford University Press, 2013).

59   Osama bin Laden, "Terror for Terror," Interview with Taysir Alluni, in Lawrence, *Messages to the World*, 121.

60   Bruce Lawrence, ed. "Introduction," *Messages to the World: The Statements of Osama Bin Laden* (London and New York: Verso, 2005), xviii.

61   See, in particular, bin Laden's interviews "The Saudi Regime" and "Terror for Terror," and open letter "To the Allies of America" in *Messages to the World*.

62   "The Example of Vietnam," Lawrence, *Messages to the World*, 141.

63   "Terror for Terror," Lawrence, *Messages to the World*, 117.

64   Qtd. by Rahul Mahajan, "'We Think the Price is Worth It,'" *FAIR*, November 1, 2001, accessed June 24, 2017, http://fair.org/extra/we-think-the-price-is-worth-it/.

65   "Terror for Terror," Lawrence, *Messages to the World*, 119.

66   "Terror for Terror," Lawrence, *Messages to the World*, 119.

67   "Terror for Terror," Lawrence, *Messages to the World*, 119.

68 For a list of the occupants of the WTC, see "A Look at Former World Trade Center's Tenants," *Wall Street Journal Online*, updated January 18, 2017, accessed June 25, 2017, http://interactive.wsj.com/public/resources/documents/Tenant -List.htm.

69 "To the Americans," Lawrence, *Messages to the World*, 164–165.

70 "To the Americans," Lawrence, *Messages to the World*, 166.

71 Scheuer, *Osama Bin Laden*, 113.

72 Scheuer, *Osama Bin Laden*, 112.

73 "Terror for Terror," Lawrence, *Messages to the World*, 114.

74 Following its release, the film became an instant box office success in the key "metro cities" of Delhi, Mumbai, Chennai, Kolkata, and Bangalore, and was thereafter distributed in international markets such as the UK, Middle East, Australia, South Africa, and Mauritius. While the Pakistani government banned the film—claiming that it would provoke terrorist attacks—pirated copies are readily available in the country.

75 Riz Khan's show *"Is There Room for Humour in the War Against Terror?"* aired September 10, 2010 on Al Jazeera, accessed August 12, 2017, http://www.aljazeera .com/programmes/rizkhan/2010/09/2010968455534861.html.

76 The classic text here is Judith Butler's *Gender Trouble: Feminism and the Subversion of Identity* (New York: Routledge, 1990).

77 Lashkar-e-Taiba, based in Pakistan, is the military arm of the Islamist organization Markaz-ad-Dawa-wal-Irshad, which seeks to liberate Jammu and Kashmir from India and to establish an Islamic state across South Asia. It has been linked to a number of deadly terrorist acts in India, including the 2001 assault on parliament and the 2008 attacks in Mumbai. The Indian government and security experts allege that the organization has ties to Pakistan's ISI, though the Pakistani government denies such ties.

78 For more on South Asian taxi drivers and their organizing attempts, See Manisha Das Gupta's *Unruly Immigrants: Rights, Activism, and Transnational South Asian Politics in the United States* (Durham: Duke University Press, 2006).

79 Louis Althusser, "Ideology and Ideological State Apparatuses (Notes towards an Investigation)," *Lenin and Philosophy, and Other Essays*. Trans. Ben Brewster (New York: Monthly Review Press, 1972 [c 1971]).

80 *Confronting Empire*, the transcripts of David Barsamian's interviews with Eqbal Ahmad, has references to the political economy of US foreign policy throughout its pages (Cambridge, MA: South End Press, 2000). For additional critiques of US foreign policy in terms of the scramble to control resources, see Noam Chomsky's *On Power and Ideology: The Managua Lectures* (Boston: South End Press, 1987) and Howard Zinn's classic, *A People's History of the US* (New York: Harper Collins, 1980). On the topic of the US attempting to gain leverage over the growing economies of Asia and Europe by controlling access to energy resources, see David Harvey's *The New Imperialism* (Oxford: Oxford University Press, 2003). It is worth noting, however, that considerations over petroleum reserves have a much longer history in geopolitics, dating back to the early twentieth century. Consider, for example, conflicts between the Mexican government and foreign companies such as Mexican Eagle Company (a subsidiary of Royal Dutch/Shell Company) and Jersey Standard and Standard Oil Company of California (now Chevron) over petroleum in the 1920s, as well as the role of corporations such as Standard Oil, Anglo-Persian Oil Company (active in what is today called "Iran" and southern

Russia, and the antecedent to British Petroleum Company), and Royal Dutch Shell (a major player in Indonesia and southeast Asia) and their collusion with various imperial powers.

81 The literature on the New Great Game is voluminous: Mohammed Ahrari and James Beal's *The New Great Game in Muslim Central Asia* (McNair Paper 47, Washington DC: Institute for National Strategic Studies, January 1996); Shareen Brysac and Karl Meyer's *Tournament of Shadows: The Great Game and the Race for Empire in Asia* (Washington, DC: Counterpoint, 1999); Lutz Kleveman's *The New Great Game: Blood and Oil in Central Asia* (New York: Grove Press, 2004); Rein Mullerson's *Central Asia: A Chessboard and Player in the New Great Game* (New York: Columbia University Press, 2007); Ahmed Rashid's *Taliban: Islam, Oil and the New Great Game in Central Asia* (London: I.B. Tauris, 2000).

82 For a detailed analysis of Powell's UN testimony, see Hugh Gusterson's "The Auditors: Bad Intelligence and the Loss of Public Trust," *Boston Review*, November/December 2005. See also Jonathan Schwarz's "The U.N. Deception: What Exactly Colin Powell Knew Five Years Ago and What He Told the World," *Mother Jones*, 5 February 2008, accessed August 12, 2017, http://www.motherjones. com/mojo/2008/02/un-deception-what-exactly-colin-powell-knew-five-years -ago-and-what-he-told-world. For more on Powell's retraction of his testimony, see CNN's "Powell: Some Iraq Testimony not Solid," CNN.com, April 3, 2004, accessed August 12, 2017, http://www.cnn.com/2004/US/04/03/powell.iraq /index.html. In a September 2012 address to the UN, Israeli Prime Minister Benjamin Netanyahu held up a cartoonish drawing of a bomb to dramatize Iran's impending nuclear capability. See Rick Gladstone and David E. Sanger's "Nod to Obama by Netanyahu in Warning to Iran on Bomb," *New York Times*, September 27, 2012, accessed August 12, 2017, http://www.nytimes.com/2012/09/28 /world/middleeast/netanyahu-warns-that-iran-bombmaking-ability-is-nearer. html?pagewanted=all&_r=0.

83 I am grateful to Barbara Harlow for remarking on the ambiguity of the name "Operation Enduring Freedom." Since September 11, 2001, the US has initiated three operations: Operation Enduring Freedom (primarily focused on Afghanistan, but also targeting smaller operations in areas ranging from the Philippines to Djibouti); Operation Noble Eagle (aimed at enhancing security at US military bases); and Operation Iraqi Freedom (renamed Operation New Dawn in 2010 when the US transformed its role to an advisory function).

84 See Harlan Ullman and James Wade, Jr., *Shock & Awe: Achieving Rapid Dominance*, October 1996, accessed August 12, 2017, http://www.dodccrp.org /files/Ullman_Shock.pdf.

85 United Nations Assistance Mission in Afghanistan, *Afghanistan: Annual Report 2011: Protection of Civilians in Armed Conflict*, February 2012, accessed August 12, 2017, http://photos.state.gov/libraries/usnato/562411/PDFs_001/UNAMA%20 POC%202011%20Report_Final_Feb%202012.pdf; Susan B. Chesser, "Afghanistan Casualties: Military Forces and Civilians," Congressional Research Service, 7-5700, R41084, July 12, 2012, accessed August 12, 2017, https://fas.org /sgp/crs/natsec/R41084.pdf.

86 C.J. Chivers, "Afghan Conflict Losing Air Power As U.S. Pulls Out," *New York Times*, July 6, 2012. A1+.

87 Qtd. by C.J. Chivers.

88 Chivers.

89 Christopher Drew, "Drones Are Playing a Growing Role in Afghanistan," *New York Times*, February 19, 2010, accessed August 12, 2017, http://www.nytimes .com/2010/02/20/world/asia/20drones.html. Until 2016, the CIA ran the drone program in Pakistan, whereas the military was in charge of the drone program in Afghanistan. The Obama administration sought to make the Pentagon in charge of drones, but the Trump administration has expanded CIA drone operations, particularly in Africa. In 2016, both the CIA and military were operating drones in Pakistan. See the Bureau of Investigative Journalism, "Drone Warfare: Pakistan, Reported US Strikes 2018," no date, accessed December 30, 2018, https://www .thebureauinvestigates.com/drone-war/data/pakistan-reported-us-strikes-2018.

90 Qtd. by Christopher Drew.

91 Crawford, "Costs of War."

92 For more on the costs of US military operations in the Global War on Terror, see Amy Belasco's CRS Report, "The Cost of Iraq, Afghanistan, and Other Global War on Terror Operations Since 9/11," Congressional Research Service, 7-5700, RL33110, December 8, 2014, accessed August 11, 2017, https://fas.org/sgp/crs /natsec/RL33110.pdf.

93 *Rethink Afghanistan*, directed by Robert Greenwald, produced by Jason Zaro and Robert Greenwald (2009; United States: Brave New Foundation).

94 See, for example, "Real Proof the Government Released a Fake Video of Osama Bin Laden!" May 19, 2009, accessed August 12, 2017, http://www.youtube.com /watch?v=1W6QLfXE3wA; "CIA Admits Faking BinLaden [sic] Video: Interview with Alex Jones," accessed August 3, 2012, no longer available, http://www .youtube.com/watch?v=V4a14_LVFtc; "Tim Osman aka Bin Laden," accessed August 3, 2012, no longer available, http://www.youtube.com/watch ?v=fBIthwLNoiI; "Former CIA Officials Admit to Faking Bin Laden Video," May 2, 2010, accessed August 12, 2017, https://www.prisonplanet.com/flashback -former-cia-officials-admit-to-faking-bin-laden-video.html; and "Bin Laden's Son Says Video Are Faked," December 19, 2008, accessed August 12, 2017, http://www .youtube.com/watch?v=3jXzK5LD3kE&feature=related.

95 "Could the Bin Laden Video Be A Fake?" *BBC News*, December 14, 2001, accessed August 12, 2017, http://news.bbc.co.uk/1/hi/1711288.stm.

96 For an analysis of the significance of caves in Islam, along with Osama bin Laden's manipulation of the media, see Faisal Devji's *Landscapes of the Jihad: Militancy, Morality, and Modernity* (London: Hurst & Company, 2005).

97 "The Power of Nightmares: The Shadows in the Cave," BBC Online, January 14, 2005, accessed August 12, 2017, http://news.bbc.co.uk/2/hi/ programmes/3970901.stm.

98 For an account of discussions within the Bush administration in the immediate aftermath of 9/11 about linking the attacks to Saddam Hussein and Al Qaeda and the security assessments that disputed such ties, see *The 9/11 Commission Report: Final Report of the National Commission on Terrorist Attacks Upon the United States*, particularly section 10.3 "'Phase Two' and the Question of Iraq" (New York: W.W. Norton & Company, 2011). Bob Woodward's *Plan of Attack* details differences among Bush's cabinet members regarding the plausibility of Iraq possessing WMD; he provides an analysis of the exaggerations and contradictions in the 2002 National Intelligence Estimate on "Iraq's Continuing Programs for Weapons of Mass Destruction" (New York: Simon & Schuster, 2004).

99   "Ali Zafar Interview: Part I," *Dawn,* June 26, 2010, accessed August 12, 2017,
     http://www.youtube.com/watch?v=Tms2HlBVomE&feature=related.
100 Ali, *The Clash of Fundamentalisms,* 3.

Notes to the Postscript

1   For monthly and yearly figures of US troops deployed in Afghanistan and Iraq,
    see Amy Belasco, "Troop Levels in the Afghan and Iraq Wars, FY2001-FY2012:
    Cost and Other Potential Issues," Congressional Research Service (7-5700,
    R40682) July 2, 2009, accessed July 25, 2018, https://fas.org/sgp/crs/natsec
    /R40682.pdf.
2   For a record of Donald Trump's tweets on Afghanistan prior to assuming office, see
    Stef W. Kight, "Trump's Years of Tweets Calling for U.S. to Leave Afghanistan,"
    AXIOS, August 21, 2017, accessed July 25, 2018, https://www.axios.com/trumps
    -years-of-tweets-calling-for-us-to-leave-afghanistan-1513304975-e76e4aa5
    -d359-4423-9af0-8bff1ad67329.html.
3   Heng, "Heng on Trump's Afghanistan Strategy," *New York Times,* August 24,
    2017, accessed July 23, 2018, https://www.nytimes.com/2017/08/24/opinion
    /heng-on-trumps-afghanistan-strategy.html.
4   Ashley J. Tellis and Jeff Eggers, "U.S. Policy in Afghanistan: Changing Strategies,
    Preserving Gains," Carnegie Endowment for International Peace, May 22, 2017,
    accessed August 2, 2018, https://carnegieendowment.org/2017/05/22/u.s.-policy
    -in-afghanistan-changing-strategies-preserving-gains-pub-70027.
5   Donald J. Trump, "Remarks by President Trump on the Strategy in Afghanistan
    and South Asia," August 21, 2017, accessed July 23, 2018, https://www.whitehouse
    .gov/briefings-statements/remarks-president-trump-strategy-afghanistan-south
    -asia/.
6   David E. Sanger, "THE 2000 CAMPAIGN: FOREIGN POLICY; A Delicate
    Dance of the Interventionist and the Reluctant Internationalist," *New York Times,*
    October 12, 2000, https://www.nytimes.com/2000/10/12/us/2000-campaign
    -foreign-policy-delicate-dance-interventionist-reluctant.html.
7   Associated Press, "A Timeline of U.S. Troop Levels in Afghanistan Since 2001,"
    Military Times, July 6, 2016, accessed July 25, 2018, https://www.militarytimes
    .com/news/your-military/2016/07/06/a-timeline-of-u-s-troop-levels-in
    -afghanistan-since-2001/.
8   Belasco, "Troop Levels," Figures for Afghanistan are on page 29 and for Iraq on
    page 35.
9   Associated Press, "A Timeline of U.S. Troop Levels in Afghanistan Since 2001,"
    MilitaryTimes, July 6, 2016, accessed September 6, 2018, https://www
    .militarytimes.com/news/your-military/2016/07/06/a-timeline-of-u-s-troop-levels
    -in-afghanistan-since-2001/.
10 The 14,000 figure is cited by Rod Nordland and Fahim Abed, "Jim Mattis Visits
    Afghanistan Amid Push for Peace Talks," *New York Times,* September 7, 2018,
    accessed September 7, 2018, https://www.nytimes.com/2018/09/07/world/asia
    /mattis-afghanistan-ghani-taliban-talks.html.
11 Thomas Gibbons-Neff and Mujib Mashal, "U.S. to Withdraw About 7,000 Troops
    from Afghanistan, Officials Say," *New York Times,* December 20, 2018, accessed
    December 31, 2018, https://www.nytimes.com/2018/12/20/us/politics
    /afghanistan-troop-withdrawal.html?module=inline.

12 George W. Bush, "State of the Union Address—January 29, 2002 (Print Format)," accessed July 7, 2018, www.PresidentialRhetoric.com.

13 George W. Bush, "Remarks to the George C. Marshall ROTC Award Seminar on National Security," Virginia Military Institute, Lexington, Virginia. President Outlines War Effort, April 17, 2002, accessed July 25, 2018, http:// teachingamericanhistory.org /library/document/president-outlines-war-effort/.

14 Qtd. by Lara Olson and Andrea Charron, "The Afghanistan Challenge: Hard Realities and Strategic Choices," *The Afghanistan Challenge: Hard Realities and Strategic Choices*, ed. Hans-Georg Ehrhart and Charles C. Pentland (Montreal and Kingston, McGill-Queen's University Press, 2009), 84.

15 For an excellent critique of the blending of military and reconstruction efforts for the problems they pose for NGOs and international law, see Jamie A. Williamson's "Using Humanitarian Aid to 'Win Hearts and Minds': A Costly Failure?" *International Review of the Red Cross* 93, no. 884 (December 2011) 1035–1061.

16 President Barack Obama, "Remarks by the President on a New Strategy for Afghanistan," *The White House: President Barack Obama*, March 27, 2009, accessed August 28, 2018, https://obamawhitehouse.archives.gov/video/A-New-Strategy-for -Afghanistan-and-Pakistan#transcript.

17 General David Petraeus and Lieutenant General James F. Amos, "Foreword," *Counter Insurgency Field Manual*, U.S. Army Field Manual No. 3-24 (Chicago: The University of Chicago Press, 2007), xlvi.

18 Petraeus, *Counter Insurgency*, xlvi.

19 Petraeus, *Counter Insurgency*, 55–56.

20 Petraeus, *Counter Insurgency*, 55.

21 See Fariba Nawa, *Afghanistan, Inc.: A Corpwatch Investigative Report*, (May 2, 2006), 28. Also available at: http://www.corpwatch.org/article.php?id=13518; Joel Brinkley, "Money Pit: The Monstrous Failure of US Aid to Afghanistan, *World Affairs*, January/February 2013, accessed September 4, 2018, http://www.worldaffairs journal.org/article/money-pit-monstrous-failure-us-aid-afghanistan; and Catherine Lutz and Sujaya Desai, "US Reconstruction Aid for Afghanistan: The Dollars and Sense," The Watson Institute for International Studies at Brown University, Working Paper No. 2014-22, (August 21, 2014): 7.

22 Lutz and Desai, "US Reconstruction," 2.

23 Lutz and Desai note that the departments of Agriculture, Justice, and Treasury also administer some of this 30% of reconstruction aid, "US Reconstruction," 13.

24 See Brinkley, "Money Pit," on troop literacy rates and Lutz and Desai on allocations of reconstruction aid, 3.

25 Ben Jones, "Despite Obama's New Executive Order, U.S. Drone Policy May Still Violate International Law," *Washington Post*, July 7, 2016, accessed July 23, 2018, https://www.washingtonpost.com/news/monkey-cage/wp/2016/07/07/obamas -new-executive-order-on-drones-means-the-u-s-may-still-violate-international -law/?utm_term=.8db279de034c. For more on RMA and Defence Transformation, see Mary Kaldor's *New and Old Wars: Organized Violence in a Global Era* (Stanford: Stanford University Press, 2012 [Third Edition]), 153.

26 Jones, "Despite Obama's."

27 Ian Shaw and Majed Akhter, "The Dronification of State Violence," *Critical Asian Studies* 46, no. 2 (2014): 211.

28 Anne Daugherty Miles, "Perspectives on Enhanced Interrogation Techniques,"
    Congressional Research Service, 7-5700, R43906, January 8, 2016, accessed August 3,
    2018, https://fas.org/sgp/crs/intel/R43906.pdf.

29 Jennifer Williams, "From Torture to Drone Strikes: The Disturbing Legal Legacy
    Obama is Leaving for Trump," *Vox*, January 10, 2017, accessed August 4, 2018,
    https://www.vox.com/policy-and-politics/2016/11/14/13577464/obama-farewell
    -speech-torture-drones-nsa-surveillance-trump.

30 No author, "Donald Trump on Waterboarding: 'I Love It,'" *MSNBC*, April 21,
    2016, accessed August 4, 2018, https://www.youtube.com/watch?v
    =Yx1DQY5a8So.

31 Annabelle Timsit, "What Happened at the Thailand 'Black Site' Run by Trump's
    CIA Pick," *The Atlantic*, March 14, 2018, accessed August 4, 2018, https://www
    .theatlantic.com/international/archive/2018/03/gina-haspel-black-site-torture
    -cia/555539/.

32 Hina Shamsi, "What Gina Haspel Got Wrong About the Torture Tapes She
    Helped Destroy," *ACLU*, May 9, 2018, accessed August 4, 2018, ttps://www.aclu
    .org/blog/national-security/torture/what-gina-haspel-got-wrong-about-torture
    -tapes-she-helped-destroy.

33 Panetta's review is described in the *Frontline* episode "Secrets, Politics, and
    Torture" Season 33, Episode 9, May 19, 2015, accessed July 20, 2018, https://
    www.pbs.org/wgbh/frontline/film/secrets-politics-and-torture/. Select Senate
    Committee on Intelligence, "Committee Study of the Central Intelligence Agency's
    Detention and Interrogation Program," Declassification Revisions, December 3,
    2014, accessed July 24, 2018, https://www.amnestyusa.org/pdfs/sscistudy1.pdf.
    Elaine Scarry *The Body in Pain: The Making and Unmaking of the World* (New
    York: Oxford University Press, 1985).

34 Mujib Mashal, "C.I.A.'s Afghan Forces Leave a Trail of Abuse and Anger,"
    New York Times, December 31, 2018, accessed December 31, 2018, https://www
    .nytimes.com/2018/12/31/world/asia/cia-afghanistan-strike-force.html.

35 Bob Meola, "Interview with Drone Tech Cian Westmoreland," *Courage to Resist*,
    September 21, 2016, accessed September 3, 2018, https://couragetoresist.org
    /obama-vs-trump-drones-whats-changed/.

36 Aaron Blake, "Sarah Huckabee Sanders Uses a Debunked Story to Blame the Media
    for Damaging the Hunt for Bin Laden," *Washington Post*, August 1, 2018, accessed
    August 3, 2018. https://www.washingtonpost.com/news/the-fix/wp/2018/08/01
    /sarah-huckabee-sanders-uses-a-debunked-story-to-blame-the-media-for-damaging
    -the-hunt-for-bin-laden/?noredirect=on&utm_term=.2a430b6ad83a.

37 Rod Nordland, Ash Ngu, and Famim Abed, "How the U.S. Government Misleads
    the Public on Afghanistan," *New York Times*, September 8, 2018, accessed
    September 19, 2018, https://www.nytimes.com/interactive/2018/09/08/world
    /asia/us-misleads-on-afghanistan.html.

38 Nordland, Ngu, and Abed, "How the U.S. Government Misleads."

39 Human Rights Watch, "Afghanistan: Weak Investigations of Civilian Airstrike
    Deaths," May 16, 2018, accessed December 31, 2018, https://www.hrw.org
    /news/2018/05/16/afghanistan-weak-investigations-civilian-airstrike-deaths#.

40 Kaldor, *New and Old Wars*, 218–19.

41 On financing the insurgency, see Douglas A. Wissing's *Funding the Enemy: How
    US Taxpayers Bankroll the Taliban* (New York: Prometheus Books, 2012).

Index

Abdul Khan, Samer Mohammad, 85
Abraham, Stanley, 177–78n43
Abu-Lughod, Lila, 60, 61
accumulation by dispossession, 6, 61, 169
aerial bombardment, 131, 153–54, 168
Afghanistan: aerial bombardment in, 131, 153–54, 168; COIN in, 163–64, 165; covert operations in, 21–22, 23, 26–32, 33–35, 68; drug and arms trade in, 119–20; private contractors in, 4; reconstruction in, 12–13, 164–65, 166–67, 168–69; Soviet occupation of, 44–45, 67–68. *See also* premature-withdrawal narrative; Specialized Search Dogs in, 113; Trans-Afghanistan Pipeline and, 11; US armed forces and bases in, 4, 8–9; US invasion of, 144–45. *See also* Afghan war
Afghanistan—The Bear Trap (Yousaf): "Afghan warrior" in, 39–42, 48; agency in, 39–40, 45–49; anxiety in, 54; CIA in, 45–48; hegemonic masculinity in, 23, 39–49; ISI in, 23, 45–46, 48–49; "modern Soviet soldier" in, 39–40, 42–45; Wilson in, 38–39, 47
Afghan war: casualties for Afghans in, 1, 123, 131, 137, 145, 152–53, 168; casualties for US armed forces in, 1, 117; coverage of, 8–9, 18, 122; geopolitical fetishism and, 4–5, 7–14; invisibility of, 1–2; left-liberal counter-narrative of, 21; narratives of, 2–5, 14–17. *See also specific narratives*

Afghan women: Beauty Without Borders and, 79–80; current situation of, 91–92; as objects of white male rescue, 60–63; retributive justice and, 57–58; Taliban and, 69, 76–79. *See also* capitalist-rescue narrative
agency: in *Afghanistan* (Yousaf), 39–40, 45–49; in capitalist-rescue narrative, 58, 94; change and, 32–35; in *Charlie Wilson's War* (2007 film), 19, 32–35, 48–49; in *The Dressmaker of Khair Khana* (Lemmon), 75
Ahmad, Eqbal, 131, 151
Akhter, Majed, 165
Albright, Madeleine, 142
Alexievich, Svetlana, 185n58
Ali, Tariq, 158
Al Jazeera (media network), 131, 142, 155
Alluni, Tayser, 142
Almanac of the Dead (Silko), 202n41
Al Qaeda: G.W. Bush and, 128–31; in *Charlie Wilson's War* (2007 film), 36; counter-terrorism measures against, 9; current situation of, 4, 153–54; three-point agenda of, 144. *See also* bin Laden, Osama; premature-withdrawal narrative; September 11, 2001, attacks
Alston, Philip, 137
American dream, 105–6, 124
American Elements, 11
American exceptionalism, 18, 124

211

About the Author

PURNIMA BOSE is Associate Professor of English and International Studies at Indiana University. She directed the Cultural Studies Program for eight years in the College of Arts & Sciences and currently chairs the International Studies Department in the Hamilton Lugar School of Global and International Studies. Bose's previous publications include *Organizing Empire: Individualism, Collective Agency & India* and essays in the *Journal of South Asian History and Culture*, *The Global South*, and the *Indiana Journal of Global Legal Studies*, among others. Along with Laura E. Lyons, she co-edited *Cultural Critique and the Global Corporation* and a special issue of the journal *Biography* on "Corporate Personhood."